DATE DUE

PRINTED IN U.S.A.

DISCARD

DEC 10 2015

Transforming Teaching and Learning with Active and Dramatic Approaches

How can teachers *transform* classroom teaching and learning by making pedagogy more socially and culturally responsive, more relevant to students' lives, and more collaborative? How can they engage disaffected students in learning and at the same time promote deep understanding through high-quality teaching that goes beyond test preparation?

This text for prospective and practicing teachers introduces engaging, innovative pedagogy for putting active and dramatic approaches to learning and teaching into action. Written in an accessible, conversational, and refreshingly honest style by a teacher and professor with over 30 years' experience, it features real examples of preschool, elementary, middle, and high school teachers working in actual classrooms in diverse settings. Their tales explore not only how, but also why, they have changed the way they teach. Photographs and stories of their classroom practice, along with summarizing charts of principles and strategies, both illuminate the critical, cross-curricular, and inquiry-based conceptual framework Edmiston develops and provide rich examples and straightforward guidelines that can support readers as they experiment with using active and dramatic approaches to dialogue, inquiry, building community, planning for exploration, and authentic assessment in their own classrooms.

Brian Edmiston is Professor of Drama in Education, The Ohio State University, Department of Teaching & Learning, USA.

Transforming Teaching and Learning with Active and Dramatic Approaches

Engaging Students
Across the Curriculum

Brian Edmiston

Routledge
Taylor & Francis Group

NEW YORK AND LONDON

First published 2014
by Routledge
711 Third Avenue, New York, NY 10017

Published in the UK
by Routledge
2 Park Square, Milton Park, Abingdon, Oxon OX14 4RN

Routledge is an imprint of the Taylor & Francis Group, an informa business

© 2014 Taylor & Francis

Library of Congress Cataloging-in-Publication Data
Edmiston, Brian, author.
  Transforming teaching and learning with active and dramatic approaches: engaging students across the curriculum / Brian Edmiston.
    pages cm
  Includes bibliographical references and index.
  1. Active learning. 2. Drama in education. 3. Interdisciplinary approach in education. 4. Communication in education. I. Title.
  LB1027.23.E34 2013
  371.39–dc23
  2013002603

ISBN: 978-0-415-53098-9 (hbk)
ISBN: 978-0-415-53101-6 (pbk)
ISBN: 978-0-203-11653-1 (ebk)

Typeset in Sabon
by Cenveo Publisher Services

Never forget
To remember
What you'd forgotten
You knew

To the memory of decades of dialogue with
Dr. Dorothy Heathcote, MBE
1926–2011

Know what you know
Know what you don't know
Know that you know more than you think you know
Know that you can't know all that you don't know

Brief Contents

Contents

Foreword

Shirley Brice Heath

For me, this is a book about experimenting, making mistakes, and rethinking. This is a courageous book. Here we are reminded that being creative will make us vulnerable at times. Yet it is our creativity that supports true openness and the ongoing generation of new ideas and alteration of past approaches.

If you are a teacher or teacher educator, you have read a hundred or more books about successful teaching. I have, and I often close the last page of these books with a sigh. I feel inadequate, for I am certain that I can never be such a perfect teacher as those portrayed in the pages of success stories of teaching. I know that I have often been wrong, unyielding, and resistant, even while I try to convince myself otherwise.

Transforming Teaching and Learning with Active and Dramatic Approaches: Engaging Students across the Curriculum is far from being yet another unabated success story. It is instead a volume that comes in truth from a topic the author knows well: the world of drama and dramatic pedagogy. Every theatre company in the world knows that playing roles, bringing text to life through players, and portraying stories comes with knowing what it feels like to be wrong, make mistakes, and have to rethink and redo. In fact, most of the best-known pieces of dramatic art from world cultures center on learning life's lessons and moving forward.

In every chapter of this book, we see ourselves when we have made foolish decisions in our teaching and learning, when we have misjudged what will go over well with a class, or when we have simply tried to hammer our way through our plan for the day's events. Edmiston does not shrink from sharing what he terms "mis-takes" with his readers, for he writes out of full awareness that central to live theatre is the reality that (aside from being captured on film) no performance is repeatable. Such is certainly the case with every class and each day of teaching and learning. Such is the drama of life's learning. This tension keeps audiences returning again to see a play they have seen on stage many times before: each performance is new.

Thus for all learners—teachers and their students alike—each performance allows us to start again and to perform differently the next time from the time before. Central within this book is the notion of trust. Learners put together in any space, whether a classroom or a rehearsal space, have to trust one another, or nothing is likely to happen. It is no accident that one of the first exercises any theatre group undertakes is the 'trust fall' in which one person falls backward, trusting that the actor standing behind is alert and ready to catch the dead weight of a falling body. Edmiston emphasizes again and again the need for learners to trust one another.

As we do so, we ask questions, enter into the spirit of another, and make small inner movements. The great English director, Peter Brook, tells us that "Acting begins with a tiny inner movement so slight that it is almost completely invisible." This small movement may be only a flicker at the outset, but for the flicker to pass into the whole organism, "a total relaxation must be there" (1968: 209). The same is true of learning that holds, for flickers of recognition have to move into motivation, embrace, and the urge to do and learn more. Relaxation that comes from trust makes this movement possible. Achieving this kind of relaxation comes more easily for young learners than for those who remain on guard against trust and full embrace. These learners fear making mistakes.

On some occasions in my teaching career, I have worn a mask to class. In addition, I take in a basket of masks from which students may select one. I have done my mask class in those cases where I felt the friction between the students and my way of doing things had reached an impasse. Initially, when I enter the room, students react with shock. They giggle, whisper to one another, and show how uneasy they feel. As the basket passes among the students, those who wish to do so make their choice. We talk about how masks allow us to take risks we are unwilling to take when we have no mask.

I explain that I am eager for students to create the character they want to reveal from behind the mask and to say to my masked character what their character is thinking and feeling. My learning and theirs shifts, and once we've had a 'mask day,' we have a shared unique experience as point of reference. Most of the time, what I hear from the masked voices is that we have not made clear the core values of who we are as a community. Edmiston often attributes this mis-take to himself as a learning teacher, but we can never hear this caution too many times. In particular, when we feel especially good about the *content* of what is to happen in the classroom on a particular day, week, or term, we overlook the fact that content means nothing if it does not link with values central in interactions and communications among learners.

Much of what happens in this volume centers around two aspects of classroom life: bodily movement and the vital importance of experiences students believe can explain particular areas of expertise they have gained in life. Every lesson that Edmiston lays out in this volume involves the embodiment of emotion, space, and sequencing.

Though learners may not be able to express verbally the "what about?" or "what if?" questions they say to themselves, they have had prior experiences that have taught them about the fact that "things happen." From an early age, children know that what is planned is not what always happens, and in creating drama, they have to bring to bear in their gestures, emotions, and bodily movements some of the possibilities that may alter outcomes. Since Edmiston uses works of literature throughout the book as the basis for the children's dramatic performances, these variables of intervention are often within illustrations. The children who can most effectively embody these conditions show that they "know" from experience what is taking place. They have some expertise about "things happening." They use gestures, pointing, and explanations that bring others into the experiences they have had that relate to the current text before the group. Moving the body, enacting emotions through gestures and facial or bodily expressions, reinforces for all learners, especially young children, abstractions such as "compassion." Embodying knowledge gives an efficient channel for memories past and into the future.

But what of works of literature that introduce characters, places, and conflicts learners may not be able to link with their own past experiences? Bringing to the minds of learners parallel situations, types of individuals, and scenes can help, to be sure. More is needed, however, and Edmiston makes clear that finding ways to bring this "more" into lessons may be among the most difficult challenge for any teacher. We cannot know, of course, what past experience has held for students, and our classrooms today will often be filled with learners from a wide array of social class, cultural, and linguistic backgrounds. Edmiston does not let readers shirk from what is needed therefore in the endless amount of preparation outside of class that characterizes good teachers. Visual props such as films, photographs, and three-dimensional models work as tools of memory support for learners. These props provide the best possible means of creating shared experience in the here-and-now. Therefore, as such tools are examined and entered into conversations in classrooms, the varied types of past experience—indeed expertise—within the group becomes clear on turf that is neutralized through these props.

In this way, all learners become identified with the props currently before every viewer. Such props can then enable learners to express their expertise in terms of recalled emotions that may be highly relevant to the group as they work together in ensemble to bring texts to life for everyone. Before students can gain deep and memorable engagement with texts containing material decontextualized in times, places, and motives far from their own experiences or expertise, they have to ground their conceptual understanding in relation to their own intuitive knowledge. Only then can they reorganize pieces of knowledge they hold in line with the necessary additional information that comes in new texts. Learners have to do this kind of coordination for themselves. They can make new ideas and information portable only once they envision and test them against intuitive ideas and ground them in dramatic action and reflection.

Relish this volume. Do so for many reasons. My reason for doing so lies in the passion and conviction with which Edmiston and the learners we meet through him tell us that art can never be simply an appendage on living and learning. When learners—whether students or teachers— who have been players within drama leave their classrooms, they are never quite the same as when they entered. This is because drama is play, and playing is never possible without truth that is on the move. Again the words of director Peter Brook say it all:

> In everyday life, 'if' is a fiction, in the theatre 'if' is an experiment.
> In everyday life, 'if' is an evasion, in the theatre 'if' is the truth.
> When we are persuaded to believe in this truth, then the theatre and
> life are one.
> This is a high aim. It sounds like hard work.
> To play needs much work. But when we experience the work as play,
> then it is not work any more.
> A play is play.
>
> (Brook, 1968, pp. 140–141)

Preface

I invite you to accompany me as I journey into classrooms where teachers and I use active and dramatic approaches for dialogue and inquiry with students, so teaching and learning become more engaging, complex, and challenging yet also more meaningful, rewarding, and joyful. The point of this book is to illustrate, explain, and analyze this pedagogy, to make it come alive for you so that you may try out some of these approaches to transform your own classroom.

The ideas in this book can be conceptualized as transformative in two ways. First, a teacher's understanding of being a teacher may change. Second, ideas about teaching and/or teaching practices may change not only in terms of how young people understand content but also how they relate to teachers and their peers as learners or students. Both types of transformation take time and both are interrelated: by changing what it means to teach, it is also possible to change how to teach, and vice versa.

Teaching and learning are complex active processes with dialogue at the center of both. In this book I explore a view of learning as making connections in dialogue between, on the one hand, new ideas and insights and, on the other hand, networks of prior understandings and shared assumptions. Learning connects the new with the old. Learning is authoring understanding. Teaching is making a difference in young people's learning. At the heart of teaching is dialogue, and over time inquiry, in which students create connections that make sense to them about topics that we believe are important.

Running through every chapter are descriptions and photographs of classroom teaching that may be read independently in order to provide a sense of active and dramatic approaches in actual teaching and learning contexts. In particular, these provide contextualized illustrations of teaching strategies along with some of my core understandings about how to use strategies effectively. At the same time, I analyze every example in order to develop the theoretical framework that explains why and how I teach in the ways I do. My purpose is not to provide an array of alternative educational theories but rather to illustrate, synthesize, and extend those frameworks that have helped me understand the planning and assessment of the pedagogies I outline in this book. Knowing that different readers resonate with different formats I develop and present ideas in multiple ways via stories, prose, analysis, photographs, textboxes, diagrams, and tables.

Grounding this book are stories from my own and other teachers' experiences with planning and interpreting our students' ideas through active and dramatic approaches to learning. I present and analyze these narratives not as templates to follow but as honest tales from the classroom that illustrate how teachers grow when we revisit personal stories and connect them with tales and experiences of new approaches that lead to new insights and deeper learning.

As I crafted the manuscript of this book I wrote with multiple readers in mind—I imagined my words being read by student teachers, full-time teachers, and teacher educators with varying amounts of classroom experience working with students of any age. At the same time I envisioned readers along a continuum between those who know little to a great deal about using active or dramatic pedagogies across the curriculum. Whether you are a beginning or a seasoned professional, I see us on parallel journeys to becoming better teachers. I imagine you reading this book as a colleague who, like me, has chosen the vocation of teaching. For over thirty years I've worked in classrooms with students of all ages from preschool to college: six as a full-time English and drama teacher in England, two as an elementary teacher in Ohio, and for over twenty years as a college professor and parent of two children who is also a frequent guest teacher and consultant in schools.

If you are a reader largely unacquainted with active approaches or with educational uses of drama then I aim to introduce you to expansive and generative pedagogies. If you are a reader with expertise in teaching through drama but with little knowledge of learning theory then this book may help you develop and understand more about your own practice. As much as is possible through the medium of print, I desire to be in dialogue with you whether you are venturing into a classroom for the first or umpteenth time and whether you are a student or a teacher educator who may be teaching courses in pedagogy or in drama education.

I don't anticipate you will necessarily read the book in a linear way. If you are anything like me as a reader you'll skip around, read ahead, return to certain sections, and make the text work for you by applying ideas in your own classroom and reflecting on their effectiveness. If you have an ongoing imagined conversation with me, as well as with the voices of the teachers, students, and theorists whose ideas fill each chapter, then the text could become a teacher for you as it has been for me in preparing it. Rather than just accept what I present, you might want to talk back, for example, by writing in the margin and by comparing my experiences with yours. Just as I developed and revised my understandings in writing this book so might you in reading it. Knowing how useful it is for me to do so, I encourage you to read with a colleague and have conversations about your classroom experiences. I also invite you to contact me via email if you have classroom examples to discuss. Such practices will lead you to engage in the sort of dialogue and authoring of understanding described by the Russian theorist Mikhail Bakhtin, and so central to this book.

In this book I share some of the significant ways I have developed as a teacher as I have reevaluated what matters to me in classroom life over the course of more than thirty years. I value being active with students in intellectual, social, and physical tasks because I want students to go beyond superficial learning to create depth of understanding of whatever information, skills, or ideas we explore and apply from any given texts or curriculum. I seek dialogue so that we may form and transform our conceptual understandings and viewpoints on the world and on our selves through collaborative, critical inquiry. I value being dramatic with students not only because this is often a route to more meaningful learning but also because imagined places suddenly become accessible to us, opening vast landscapes for learning and teaching.

Overview of the Book

The book begins with principles of dramatic approaches to learning, continues with concepts and practices that support planning, then examines detailed examples of teaching, and concludes with chapters on assessment and a review of key principles that affirm the value of active and dramatic approaches to learning.

I introduce core principles of learning: be active, be dramatic, and be dialogic in Chapter 1. I show how to engage in authentic dialogue with students through the intersections of four active learning modes and related dramatic learning modes.

In Chapter 2 I explore the relationship between social and academic learning as I describe how we might build a classroom community of trusting, collaborative learners who work together for shared purposes, as an ensemble.

Chapter 3 introduces a process of planning for possible tasks on a shared journey of exploration.

In Chapter 4 I consider how to organize for authentic teaching across time through increasingly critical and dialogic dramatic inquiry.

Introducing four teaching modes, in Chapter 5 I introduce and apply the concepts of strategic and tactical teaching to classroom examples.

I consider how meaningful assessments intersect with planning, teaching, learning, and values in Chapter 6.

I close, in Chapter 7, by adopting a paradoxical viewpoint as I note both the complexity and simplicity of active and dramatic approaches to teaching and learning.

Acknowledgments

I could not have written this book without the young and adult learners and teachers whose thoughts, actions, and dialogue about texts, ranging from nursery rhymes and Shakespeare to factual accounts and mythic tales, are described across these pages. In particular, I want to acknowledge the generosity and openness of the many preschool through college teachers who have shared and dialogued with me about how insights on their own learning journeys intersect with the tales and ideas in this text. They include the following: Megan Ballinger, Tracey Bigler-McCarthy, Jennifer Lee Fong, Megan Rogers Frazier, Lorraine Gaugenbaugh, Geoff James, John Jordan, Linda Mahan, Amy McKibben, Amy McMann, Chris Ray, Amy Rush, Jill Sampson, Becky Searls, Laura Sobjack, Tim Taylor, Becky Wanless, Meredith Whittaker, Emily Foster Whittaker, and Melissa Wilson. Thank you for sharing paths on our pedagogical journeys.

Most important, without the love, assistance, and unwavering support of Pat Enciso, and our children Michael and Zoe, this journey would have been a lonely one. Thank you for always being there to enrich and deepen the dialogue and our growth as whole people within our precious family.

Chapter 1

Be Active and Dramatic in Dialogue to Transform Learning

To live means to participate in dialogue: to ask questions, to heed, to respond, to agree, and so forth. In this dialogue a person participates wholly and throughout his whole life: with his eyes, lips, hands, soul, spirit, with his whole body and deeds. He invests his entire self in discourse ...

(Bakhtin, 1984, p. 293)

People are in dialogue. The people in the following photographs are attending to one another, making meaning together about a topic of importance to them as they respond to what the other has just said and done. They are listening carefully to one another, to find out what the other is feeling and thinking about an event that concerns them. All are deeply engaged in a task with a shared goal. All are communicating both verbally and non-verbally though neither pair shares the same first language.

Photograph 1.1 shows teachers, who work in different countries with students of different ages, struggling to author words that an administrator would understand. They are trying to explain why active and dramatic words and movement in the classroom can be transformational for learning. Photograph 1.2 shows people collaboratively working out how to use a stethoscope to listen to the breath and heartbeat of an injured man.

The photographs show people being physically, mentally, and socially active while also being dramatic. The two adults have been taking turns imagining that one is the principal of their school. The adult and child are in the midst of pretending that someone has hurt his head badly and needs help.

The photographs show teachers and learners. When I was a young teacher I would have looked at these photographs differently. In identifying the child as a student I would have positioned him as the only learner. Now I see people as learners when they are making meaning together, and people as teachers when they are making a difference in someone

Photograph 1.1 Adults Dialogue.

Photograph 1.2 Adult and Child Dialogue.

else's learning. When I was starting out in the classroom, I believed that differences in age and social role created a significant divide between teachers and students. Now I know that whatever our age, in dialogue we can author meaning together. Whatever our given social role we may adopt other roles when we dramatize events, allowing us to imagine the world, our social position, and our possible lives quite differently. As adults there is much we can learn from young people about how to be active and dramatic while learning and teaching.

Over the years I have developed theoretical understanding in dialogue with the ideas of people whose written and practical work I value extensively and to whom I refer throughout this book. No one has been more significant for me, as a scholar of dialogue than the Russian philosopher, Mikhail Bakhtin (1981; 1984; 1986; 1990; 1993), whom I cite above and whose theories are central to this book.

Bakhtin is clear that without participation in dialogue we must accept other people's "ready-made truths" as explanations of life and our potential voice in the world rather than grow in our understanding by developing meaning in discourse with other people: "truth is born between people collectively searching" (1984, p. 110). In this book I share some of the growing 'truths' about teaching and learning that I've discovered and lived throughout my ongoing search with people of all ages.

Following Bakhtin, I aim to place dialogue at the heart of both active and dramatic approaches to teaching and learning about topics, texts, the world, and our selves. Dialogue is *active* when meaning is made continually *with* young people rather than expecting them passively to receive or regurgitate information or ideas. Dialogue becomes *dramatic* when we create understanding *as if* we were elsewhere or were other people, especially when we imagine we are characters in stories or people referred to in any narrative text.

Dialogue with students is now my primary practice as a teacher. I greet young people, get to know them, listen to them, communicate, explore narratives, imagine together, develop understandings, and then say farewell, all in dialogue. It's through dialogue that we can organize, question, joke, instruct, and change what we're doing. Without dialogue I would be left lecturing in monologues and learning nothing about the content, other people, or my self as a teacher.

Another central influence on my thinking and practice has been Dorothy Heathcote (Johnson & O'Neill, 1984; Heathcote & Bolton, 1995). Heathcote was one of the pioneers of using dramatic approaches for educational purposes; her philosophy, practice, and theorizing pervades my understanding of dramatic pedagogy.[1] She stresses that adults and young people share the same capability to imagine and dramatize: "the ability of humans to 'become somebody else', to 'see how it feels' ... to 'put yourself in my shoes' [is a capacity that] humans employ naturally and intuitively all their lives" (1969/1984, p. 54).[2]

My ideas have also been informed by dialogue with theorists and practitioners in other fields. For example, the cognitive psychologist Jerome Bruner (1987) characterizes a core process of understanding in which our "actual minds" create "possible worlds" as actively making meaning about oral or written narratives and the ideas contextualized by them explicitly and by inference. Bruner suggests we understand life and texts in terms of our own and others' stories. Using social imagination, any fictional or factual text may begin to come alive mentally and socially for a group when people talk, move, and interact collaboratively *as if* they are living within an event in the world of the narrative. This is what I call dramatic learning. Similar resonances arise in the work of the anthropologist Dorothy Holland (Holland et al., 1998). Holland stresses that, like fictional story worlds, the "real world" can be understood in terms of our experiences and understanding of shared narratives and that our social position in relation to those narratives is socially and culturally co-constructed; this is what I call active learning.

In active and dramatic dialogue about narrative worlds people not only make meaning about texts but also may change their understanding of who they are, and who they might become, both in the classroom and in the world beyond the school. Using Bakhtin's global concept, teachers as well as students may become more aware of their "authorship" (Morson & Emerson, 1990, pp. 123–268). When I author meaning I improvise acts that can affect my social position and understanding of my self in the world, which from a Bakhtinian viewpoint, as Deborah Hicks (1996) argues, is at the core of learning.

Learning is making meaning and authoring understanding in dialogue

I use the following terms as broad synonyms: authoring, creating, constructing, developing, and making. Similarly, I use understanding, meaning, and knowing interchangeably. I tend to use 'meaning-making' to refer to learning in-the-moment and 'authoring understanding' to describe the longer-term process of creating conceptual understanding.

The terms 'utterance' and 'words' foreground verbal dialogue whereas 'act', 'action,' and 'deed' highlight related non-verbal movement. Because the processes of learning are social practices learning may also be characterized as dialogic, coauthoring, co-creating, or the co-construction of meaning and understanding.

When I taught a week-long class for graduate and undergraduate students at The Ohio State University in June 2011, my teaching, and the teachers' learning, was active and often dramatic. Over that week, the sixteen practicing, former full-time, and pre-service teachers, and myself engaged in extended dialogue about an essential inquiry question: "How and why might you use active and dramatic approaches for teaching in your preschool-college classrooms?"

To make our learning more authentic and substantive I wanted students to learn through direct practical work with young people.

To this end, during the week we worked with two groups; one a group from a local middle school and the other a group of preschoolers. Later in this chapter I will describe what happened when the middle level students came to class with their teacher. First, I will look at the work with the preschool children.

One morning, in collaboration with Amy Rush, a teacher in our university childcare center who was a graduate student in the class, I led an hour-long session at the center with eighteen three- and four-year-old children and their adult caregivers. About half of the children came from five different countries beyond the United States.

In dialogue with very young people, many of whom did not speak English as their first language, the children authored meaning about this simple, though not simplistic, text:

Jack and Jill went up the hill
To fetch a pail of water.
Jack fell down, and broke his crown
And Jill came tumbling after.

Up Jack got and home did trot
As fast as he could caper.
He went to bed to mend his head
With vinegar and brown paper.

Amy and I had met in advance of working with the preschool children in order to agree on curricular goals. These were related to an appropriate early childhood academic concept, why people need water, and a core social practice, how and why people help one another. Additionally, from a literacy perspective we had a particular learning objective: we wanted the children to recite and form some understanding about the *Jack and Jill* nursery rhyme that none of the children had previously encountered. Our planning and teaching were guided by the following inquiry questions: why might Jack and Jill have needed water, and how could we help heal Jack's head?

For nearly an hour, in a sequence of tasks the children dialogued about a narrative event: Jack went up a hill and hurt his head when he fell down. The following photographs illustrate one moment of dialogue about five minutes after we first met. Photograph 1.3 shows Amy and me actively showing and narrating the actions of the people that we are both imagining. As we recite the first stanza of the nursery rhyme, Amy-as-Jill and I-as-Jack fall down as we each pretend to hold a pail of water.

In Photographs 1.4 and 1.5, the children can be seen responding as everyone embodies and collectively recites the first two lines of the rhyme.

Photograph 1.3 Amy-as-Jill and Brian-as-Jack.

Photograph 1.4 Jack and Jill Went Up the Hill.

Photograph 1.5 Jack Fell Down.

People Dialogue with Words and Deeds

In the classroom, as the story of these preschoolers demonstrates, dialogue is not simply talking, but rather back-and-forth substantive meaning-making between two or more people whose *intended action* may involve non-verbal and well as verbal communication. Everyone was moving while talking. Dialogue is *active* meaning-making using words and/or deeds. Dialogue is *dramatic* when people act and communicate as if they are other people and/or as if they are elsewhere. Everyone was pretending to go up a hill to get water. When people dialogue they create understanding as they choose to act and communicate about something important to them. The children loved pretending to carry water and fall down.

Bakhtin assumes that dialogue always involves both verbal and non-verbal aspects of communication working together. He refers to "utterances" as "links in a chain of speech communication" (Bakhtin, 1986, p. 84). Yet an utterance is never just the words spoken but always accompanies, or substitutes for, a physical deed. When teachers say, "Use your words," they want children to use verbal language but the words still affect the person being addressed. Likewise, when they say, "Show us what you mean," they don't mean to stop using words. As Josh, one of the children, approached me, I was unsure what he wanted. I asked,

"What's happening?" He said, "water everywhere" as he moved his whole body while pretending to fall down and spill water on me. I giggled, acted surprised, and we repeated our exchange again, and again.

People communicate verbally in, and understand, utterances. We don't dialogue in complete sentences. For Bakhtin, an utterance is each unique contextualized, purposeful, and value-laden unit of speech directed, or "addressed," by one person to another, who is likewise expected to respond, or "answer." In contrast, a "sentence" has an abstract meaning repeatable out of context that may confuse more than communicate (for example, repeating a sentence from a nursery rhyme without talking about its meaning.

As Morson and Emerson (1990) clarify, "abstract meaning is 'pure potential' to mean—but only when the potential is exploited for a particular purpose on a particular occasion is there real meaning ... that always belongs to (at least) two people, the speaker, and his or her listener" (pp. 127, 129).

In summary, dialogue is not optional if we want people to understand and thus learn. Unless young people, and adults, genuinely listen and respond to what others have said and done and seek to understand one another's views then there is little substantive learning going on in classrooms. Teaching is primarily about engaging in and facilitating productive dialogue with and among students to mediate their authoring of meaning about texts and their understanding over time about life and their selves. Of course, it is easier said than done. This book illustrates some of the ways I, and others, have used active and dramatic approaches to promote dialogue that transforms learning, and teaching.

Dialogue transforms learning when ...

Dialogue is not mere talk
It is active back-and-forth
open-ended substantive meaning-making with others
authoring understanding in words and deeds
as one consciousness, voice, or perspective answers another
searching for meaning
while connecting with prior understanding
in the real world and/or in a real-and-imagined world

As this story from Amy's classroom illustrates, even very young children are active meaning-makers provided they dialogue. Like all learners, they must be able actively to shape and answer an utterance addressed to them, in ways that are meaningful for them. Literacy scholars agree that when young children make sense of texts in ways that are understandable for them their literacy can develop from infancy (Neuman & Dickinson, 2011). However, to be meaningful, children's utterances are likely to include actions like whole body movement, pretending, singing, touching, and making artifacts, along with speaking to adults or peers.

Our verbal and non-verbal language is always, using Bakhtin's (1981) phrase, "half someone else's" in the sense that to author understanding we are always actively using ideas and ways of making meaning that we and others have used before us. Bakhtin continues:

> [Language used in the moment] becomes "one's own" only when the speaker populates it with his own intention, his own accent, when he appropriates the word, adapting it to his own semantic and expressive intention.
>
> (p. 293)

This "double-voiced" nature of language is very apparent when we pretend. When I act to speak and move as if I am another person (like Jack), in a sense there are always two authoring voices present: I-as-myself choose particular verbal and non-verbal language with the intention of making meaning from the viewpoint of I-as-other. This is just as true for children.

As a teacher-leader I may address a group both when I speak and move as 'myself' in the real world and when I embody the deeds and speak the words of others not actually present. Young people can do the same.

How we respond to and answer one another, whether or not we are pretending, affects the quality of our dialogue and thus the meaning we actively create, or author, about all of the following: the *topic* of our exchange (e.g. the meaning of a rhyme), the *process* of meaning-making (e.g. being safe when we fall down), and about our *selves* (e.g. how we are feeling about someone being hurt).

In summarizing Bakhtin's ideas about authoring understanding in dialogue, Morson and Emerson (1990) make clear the distinction between mere talk and the highly demanding active social practice of creating meaning with others (using ideas that I reference throughout this chapter):

> In an act of active understanding ... the listener must not only decode the utterance, but also grasp why it is being said, relate it to his own complex of interests and assumptions, imagine how the utterance responds to future utterances and what sort of response it invites, evaluate it, and intuit how potential third parties would understand it.

Above all, the listener must go through a complex process of preparing an [active] response to the utterance.

(pp. 127–128)

In the *Jack and Jill* session young people authored meaning in their actions as they shifted back-and-forth from answering in response to utterances that were addressed to them by teachers and peers to addressing adults expecting to be answered. I consider their learning was transformed in dialogue that was:

- active and dramatic;
- in and about a narrative event in
- an authentic conversation that was
- open-ended and dialogic,
- substantive,
- polyphonic,
- experiential, performative, and reflective
- dramatic inquiry.

Active and Dramatic Learning

Everyday conversations often occur sitting down, but dialogue can also be physically active, when we stand up and move around, and dramatic, as we imagine we are interacting as and with other people in a narrative world.

Working with young children, almost invariably I find moving and pretending *with* them promotes richer dialogue than just having a sit-down conversation. All of the preschoolers followed the lead of a few boys eager to move like fish and other animals in water. Rather than abstractly talk about water or fetching it they desired experience of ideas in an imagined context. As shown in Photograph 1.6, soon we had swimming ducks, walking flamingos, and biting crocodiles!

Intending to move in imagination into the world of the rhyme, I picked up, and carried, a plastic bucket as I said, "I know a story about some people who went to fetch some water in a pail, in a bucket like this." That was when Amy and I first pretended to be Jack and Jill and the children joined us in carrying the plastic buckets that Amy had brought in (shown in Photographs 1.3 to 1.5).

When I began to pretend to drink water they did too. After asking, "I wonder what else we need water for?" some responded verbally and there were soon many children sharing prior knowledge as they pretended to wash their hands, brush their teeth, and even bathe a dog!

I sat down with the children to check in informally and reflect with them, and their caregivers, about how they were experiencing the process.

Photograph 1.6 Pretending to be Animals Swimming.

I asked, "Are you enjoying pretending?" "Yes!" The mood in the room had changed from one of reserve with strangers to joyful exuberance through collaborative dramatic play.[3]

Joining in and pretending with young people

- When I first used dramatic approaches, knowing that I didn't have to stay 'in' but could always step 'out' of an imagined space to talk as myself provided me with feeling I had a huge safety net.
- I find it relatively easy to play with very young children. I usually ask if they'd like me to join in and begin by following their lead. I also ask who they'd like me to be and engage in dialogue as if I am that person.
- With older children I find that brief collaborative games are invariably an effective way into imagining we are elsewhere.

Our dialogue continued when I reintroduced the first stanza of the nursery rhyme and again encouraged the adults to join and recite the words as everyone pretended to be the characters. Meanwhile I was singing the words, using a tune I had learned in childhood. All over the room, children and adults were all, to some extent, pretending to go "up the hill" to "fetch" water in "pails" and use water. The children were having a lot of fun talking and moving with peers and adults as they imagined drinking, washing hands, and brushing teeth.

When I asked the children how else we might use water, one of the teachers suggested "dumping it on a friend's head." Photograph 1.7 shows how delighted the children were in pretending to do just that!

I was glad to see that ten minutes into the work I had been included, and addressed, as a "friend." Further, from a learning objective view-point, through our dramatic playing the children had shared and coau-thored some meaning about the words in the rhyme and in particular about water and how it is used in tasks I had introduced but in which everyone had voluntarily participated.

As Figure 1.1 suggests, through dialogue we had begun to create a circle of trust in the room as we moved seamlessly back-and-forth from active learning in the real world of the classroom (as we talked and moved as ourselves) to dramatic learning in a socially imagined world (as we collaboratively imagined we were elsewhere). If we had not been pretending, the children would not have been so actively involved in dialogue and learning.

Photograph 1.7 Dumping Water on a Friend's Head.

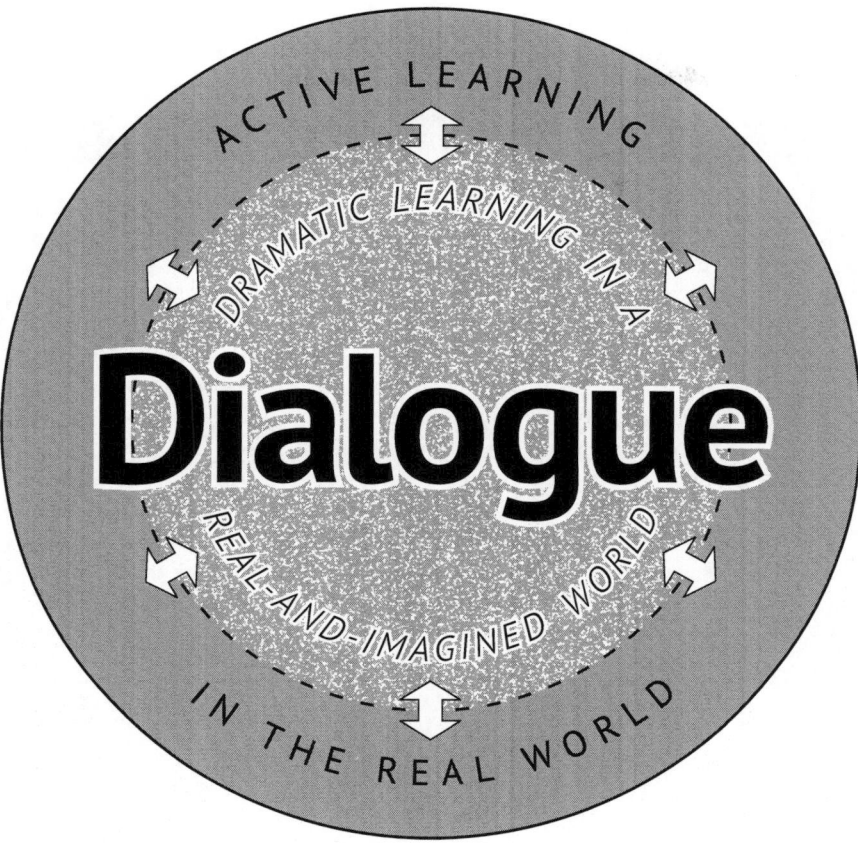

Figure 1.1 Active and Dramatic Learning.

Real Spaces and Real-and-imagined Spaces

The real world of the classroom had begun to contain fictional spaces that through our dialogue over the next hour would blossom into socially imagined spaces in the real-and-imagined world of the narrative *Jack and Jill*. I borrow the terms "real-and-imagined" and "space" from the social geographer Edward Soja (1996) in order to emphasize the *layers* of meaning that are created socially by participants and that accumulate for them over time. For Soja, space is a lived, perceived, and conceived reality that is temporal as well as spatial. In dramatic playing participants can transform their experience of space, in social imagination, so that they may experience the actual classroom place as if they were elsewhere. When I use the word 'context' I am referring more to the *immediate* social situation in which people interact. As Soja notes, some scholars use the terms place and space interchangeably; when I refer to 'place' in relation to the classroom I mean only the physical space.

Adapting the physical space
• Rather than move to another room to use more active or dramatic approaches I have found it less disruptive when I adapt the existing physical classroom space. • These are my minimum spatial requirements: people are able to see one another when sitting, could move out of their chairs if they chose to do so, and could talk with one another in small groups. Ideally, they could also gather together as a whole group. • When young children are used to sitting together on a carpet I sit with them to begin. • Unless it seems too disruptive, with older students I move their chairs or desks into a circle or a horseshoe. I consider moving chairs toward the edge of the room leaving a space in the middle. • Some teachers I know institute a procedure whereby the students learn how to move desks collaboratively and quickly with minimal talking and later return them to the usual layout.

The first ten minutes were playfully open-ended. The connection to the rhyme was mostly thematic as people drew on what they already knew to pretend we were people using water. In the next forty-five minutes, people extended their understanding of water in tasks related to the world of the narrative. I performed the entire rhyme several times and then, working with adults and peers, the children spent time using tools to help one of the adults who pretended to be Jack.

What Bakhtin says about reading can also be understood to apply to our dramatic playing:

> I actively enter as a living being into an individuality, and consequently do not, for a single moment, lose myself completely or lose my place outside that individuality.
>
> (Quoted in Morson & Emerson, 1990, p. 54)

Playing, like reading, is never completely losing your self in another world but rather actively and intentionally creating an alternative reality where you can *experience* the world *as if* you were other people. Playing is choosing words and deeds to play with possibilities, trying out ways of acting in and on the world (Edmiston, 2008).

Shirley Brice Heath (2012), the anthropologist and international scholar of arts, language, and literacy in education, has shown the significance of dialogue in collaborative play over time in her thirty-year-long ethnography of 300 Black and White working-class families. She stresses that, "an assessment of consequences of one's current actions relies on an ability to distance the self from emotional involvement and perceived self-interest" (p. 117). She illustrates how this ability can only be learned by extrapolating from questions of "what if?" and "what about?", stances that are inherent in collaborative dramatic play, games, stories, and open-ended conversations with adults. The individual and social consequences are vast:

> For visions [of the future] to be realized, individuals have to know how to narrate and question internally their course and to factor into what they envision, the possibility of accidents, ill health, and unscrupulous actions by those in power.
>
> (p. 103)

The significance of dramatic playing for preschool children in achieving more self-control by developing their "executive function" has been documented by the research of Elena Bodrova (Bodrova & Leong, 2006), but the social and individual benefits of play go much further, and do not end in early childhood, especially when playful experiences are transformed with discipline into art and science. As Heath (2012a) put it recently in a keynote address connecting play, the arts, and science:

> sociodramatic play and opportunities for young people to play roles and say the words of others ... helps develop [not only] what psychologists call 'a theory of mind' or recognition of the intentions, plans, and desires of others ... but also the foreshadowed thinking that comes with all types of art performances and exhibitions that help [people] wisely put action behind their intentions and consider consequences.
>
> (n.p.)

Dramatic Playing and Dramatic Performance

Young children are adept at embodying and inhabiting multiple perspectives in dramatic playing. As Lev Vygotsky puts it, the preschool child "can be somebody else just as easily as he can be himself" (cited in Holzman, 2010, p. 38). Vygotsky, the Russian psychologist whose theories are central to understanding the social, cultural, and imaginative dimensions of learning and teaching, famously states that "play is imagination in action" (1933/1976, p. 539) and argues that, "In play a child always behaves beyond his average age, above his daily behavior; in play it is as though he were a head taller than himself" (1978, p. 102). Playing *with* others is so important for learning because, "Learning awakens a variety of internal development processes that are able to operate only when the child is interacting with people in his environment and in cooperation with his peers" (ibid., p. 90). The highly significant implication is that "play is the leading source of development" (Vygotsky, 1933/1976, p. 537). Whereas Vygotsky only wrote about play in relation to young children, others, notably Goncu and Perone (2005), extend Vygotsky's understanding to argue that pretend play is "a life span activity":

> At all stages of development pretend play enables us to develop rep-resentations of experiences with affective significance. In the free, spontaneous, social, imaginative, fun, and improvisational world of play, what was initially intuitive and considered personal becomes symbolic and dialogic. This process simultaneously leads to the con-struction of knowledge and awareness about self and its relationship to the community.
>
> (p. 145)

In other words, adults, and young people of all ages, are able to experi-ence and learn about self and the world through collaborative dramatic playing (that includes many active games) in ways beyond what they are able to do when they are not playing or when they play alone.

For about the first ten minutes of our session at the childcare center adults and children were mostly playing together. In pretend play, most of the children were acting "a head taller." For example, they were acting more like adults carrying buckets of water carefully rather than as pre-schoolers who would likely have spilled actual water. At the same time they were learning both about how to use water and how to act in more adult ways.

Along with those adults who joined in, I had also moved into several brief dramatic performances in order to address the children. Gavin Bolton (1986), a major scholar of the use of drama in education, has long recognized the experiential overlap and social difference between dra-matic playing and dramatic performance (that he views on a continuum).

> The critical distinguishing feature between these two modes is that of *intention*, between being in the 'as if' mode for oneself and one's fellow participants as opposed to being in the 'as if' mode for other people. In the former one submits oneself to the experience; in the latter one projects what one has already determined.
>
> (p. 14)

Dorothy Heathcote (1978/1984) emphasizes the relationship between dramatic performer and spectator: "The point at which we move from being a participant in, to a spectator on, an event is critical: as soon as there are 'those who do' and 'those who watch' the event" (p. 105).

I moved into dramatic performance mode when, with Amy, I showed the children Jack's movements while speaking the words from the rhyme (as illustrated in Photograph 1.3) just as I had done at the beginning of the session when I used movement to represent the meaning of words like 'swimming.' I was more intent on showing the meaning, or projecting for the watching children my prior understanding, of the language I referenced, and I did so as if I was elsewhere. When the children responded through dramatic playing, for Bakhtin they were beginning to "decode the utterance and grasp why it is being said." They did so as they were collectively "submitting to the experience" and thus to the meaning of the words, experienced in motion, which I affirmed in our dialogue. But they needed more.

Just saying the words from the rhyme, especially the second stanza detached from the first, would have been a very opaque utterance for the children, especially for the non-native English speakers.

Brief adult dramatic performances created and embodied visible images that actively illustrated the words we were speaking, which could then be viewed and interpreted by the children. This was highly significant for the children since as Bakhtin (1990) stresses, "play images nothing it merely imagines" (p. 75). A primary value of playing is to *experience* in imagination. But to make reflective meaning people must be able to be spectators of created and visible *images* of their own or others' related imagined action and/or ideas. Experience is meaningful but reflection gives us distance from experience allowing us actively to create meaning about images of experience. As the Reggio Emilia approach stresses, not only do we have to "make thinking visible" (Project Zero and Reggio Children, 2001), we also have to "make teaching visible" to children and to ourselves (Project Zero et al., 2003). Dramatic performance is one way to do both.

Dramatic playing and brief dramatic performances were insufficient for sharing a meaning of the narrative as a whole to all of the children: I needed to shift into a more extended dramatic performance mode. Photographs 1.8 and 1.9 show how I strove to make the language of the whole narrative more understandable and accessible to all, using dramatic performance. I used blocks, a couch, blankets, and my body to create a sort of **puppet show** of the story as a dramatic strategy to mediate the children's understanding of the narrative. (Active and dramatic strategies are **bolded** throughout the text when their use is described; dramatic strategies are also **italicized**.) This culminated in the discovery of graduate student Justin Debrosse as if he were Jack lying on the ground with an apparently bloodied and bandaged head (the 'blood' was in fact

Photograph 1.8 A Puppet Show Using Blocks.

Photograph 1.9 Discovering Justin-as-Jack in Bed.

red paint). We had carefully prepared to use this *teacher-in-role* strategy. I had helped Justin put on the bandages and rehearsed with him what he would do and say when he took on the 'role' of Jack who had gone "to bed to mend his head."

The photographs show only two moments from a one-minute dramatic performance of the tale that I repeated twice. As I said the words of the first stanza I moved the blocks as if they were Jack and Jill going up the hill. On the line "up Jack got" I got up and moved around the children as I said "and home did trot …" By the time I got to "He went to bed to mend his head" I was standing looking at Justin. It may sound complicated since I was both narrator and performer but since I was showing the meaning while saying the words it was not confusing to the adults and children who were spectators to images tied to my words and imagined deeds.

Dramatic Reflection

As I repeated the words "He went to bed to mend his head," I pointed to Justin saying, "Jack's in bed. What do you think is wrong with his head if it needs mending?" This was enough to initiate some *reflective* dialogue with and among the children about what might be wrong and what we might *do* in response to help Jack. I asked Justin-as-Jack how he was feeling and encouraged some of the children to talk with him. Those who looked at Jack and spoke with him foregrounded a different mode. They answered Justin-as-Jack as spectators of his dramatic performance as if he was Jack in bed. As Bakhtin (1990) stresses, "the imagined life becomes an imaged life only in the active and creative contemplation of a spectator" (p. 75). Now they had something to look at, make sense of together, and respond to in action.

In dramatic reflection mode, the children did more than understand the meaning of individual words as they had done previously by playing in response to my dramatic performance of swimming. As spectators they were also in a position to interpret images and, significantly for authoring meaning, *evaluate* Jack's utterances, as if they were talking with Jack, responding appropriately and meaningfully within the context of this event in Jack's life. The children continued to dialogue in dramatic reflection mode when they talked about Jack's problem with other adults or their peers. As Heathcote (1976/1984) has stressed, dramatic reflection feels quite "normal" because

> all it demands is that children shall think from within a dilemma instead of talking about the dilemma … you bring them to a point where they think from *within* the framework of choices instead of talking coolly *about* the framework of choices.
>
> (p. 119, my emphasis)

Children in dramatic reflection mode can also be playing as they explore possible choices of how to respond. Many of the preschool children did so when they interacted physically with Justin-as-Jack in response to his moaning and talking.

In contrast to the relationship of actors to spectators or an audience in the theatre, in the classroom participants are able to interact with those who are performing. Augusto Boal's (1979/1985) term "spect-actor" is useful for conceptualizing the relationship between those watching and interpreting (like the children) and those showing and telling (like Justin). Reflection is active meaning-making not passive reception. And part of active understanding is a responsive utterance that might involve talk, movement, and the use of physical objects as participants join the performers in the event.

Amy had artifacts available in the room that could be used as tools to make images and meaning about the imagined world: band-aids, bandages, plastic syringes, X-ray negatives, and stethoscopes that the teachers made available to the children so that they could use them in context to create and embody their possible 'answers' to Jack's problem. We also had actual "vinegar and brown paper" but no one was interested in using them. Those words remained just 'words' with no apparent meaning for any of the children.

As Justin moaned and held his bandaged head he answered any children who addressed him. He was embodying the consciousness of Jack, keeping it visible and present for the children in images once the words of the rhyme had been said and had likely dissipated mentally. Photographs 1.10 and 1.11 show the degree of concentration, focus, and mutual respect in the ongoing active and dramatic dialogue among children and adults.

Some children can be seen actively working out how to give shots and how to put on adhesive bandages. At the same time, other children and adults are shown using actual stethoscopes to listen to the beat of a heart. Everyone was engaged in respectful dialogue as they shifted seamlessly among the modes of dramatic playing, dramatic reflection, and dramatic performance.

As spectators of Justin's dramatic performance, the children reflected on how to tell if Jack's head was "broken." In response, like spect-actors, as many moved into dramatic playing, their actions led to more reflective dialogue; one child wanted to take an X-ray, which he did in imagination when an adult joined him in dramatic playing. Whenever children showed prior or new understanding to adults or peers they shifted briefly into their own dramatic performances. For example, when another adult asked how to tell if Jack was hot, a child showed this by putting a hand on Justin's forehead. Adults and children learned something about *how* to do those medical procedures in dramatic dialogue as they talked about

Photograph 1.10 Helping Jack.

Photograph 1.11 Using Stethoscopes.

and pretended to actually *do* them, showed what to do, and reflected on images of the meaning of what they were doing.

The children were actively and dramatically using mediating tools to make meaning with adults in tasks with shared goals that they chose to engage in for ten to fifteen minutes, a long period of time for such young children. In dialogue they were authoring understanding about what it might mean to help Jack or someone else who might have hurt him- or herself.

Using dramatic performance to mediate young people's dramatic reflection

- A mis-take I made early on was expecting students to pretend they were other people while I remained outside the imagined world in the role of teacher.
- I find that young children love to see parts of stories performed as well as told. Then they have images to reflect upon.
- Having a colleague or parent in role provides a strong focus for reflective dialogue allowing me to be able to shift among different learning modes with the students.
- Once I realized that I might only do so for a few moments, I found it relatively easy briefly to pretend to be a character when reading a narrative so that the children could ask me questions. Hotseating (see page 54) is a more formalized version of this strategy.
- I didn't realize early on that expecting students to perform is likely to feel very exposing for them whereas watching and talking with me- or another adult-in-role feels much safer.

Dialogue When Shifting Among Dramatic Learning Modes

Actively moving around the room, using physical artifacts, and dramatically embodying, performing, and reflecting from different perspectives, did not limit or restrict dialogue. On the contrary, there was an enhanced, deepened, ongoing active and dramatic conversation about the meaning of the nursery rhyme as everyone imagined it together from different viewpoints. Adults addressed young people who answered, addressing adults and sometimes other children, and were in turn addressed again.

As Figure 1.2 represents, dialogue was at the center of the work as adults and children authored meaning about the narrative world of *Jack and Jill* shifting seamlessly back-and-forth from active learning in the real world of the classroom to dramatic learning in a real-and-imagined world

Figure 1.2 Dialogue When Shifting Among Dramatic Learning Modes.

and among the modes of dramatic playing, dramatic performance, and dramatic reflection.

Tools Mediate Learning

The stethoscopes, band-aids, and other physical artifacts were powerful tools for mediating learning by children, and adults, about the imagined world. Making meaning was more extensive because those artifacts were available for active and dramatic learning.

However, people mediate meaning-making using more than physical objects as tools. Mediating tools can be any artifact made by us or someone else; tools can be mental, social, and cultural as well as material or physical. Thus, using words, gestures, drawings, photographs, visual images, mental images, social practices, conceptual understandings, cultural assumptions, etc., are all potential tools for making images and meaning. Active and dramatic strategies are also mediating tools. As the children moved among learning modes, the language, movements, and objects used by me, Justin-as-Jack, the other teachers, and their peers, were all mediating tools.

Vygotsky's (1934/1986) theory of learning argues that ideas and information cannot transfer directly from one person to another. Rather people *mediate* their creation of understanding actively using multiple tools; for example, the objects used in dramatic playing, and especially the language used to name and animate those objects. Whatever tools are available (or not available) affects the potential for meaning-making, since every tool has different "affordances" (Holland & Cole, 1995). Thus, the children in dialogue with an adult as they used stethoscopes in dramatic playing created more complex meaning than if they had been listening to a teacher talk about a picture of medical instruments.

For Vygotsky (1934/1986), when we *use* a tool in a particular social context it is also a psychological tool enabling us to move beyond perception of physical reality, to the "higher" mental, social, and cultural functions like abstract thinking and control of the will. Tools are symbolic and become "signs" with "semiotic" meaning when people culturally accept that they stand for something else and use them accordingly to perform mental and physical operations. Thus, the stethoscope was both an artifact that allowed children to hear their heart and had meaning for the teachers (and perhaps for some children already) as a medical implement that physicians use to treat patients. For Vygotsky, the "tool of tools" for mediating meaning is language, which is inherently symbolic since words only make sense when we know what they stand for (Cole, 1996).

Similarly, from a Bakhtinian viewpoint, language is the primary tool people actively use to enter into, and experience another consciousness, or to perform an understanding, or to reflect to make meaning. Thus, dialogue is not only a mode of authoring understanding, it is also a source of language that young people can then use with others to mediate their meaning-making and author understanding. For example, some of the children began to use words in context like stethoscope that they may not have previously encountered.

Movement is a tool that becomes a sign when it's meaningful to participants as action in a social context. For example, when we use a stethoscope, in conjunction with appropriate speech and movement, we can make meaning about heartbeats, and about caring for other people in general, beyond any meaning we make about how to physically use the object. As an adult I can bring to my dialogue with children any social and cultural 'semiotic' understanding of a stethoscope and how physicians use it that I have authored previously. In dialogue we 'teach' in the sense that each person is sharing their prior understanding using mediating tools to affect learning and we 'learn' when we use tools actively to create some new understanding that extends our prior knowledge. In any genuine classroom dialogue, adults and young people are to an extent both teaching and learning, though they may be focused on different purposes. Their actions may be physical but when they are learning they are always mentally and socially making meaning.

Mediating tools include talking, moving, writing, drawing, and listening to or reading words (as ourselves as well as if we are other people) as well as using artifacts made by others (like stethoscopes), or by students themselves (like a drawing of a stethoscope or a piece of paper folded to represent it). As Vygotsky (1978) argues, used over time, tools collectively acquire social and cultural abstract meaning as semiotic "sign systems" that allow us to communicate in increasing complexity about abstractions (like the meaning of a rhyme or what it means to be a physician) as well as about concrete reality (like a person with a hurt head). Just as language is a meaning-making system, so are other semiotic systems like those used in the sciences and the arts (John-Steiner, 1987). Along with dialogue itself, each of the dramatic learning modes can thus be considered tools that when used over time with students can collectively become a sign system for mediating, and thus authoring, understanding through dialogue.

Rather than worry about what tools or sign systems young people are or are not using, whether or not dialogue is dramatic, or the particularities of tasks or strategies, I focus on two things:

- Are we having a *genuine dialogue* about something of interest to the children?
- What *tools* are we *using* (and what other tools might we use) in a task to engage in *action* that includes words and/or deeds?

It was because I asked these planning questions that I knew to gather up lots of possible artifacts that would likely be of interest to the children in preparation for our work. With older students I might have brought in photographs of springs and other sources of water, or paper for drawings, provided access to a computer to conduct research, or watched a videotape of a surgeon treating head trauma.

Choosing to use artifacts with other people as tools immediately invites dialogue. Whatever artifacts are available suggest tasks in the meaningful context of a narrative event. As Heath (2012a) stresses, people need to be to use their "thinking hands"; not to provide people in schools with artifacts has devastating consequences:

> when the young lose the opportunity to represent and to make things with their hands, they lose the opportunity for creativity—for imaginative thought itself.
>
> (n.p.)

The 'Eventness' and 'Presentness' of an Event

I have been using the term 'event' as if it has an obvious meaning. However, Bakhtin has a particular understanding of the term that I find especially useful in understanding why some events are more engaging than others for participants. Why was dramatizing a rhyme that narrates only a single event so engaging for such young children? Jack [and Jill] fall down a hill where they had gone to fetch water; Jack goes to bed to get better.

As we dialogued, and in imagination moved seamlessly into and out of the world of *Jack and Jill*, everyone was actively and dramatically engaged in experiencing what Bakhtin calls the "eventnesss" of a "live event," that is "played out at the point of dialogic meeting between two or several consciousnesses" (Bakhtin, 1984, p. 88). Following Bakhtin, I use interchangeably the terms consciousness, point of view, viewpoint, standpoint, perspective, and voice.

In a written text, the dialogue between characters in a live event can be contrasted with a text that only makes an allusion to events in reported speech or that replaces events with abstractions. When a text does not have live events (for example a pastoral poem, a sheet of factual information, or a description of an abstract concept) the meaning is more opaque and the text is unlikely to be as immediately engaging for participants unless they are sophisticated readers used to inferring elusive meaning and creating possible narratives to contextualize ideas.

The two viewpoints in the *Jack and Jill* narrative were those of the characters Jack and Jill. Adults and children could have dialogued as if we were Jack and Jill *in* the narrative event (going up the hill, falling down, running home, etc.). With older children we could also have critiqued a character's action, for example, asking why Jill didn't break her crown or, assuming they were children, why they had gone up the hill without adult supervision.

Justin-as-Jack embodied the consciousness of Jack so that each child could not only dialogue *with* him but also *about* him and the narrative event (both as 'themselves' and, when planning possible ways to use the medical equipment, like physicians).

In addition to the "eventness" of an event (whether it is experienced in real life or in a narrative), for Bakhtin there is also "presentness": "time is open and each moment has multiple possibilities ... the potential to lead in many directions" (Morson & Emerson, 1990, pp. 46–47). It is highly significant that the text does *not* tell exactly what happened to Jack or why he injured the top of his head. This ambiguity leaves open the possibility for exploration in imaginative *action* what *could* have happened or, in this case, what *might* happen *next*.

To engage very young children I have found that it's important to focus on one narrative event at a time. One of the reasons nursery rhymes like *Jack and Jill* are such accessible texts for young children is that the narrative only revolves around a *single* live event and its aftermath. Whereas older students can hold in memory more than one event, compare them mentally, and form abstract ideas in relation to events in their lives, young children focus best on the complexity of one concrete live event at a time.

Older students can engage with texts that are more complex in the sense that there are multiple competing viewpoints across intersecting events. Bakhtin and Vygotsky help me understand why. For Bakhtin, the consciousnesses of characters and readers, within and across events, intersect through dialogue. The more events, characters, and readers, the more potentially interrelated viewpoints there are on past and future possible actions and ideas. For Vygotsky, the more events someone is thinking about, the more the mental and social demands on the person. Whereas older students are able mentally to manipulate sign systems with less concrete representation (especially in abstract talk), younger children need more support in mediating their mental operations, for example representing abstractions with actual objects, representations of those objects (such as a drawing), or by people-in-role. In contrast, over time older students could have explored *multiple* events in a narrative about water (for example, a complex novel like *Moby Dick*).

Authentic Conversations

For me, the terms dialogue and conversation are synonyms. Though both may involve non-verbal as well as verbal communication, the term conversation carries important connotations of a more informal back-and-forth exchange that could continue over time, often involving more than two people. Toward the end of our session there was a conversational tone for over twenty minutes that felt more like professional physicians at work than teachers and young children in a preschool.

Whereas in everyday conversation we tend only to reference the viewpoints of other people linguistically, in dramatic dialogue we can extend conversations by embodying the deeds, using the tools, and speaking the words of others in images of events that are socially imagined.

Unlike most classroom exchanges, as Nystrand puts it, in the preschool people were "figuring things out together" (Nystrand et al., 1997, p. 3). And as Daniel Menaker (2010) stresses, despite people's different social roles (in this case, American 'teacher' and often non-American 'student'), "the main part of a conversation establishes some common ground" and then builds on that as "significant connections" are made (p. 18).

The adults were not telling the children what to do but rather dialoguing in small groups attempting to reach some shared understanding, for example, about how best to give a shot or use a stethoscope. These are examples of establishing "common ground" for conversations. As Becky Searls commented:

> In Photograph 1.11 you see me in conversation with Tom. As he was speaking Chinese, as well as talking in English about what we were doing I tried using gestures to communicate. He took the stethoscope when I showed it to him and we worked out together how to put the listening buds in our ears. I'd never held a stethoscope before. We focused on his ears first and then mine. When I held the other end over my heart Tom listened intently. It took us a few tries before we could hear his heart beat. He was so delighted. So was I! When I pointed to Jack he was keen to move and I helped him listen for Jack's heart beat.

Cathrene Connery (2010) summarizes Vygotsky's theoretical under-standing of the significance of adult mediated exchanges with young chil-dren: "we project meaning onto children and their abilities whereby we relate—and co-create—their thoughts, emotions, and preferences. These ascribed intentions are the sources of children's earliest meaning-making" (p. 89). In other words, as children talked, moved and pretended to use stethoscopes, apply band-aids, give shots, etc. they were in dialogue with adults who used appropriate language and gestures to interpret and respond to their actions as meaningful in the appropriate, though fic-tional, medical context. In doing so they were assisting the children to make meaning beyond what they could do alone in what Vygotsky (1978) has called a "zone of proximal development" or ZPD (p. 86). In criti-quing the ZPD as much more than the dominant interpretation as a teacher to student instructional context, Vygotskian scholar Lois Holzman (2010) has stressed "collective activity" in saying that, "what is key to the ZPD is that people are doing something together" (p. 29). What the chil-dren were "doing" was working collaboratively *with* adults to mend Jack's head, versus being told information about medical supplies.

For Bakhtin, authoring understanding requires that, for adults as well as children, as part of a "chain of communication ... above all, the lis-tener must go through a complex process of preparing a response to the utterance." The children had engaged in an apparently simple, but actu-ally highly complex, process. In dialogue with adults, mostly in dramatic playing mode, along with dramatic reflection in response to adult dra-matic performances and some performances of their own, for Bakhtin, the children brought their "entire self" to "ask questions" or "agree" in "deeds" that are "whole body responses." For Vygotsky, they were developing higher mental functions including abstract understanding as well as control of the will.

When I expect children to raise "authentic questions" I am more open to shifting the focus of any discussion toward matters of concern to them. In an authentic conversation there is "uptake" of one another's ideas and I treat all children's utterances as mediating "thinking devices" rather than as the transmission of information (Nystrand et al., 1997, p. 9). For example, when Tom raised implicit questions about a medical instrument of interest to him Becky shifted the focus of their interaction; they collaboratively explored how to use the stethoscope.

Active understanding requires authentic responses: young people must connect with the topic and share what they know (or don't know) as well as what they are coming to understand as they "relate it to their own complex of interests and assumptions." As a teacher I promote, support, sustain, and deepen classroom dialogue. Like Becky and other good conversationalists, I do not use my power to dominate discussion and impose meaning authoritatively. Rather, I socially position all young people as having *equal* interpretive authority over how to respond to the events of a narrative and I provide them with choice and opportunities to explore, and make sense of, something of interest to them (Harré & Langenhove, 1998). For example, the children could choose which implement to pick up, whether or not to sit with Justin, which adults or peers they wanted to work with, what to say, do, and question, and whether or not they would continue (which most did) or switch to a new focus.

A conversation is authentic when people raise and explore concerns and questions of interest and of importance to *them*. Neither young people nor teachers are feigning interest in the topic; the dialogue keeps going because of the energy between participants.

When dialogue is authentic a person does not stick with a beginning viewpoint. Rather, as I dialogue with other perspectives I author new meaning. That goes for me as an adult as well as the young people. For example, until we explored the world of *Jack and Jill* I had never really thought about the narrative from the viewpoint of physicians.

Open-ended Dialogic Conversations

Dialogue cannot have a predetermined outcome or it becomes a monologue: our discourse (like the event we focus on) must be open and not remain closed to new meaning. Using more of Bakhtin's (1981) core ideas and terminology, a conversation must be "dialogic" in the sense that it is not "monologic." One person cannot be leading the other toward an existing, fixed answer to any question under consideration. A conversation may reach some agreed outcome, or it may not, especially with older students who may agree to leave a problem unresolved. Alternatively, a group may want to feel some resolution. At the end of an hour the young children wanted to see Jack recover, so I used the dramatic strategy of *narrating* to tell the children how all our work had helped him recover, Justin-as-Jack stood up, took off his bandages, said how much better he felt, and thanked the children-as-doctors for their help.

Dialogic conversations are never interrogations but rather a meeting of equals who are addressing and answering each other. There can be no dialogue when a teacher already knows *the* answer to a question. And if I already have a response in mind I can't genuinely listen to other people or answer them.

As a young teacher I had much to learn about how to initiate and maintain authentic open-ended conversations. Vivian Gussin Paley's (2007) realization during her first years of teaching preschool is a salutary reminder of how I *don't* want to teach:

> ... the appearance of a correct answer gave me the surest feeling that I was teaching ... I wanted most of all to keep things moving with a minimum of distraction. It did not occur to me that the distractions might be the sounds of children thinking.
>
> (p. 152)

Like Paley, I began to pay attention to how I was affecting the conversations that young people wanted to have:

> The question was not *how* would I enter but, rather, *what* were the effects of my intervention? When did my words lead the children to think and say more of their problems and possibilities, and when did my words circumvent the issue and silence the actors? When did my answers close the subject?
>
> (p. 155)

For Menaker (2010), "good" conversations do not have a feeling of "direct utility" (like achieving a benchmark or a grade level indicator) (p. 11). Our attention is on the dialogue itself and the relationship with the other people rather than on any predetermined outcome (like 'getting' my meaning). That does not mean that we should not instruct, evaluate, or withhold our expertise. Rather, we should instruct as part of dialogue in response to students' authentic questions. There is a significant difference in terms of meaning-making between sharing invited knowledge that deepens a conversation and imposing information that ends it; the latter actually closes down authoring understanding.

In Photograph 1.12, Ryan can be seen exploring with Lauren Akers how best to give Jack a shot. Lauren has not asked him an evaluative inauthentic comprehension question, which could have undermined their shared exploration (e.g. What do you call this?). Nor has she begun with any instruction. Rather, as part of their mostly non-verbal conversation

Photograph 1.12 Exploring How to Give Jack a Shot.

she has been responsive to his desire to hold the syringe and in response to his implicit question about how to use it she is showing him how she holds the implement.

Lauren's answering Ryan, and showing uptake of his concern, did not mean that she simply agreed with him. Dialogue at the meeting of different viewpoints may at times feel conflicted. For Bakhtin (1981) each person's intention is refracted through language at different "angles of refraction" (p. 300). In dialogue those different angles can create a feeling of dissonance that affects how we respond (Edmiston & Enciso, 2002). Just prior to this moment, Ryan had picked up the syringe and approached Lauren when she offered to work with him. Feeling dissonance between their views on how to use the syringe, Lauren chose to challenge his initial rough attempt. She addressed him with a sharp cry of imagined pain, adding, "You might hurt Jack if you press the syringe so hard on his skin. Can you try again but this time press more gently?" Ryan responded by using the syringe again several times, and following Lauren's lead, he became more intentional and gentler with his contextualized real-and-imagined actions.

Paley stresses that authentic conversations are grounded in curiosity and respect for other people's ideas. And in any classroom respect is something we have to earn as well as exhibit for all people, whatever their age. Lauren, Becky, and the other teachers were respectful, and not authoritarian, in their dialogue with the children who were expected to be respectful in return. The adults were interested in what the children were curious about. Paley concludes with advice that I have tried to follow in classrooms from preschool to college:

> The key is curiosity, and it is curiosity, not answers, that we model. As we seek to learn more about a child, we demonstrate the acts of observing, listening, questioning, and wondering. When we are curious about a child's words and our responses to those words, the child feels respected. The child *is* respected.
>
> (p. 15)

Substantive Dialogue

Newmann (Newmann & Associates, 1996) stresses learning needs to be "substantive" in the sense that for students there are "extended conversational exchanges with their teacher or their peers ... that builds an improved and shared understanding" about the substance or ideas in a topic or text (p. 33). Dialogue is always 'about' something of importance to participants otherwise it cannot be sustained and will have little academic or social worth. Substantive dialogue is always based in *mutual* curiosity about a topic and the other's views. Though they would not have expressed themselves using these words, the children were curious about all of the following:

- How do you treat someone with a fracture?
- How do you know if they're better?
- How do you call the emergency squad?
- How do you put on a band-aid or a bandage?
- How do you use a syringe?
- How do you use a stethoscope to hear a heart beat?

These were pretty weighty topics and goals for three- and four-year-old children but ones that were important with an eye to preparing them for 'helping' in any future medical emergencies. As children, like Ryan, considered how to use a syringe and other artifacts, following Bakhtin, they could begin to "imagine how the utterance responds to future utterances and what sort of response it invites."

The preschool children could easily have continued with the conversation that we initiated that day; Amy reported that many chose to use the medical supplies the next day and some were seen pretending to be doctors on the playground.

Curiosity is not something just for young children. Curiosity is a stance toward the world that drives people to inquire about life whatever their age. As I was revising this section in August 2012, a spacecraft named *Curiosity* was landing on Mars. On its side is the signature of Clara May, a high school student from Kansas, who won the competition to name the rover. She wrote, "Curiosity is the passion that drives us through our everyday lives. We've become explorers and scientists with our need to ask questions and to wonder."

Authentic open-ended substantive conversations grounded by genuine curiosity are hard to find in public school classrooms. As Nystrand (Nystrand et al., 1997) discovered in research of nearly five hundred class sessions in over a hundred middle and high school English classrooms with diverse populations, "most schooling continues to be based on a transmission and recitation model of communication. Teachers talk and students listen" (p. xiv). Further, "Almost all teachers' questions required students to recall what someone else thought, not to articulate, examine, elaborate, or revise what they themselves thought" (p. 3).

The possibility of authentic and substantive classroom conversation is undermined by typical 'IRE' teacher–student exchanges that feel quite normal for many teachers (and did for me early on in my career): I 'initiate' with a question to which I already know the answer, students 'respond,' and then I 'evaluate' an answer as right or wrong.

When I realize I am drifting back into a monologic exchange with students of any age, often signaled by my 'teacher-talk' with an all-knowing tone of voice, I stop talking and start listening. I try asking students what they think, or I ask a genuine question that I honestly don't know the answer to, or I just watch and listen. In other words, I try to get an authentic conversation going.

Polyphonic Conversations

Extending dialogue from two people making meaning together to include the voices of more people makes a conversation polyphonic. Engaging as many people as possible in authoring understandings about a topic or text extends the meaning-making potential of each participant who answers utterances from more than one person.

In summarizing Bakhtin's view of a "polyphonic author," Morson and Emerson (1990) stress two roles: "he creates a world in which many disparate points of view enter into dialogue, and ... he himself participates in that dialogue" (p. 239). As a teacher I try to be a polyphonic author. One of my primary roles as a teacher-leader is to select narratives with events that are likely to engage the group in conversations that may become polyphonic. Another primary role is dialoguing over time with all of the young people both inside and outside an imagined world and reflecting with them on how and why we may all be more polyphonic authors.

Though there were a few instances of a polyphonic conversation with the preschool children (for example when I considered with the whole group whether or not to call the emergency squad) mostly they dialogued in small groups with adults and there was little polyphonic dialogue.

A polyphonic conversation had happened the day after we worked in the preschool toward the end of a 90-minute workshop I led with middle level students. Twelve young people, aged twelve to thirteen, joined us in the morning at the invitation of their teacher, Emily Foster Whittaker, another graduate student in the class.

We explored the theme of bravery in the Irish folktale *Brave Margaret* retold by Robert San Souci (San Souci and Comport, 2002). A core event in the narrative is this: a giant steals a castle, and other "holdings," from a woman who seeks warriors who might be able to restore the land to her. We had read the following words as if we were warriors seeing them written above the fireplace in the woman's hut:

> Only the champion whose finger fits the ring can lift down the sword of light, slay the giant, and give me back my holdings.

After working for forty-five minutes the young people were eager to participate in a whole-group encounter between the giant and the warriors. To dramatize the event I first offered participants a choice between imagining from the viewpoint of the giant or the warriors (only one of whom, according to the narrative, eventually succeeds in defeating the giant). All but three chose warriors. Photograph 1.13 shows those who wanted to embody and speak (in a *collective role*) as if they were the giant.

Photograph 1.14 shows me-as-the-giant using the *teacher-in-role* strategy in dramatic dialogue with *students-in-role* as warriors. At the same time I was supporting the three students-as-the-giant in an encounter with the other-students-as-warriors. The three young people had been reluctant to move and speak in front of their peers as if they were the giant, but they were ready to feed words to me-as-the-giant. I **amplified** utterances that they spoke as I, using another of Bakhtin's (1981, p. 299) terms, "ventriloquated" their words (but not their muted tone) to taunt and predict the death of the other students-as-warriors. I was intentionally, yet appropriately, menacing in my tone. In contrast to an everyday conversation that could have been emotionally detached, like Heathcote (1975/1984), I was using role "to teach the class that emotion is the heart of drama" and dramatic dialogue (p. 101).

Responding to threats of attack from the students-as-warriors (and using information from the narrative) I-as-the-giant reminded them that

Photograph 1.13 Student Preparing for Taking on the Collective Role of the Giant.

they were standing on the bones of the previous attackers. This gave some of the students-as-warriors pause.

Then, to move toward making the dialogue more polyphonic, I stepped out of the narrative world to negotiate shifting into dramatic playing mode in a task using the **Consciousness Threes** strategy. Everyone could now *simultaneously* be engaged in dialogue with people addressing and answering from *different* 'consciousnesses' or perspectives. Photograph 1.15 shows everyone working in threes. The person-as-a-warrior standing between two other people is faced with a *choice*: should I go fight the giant and face likely death, or stay away? His or her mind has a 'split consciousness' represented by the other two people standing either side of him ready to talk into his ears to persuade him to move toward or away from the giant.

First, I asked each person in the middle to decide if they held a sword, or another medieval weapon. Then, the other two people in the trio briefly planned how they might persuade the person what to do. One would argue in favor of fighting the giant with the other opposed.

As they began the task, all the voices, each with a different "angle of refraction," spoke at once while each warrior listened as if to an

Photograph 1.14 Teacher-as-Giant Meets Students-as-Warriors.

internal dialogue. The students-as-warriors could respond verbally and had to *move* forward or backward in answer toward or way from the end of the room representing the giant in the castle. Each was caught in a conflicting experience. The task was over for each group of three when they reached a line between chairs at the end of the room representing the castle or a line at the other end signifying a safe distance. When I stopped the task to shift the group back into the real world of the classroom, many were still in-between the two lines.

Nikulin (1998), applying Bakhtin's concepts, contrasts polyphonic dialogue with "Platonic dialogue," dominant in most classroom discourse, where "many voices display one idea" (often the teacher's). In contrast, as he puts it, "in polyphonic dialogue every voice presents its own unique idea [and] multiple voices do not try to reach a synthesis" (pp. 393–394). Depalma (2010) envisions a "polyphonic classroom" as "a discursive space into which multiple voices are invited ... to engage each other in dialogue" (p. 437).

In this task the imagined voices of giants and warriors had been invited into the classroom. Each trio was not trying to reach an agreement but rather, using opposing viewpoints, each person-as-a-consciousness was trying to change the outcome for the person-as-warrior in the middle and

Photograph 1.15 Consciousness Threes.

press for dramatic action from their viewpoint. The person in the middle was positioned to respond to conflicting utterances but was not trying to synthesize.

In dramatic learning, face-to-face dialogue is ideally always in relation to an ongoing conversation including viewpoints from the whole group and the perspectives of characters or people concerned with events in the imagined world. The Consciousness Threes task was not in isolation but rather came at the end of a sequence of other tasks (see below) that together created an ongoing dialogic, and at times polyphonic, conversation.

As I directed the group into dramatic reflection mode, people were spread across the room as they shared in their groups of three, and then with the whole group, why they-as-warriors had ended up where they were. There was no attempt to synthesize. Some of the ideas included this array of responses:

- "You miss 100% of the chances you don't take."
- "I want the story of my bravery to be told for years to come."
- "I don't want to be hambone soup."
- "I would rather stay and be with my family."
- "I want to show my family that I am brave but I don't want to die."
- "I want to have a chance to be remembered."

To an extent, following Bakhtin, the students seemed to be "intuiting how potential third parties would understand" the dilemma of the warriors. They were not locked inside the viewpoint of a single character but were rather in a position of interpreting their actions to others.

Mediating whole group polyphonic conversations so that all voices can participate in dialogue, while making sure that some voices, including mine, do not dominate, is a challenging and complex but important teaching practice to develop.

Initiating and maintaining conversations to make them as authentic, dialogic, substantive, and polyphonic as possible

- I found that dialogue could easily drift into monologues until I began to create spaces intending that over time everyone would have opportunities to share and an equal right to be heard.
- I practice, and as necessary agree with students on, basic and age-appropriate conversational expectations (e.g. listen then speak; try to agree and add on: say "Yes, and ..."; ask others what they think; be respectful of difference); when I write these down and display them then the students and I may refer to them.
- I try hard to plan and then ask genuine open-ended questions that I don't know the answer to (e.g. "How might we help Jack?").
- I strive to not let a few people dominate the dialogue, especially myself. I try to remember to ask frequently, "Has anyone not spoken who wanted to say something?"
- I aim to support young people when necessary in their articulation and sharing of ideas (e.g. "Did you hear what she just said?").
- I work to remember to check that people's ideas have been heard (e.g. "Can you say that again and we'll listen for what's different in your idea?").
- I may try to extend a conversation when I think of an alternative perspective on an event I (e.g. "I was wondering about ...").
- I seek to help people make connections between prior knowledge and other people's ideas (e.g. "Does anyone have a similar idea? ... a different idea?").
- I support people in raising further questions (e.g. "So, what have we not thought of?").
- Overall I foster keeping conversations going (e.g. by switching tasks or moving among active and dramatic learning modes).

A Model of Active and Dramatic Learning

As I have argued in this chapter, people learn actively and may extend their learning dramatically in ongoing dialogue. As I illustrate in Figure 1.3, each of the three dramatic learning modes I've outlined above can be conceptualized as grounded in an active non-dramatic learning mode: dramatic playing is experiential, dramatic performances are performative, and dramatic reflection is reflective learning.

Further, when groups have a shared goal of *inquiring* into aspects of a topic or narrative then their dialogue can be conceptualized as an additional learning mode: dialogic inquiry. And when learners dramatize their inquiries they move into a fourth dramatic learning mode: dramatic dialogic inquiry, or more simply, dramatic inquiry.[4] Just as each mode of active learning is manifested in different types of action (acts that are experiential, performative, reflective, or promote inquiry) so each mode

Figure 1.3 Four Active and Four Dramatic Learning Modes.

of dramatic learning opens up the possibility of different dramatic actions (dramatic playing, dramatic performance, dramatic reflection, and acts that promote dramatic inquiry).

In **dialogic inquiry** learners collaboratively explore the meaning, and coauthor understanding about, topics and narratives. In dramatic dialogic inquiry, or **dramatic inquiry**, learners make meaning about real and imagined worlds. Over time, inquiry opens up meaning to new possibilities as inquirers learn from and with one another in ongoing authentic, substantive, polyphonic, dialogic conversations focused by implicit or explicit inquiry questions. As a teacher I primarily assist learners to connect, and sometimes critique, the new meanings they individually or collectively create across tasks with our prior understanding and background knowledge.

In later chapters I illustrate how adults' and young people's actions, and dramatic actions, across these different learning modes may become part of the social fabric of a classroom community. Active and dramatic approaches can extend the social practices in classrooms to become additional "socially recognized ways of generating, communicating, and negotiating meanings" (Lankshear & Knobel, 2011, p. 33).

Experiential Learning

John Dewey (1897), the American philosopher of education whose theories continue to influence classroom practice over a century after his writings were first published, famously argued that people learn and grow through their own experience; other people, including teachers, can't act, move, think, feel, experience, or learn for you. For Dewey, experience "must involve interaction between the person and his or her environment," which includes people and ideas and well as the physical and natural world (Rodgers, 2002, p. 846). Thus, in a sense, an experience in itself is always dialogic. Dewey's philosophy inspired many twentieth-century classroom innovations and still provides grounding educational principles, for example, in the Experiential Education movement (Smith & Knapp, 2010).

Despite decades of research documenting mind–body connections (Heshusius & Ballard, 1996; Johnson, 1997), adults tend to separate and dichotomize mind and body especially in schools where learning is often treated as a purely mental activity only happening from the neck up. Yet, as Johnson (1997) summarizes:

> Change your brain, your body, or your environments in non-trivial ways, and you will change how you experience your world, what things are meaningful to you, and even who you are.
>
> (pp. 1–2)

The examples in this book illustrate simple but non-trivial changes in classroom environments and relationships so that young people and adults may be changed as they actively and/or dramatically embody and experience words and ideas from whatever texts are being studied.

Learning is experiential: people learn by *doing*, by acting in and on the world, having experiences in situations that are always physical and social as well as sensory, mental, and emotional. It's through repeated experiences that skills, social practices, and cultural values are able to develop when we no longer have to think intentionally about what we're doing. From learning to read to developing classroom community norms of interaction, people grow as understanding accumulates over time through sequences of situated experiences.

In the social world of the classroom we can't separate out our bodies or our interactions from our thoughts or feelings. Vygotsky (1930/2004) is clear that cognition and emotion are two sides of the same experience (cited in John-Steiner et al., 2010, p. 15). And as Bakhtin puts it, a person participates with "eyes, lips, hands, soul, spirit, with his whole body and deeds" (Morson & Emerson, 1990, p. 60).

Though young children, like those I worked with in the preschool, demonstrate daily how social interaction, movement, thinking, feeling, and learning are all interconnected, all people need to have choice about being able to move, not just when they are young or when they obviously have to, for example when learning a sport. As children grow older, it becomes 'normal' to sit still for long periods of time to think about ideas, while diminishing one's actual felt experience. As a 'student' in school I learned to control my desires to stand, move, talk, ask questions, or change activity. While being physically inactive I learned to accept long periods of listening to become 'successful' academically. But, especially as a young child, too often my experience of school was tortuous. In later life, unlearning habits that we may over-apply can be difficult. For example, in writing the manuscript of this book I had to make my self get up and move around!

Dramatic Playing

Dramatic playing is rooted in experiential learning. As Vygotsky (1930/2004) stresses, "every construct of the imagination has an effect on our feelings, and if this construct does not in itself correspond to reality, nonetheless the feelings it evokes are real feelings" (pp. 19–20). Pretending to be someone else in a real-and-imagined world extends, but does not replace, the real experience of moving, talking, feeling, and thinking with others.

Whereas young children often seem more comfortable living for long periods of time in an imaginative flexible play world rather than in the physical and socially stable real world, older students mostly show the inverse tendency. The Consciousness Threes example above illustrates how the older middle level students were able to imagine they were warriors meeting the giant, but that only happened after we had worked together for over an hour. At first I had focused on experiential tasks that allowed everyone the freedom to choose to move, talk, listen, ask questions, have fun, find out something about the other people present, while gradually beginning to imagine the world of *Brave Margaret*.

After brief introductions when the students arrived I laid out pieces of **paper on the floor** with words written on them that introduced characters, settings, themes, and significant objects from the narrative: giant, warrior, champion, ship, sea monster, castle, hut, sword, ring, hag of sorceries, old woman, young woman, young man, prince, fear, brave (visible in Photograph 1.19). I asked everyone to walk around and end up by one word that interested them; at least one person stood by each word. When I said we were going to explore a story about bravery that involved all of those things all seemed interested. Several people shared the titles of other stories they liked that they were reminded of; these included *Jack and the Beanstalk* and *The Hunger Games*.

I then moved into a mixing game that I have used successfully with all ages of students. Photograph 1.16 shows everyone actively participating in dialogue as we played **The Trading Game**.

This highly versatile collaborative game is one of my favorite ways of beginning work with older students in order to share and gather information and ideas or introduce a theme. The game also exemplifies the type of collaborative social practices that build community through meaningful shared experiences. Each person shares with another person in response to a question posed by the teacher, in this case, what does it mean to be 'brave'? Before moving on to talk with another person, and then another, each individual decides whether or not they will keep their original idea or take the other person's. Sometimes people trade but they might not. On the board I wrote down the synonyms they ended up with: courage, heroic, bold, fearless.

We then moved to stand in a circle to play another game, *Cross the Circle*. The preschool children had jumped into pretending to be sea creatures; this game is a predictable, non-threatening equivalent that I've used, especially with older students, to embody the actions of characters

Photograph 1.16 The Trading Game.

in a narrative for very short periods of time. Photograph 1.17 shows students playing the game that also functions as another social mixer. The idea is that, in answering a question, everyone can cross the circle at the same time ending up at a different spot on the perimeter. As I usually do, I began with a non-dramatic question: cross the circle if you like ice-cream. I invited the last person to find a new spot to ask the next question of the group: cross the circle if you like sports. After a few rounds I said we were going to use the words on the pieces of paper. I began: cross the circle as if you are a giant. There was much laughter as people (myself included) made roaring sounds and exaggerated gestures. Again, the last person took over as leader. Everyone crossed the circle as warriors, then as if in a ship, and momentarily wielding a sword.

The students had been learning experientially from the moment they had walked in the door. Now in experiencing brief moments of dramatic playing, in imagination they had chosen to step into, and out of, an imagined space in the narrative world we were about to begin to explore.

As Vygotsky (1933/1976) argues, using a tool can act as an imaginative "pivot" into a playful experience in an imagined world. As the pre-school children exemplified, younger children will readily dramatize narrative events by transforming artifacts and their own bodies into imagined objects, people, and events. Moving an object (like a block) and/or their body as if it is something else (like a fish) pivots the mind into constructing an alternative meaning in a space that is now real-and-imagined.

Similarly for the middle level students, choosing to take a step forward and then briefly moving across the circle as if they were a character was

Photograph 1.17 Cross the Circle.

a pivot for imagining action in another world that was also an embodied and visible "sign" of an imagined space for everyone watching.

Five minutes after playing the game, having read the words written above the fireplace in the old woman's hut as if we were warriors, we imagined "lifting down the sword of light" intending to "slay the giant." First, as I tend to do with most school-aged students, I used (and repeated later) a key phrase: "Let's step forward into the story world." And then a few seconds later, "Let's step out again into the classroom world." The step forward and the deliberate gesture of raising an arm (as shown in Photograph 1.18) were more pivots into a significant moment from the narrative. The backward step was a pivot back into classroom reality.

Performative Learning

Learning becomes performative when people change how they act, because they believe that they and their actions are being witnessed and interpreted. Kalantzis and Cope (2008) describe "performatives" as "acts of intervention as well as acts of representation, deeds as well as thoughts,

Photograph 1.18 Stepping into the World of the Story.

types of practice as well as forms of contemplation" (p. 187). In other words, people are performative when they intend, or become aware, that their verbal and/or non-verbal actions will make a difference to a social situation. In Bakhtinian terms, a performance could be thought of as a public utterance. Through dialogue with one or two other people I can play with ideas and restate what I say or revise what I think. But when others are watching rather than participating in shared action, an utterance tends to feel like a more fixed representation of 'my' view.

The moment of holding-a-sword shown in the previous photograph could have become momentarily dramatically performative if I had remained standing with my arm raised with everyone else watching to say what they noticed about the warrior I was representing. Alternatively I could have asked for volunteers or for half the group to freeze while the others looked and dialogued about the depicted moment.

Previously, after playing the **Cross the Circle** game and writing down the young people's ideas about bravery (and before the holding-a-sword event), the students all had an opportunity to perform in what I intended to be a less threatening almost entirely non-dramatic way. I had posed this inquiry question: what might a person *do* if they were being brave? I asked everyone to **Step Forward** when they had a mental image from a factual or fictional story of what a 'brave' action might look like. Then I asked each person to **Talk to Your Neighbor,** *Show Them* the action, and explain the context.

They had a brief opportunity to perform when I invited volunteers to cross the circle to *Show Us* their action and explain it. One memorable example was when Jane (in Photograph 1.19) showed an image of how she had spoken to a teacher, on behalf of the students in her class, to protest a rule that students were not allowed to go to the bathroom.

Erving Goffman (1990) conceptualizes everyday life as people's ongoing performances of different social roles in various contexts. How Jane performed as 'a student' became more apparent to the group as she told, and to an extent showed, a story about a significant event in her life at school.

Performance theory has been used in the critical pedagogy literature as "a cultural lens for examining the underlying power relations that structure our world" including the possibility of making "performativity" more visible: "the stylized repetition of acts used to control outcomes and create a culture of accountability" (Alexander et al., 2005, p. 3). Jane was using her brief performance to show her critical stance on a power

Photograph 1.19 Show Us.

relationship in her schooling that she had challenged, in relation to who had power over the "repetitive acts" of going to the bathroom. Her peers seemed impressed with what she had done.

There is a qualitative difference for young people between experiential actions that they do *not* feel are 'on show' and performative actions that they *do* feel are being observed. Performance may begin to feel emotionally unsafe if people feel that spectators are also making adverse judgments.

Performance is essential for dialogue because without performances a person's ideas cannot be crystallized and shared with a group or carried into possible action in order to extend a dialogue. If they are to learn actively and dramatically, students must become comfortable with, and more competent at, performing their ideas for peers. The preschoolers were largely unself-conscious about sharing and could easily blurt out or move to show their thinking. Like all young children they need to become more aware of the social expectations of other people who are watching and listening to them. Older students, like adolescents, have the inverse tendency. They may feel exposed and 'on the spot' when showing and/or talking about their ideas in front of a group that they believe is being evaluative. Even though she had volunteered, you can see in the photograph that Jane was somewhat self-conscious.

Dramatic Performance

Dramatic performances may create a context in which older students can feel able to share, discuss, and carry into action ideas as *images* for others to see that would otherwise be difficult to examine for emotional or physical reasons. Without performance, ideas can remain abstract and more difficult to examine. With dramatic performance, ideas are contextualized with physicality and emotion in an imagined context.

The inquiry questions facing students-as-warriors in the world of *Brave Margaret* included these: would you fight the giant to recover the stolen castle? Would Prince Simon fight to save Margaret, his betrothed, who was being held captive by the old woman who was described as a "hag of sorceries"? Would he risk his life?

A performance becomes dramatic for spectators when it is clear to them that they should interpret the actions of those being observed, not as 'students' acting in everyday life but rather as people in an imagined event. Not only do performers have to pivot into a fictional space but spectators also pivot into seeing people as actors creating images of people in an imagined world. Verbal agreement is the easiest way to mediate that initially. Having agreed to make this significant shift in how they interpret what is shown, a dramatic performance can paradoxically feel much safer emotionally for the presenters than an everyday sharing, especially when it is brief and clearly bounded as either 'inside' or 'outside' an imagined event. To this end, the use of predictable language accompanying movement (Step in … Step out) really helps. Whereas staged performances are often lengthy, I find that dramatic performances by students in the classroom are usually best when they are short and performed by groups no larger than three to four people.

Photograph 1.20 (taken soon after Photograph 1.18) shows one of the **Tableaux** (or **Still Images**) created by the students working in small groups after the moment of holding-a-sword. After we had read an extract from *Brave Margaret* the students chose words from it to use as a title for a dramatic performance of a still image that they thought could have been an illustration for the book. Working in groups of two to three for a few minutes, each group dialogued to prepare a tableau for sharing.

Here Dominic shows how Simon is given the silver ring by the "hag of sorceries," represented by Mara. Only if the ring fits will Simon be able to take down the Sword of Light to fight the giant who has stolen the old woman's castle.

Notice the seriousness and obvious selectivity of action in Dominic's dramatic performance with Mara. This was one of a series of brief, still, silent images that began to establish a mood of seriousness in the conversation about what was at stake for the warriors.

Photograph 1.20 Dramatic Performance of a Tableau.

Facilitating Performances

Part of my role as a teacher when small groups present ideas is to facilitate dialogue with presenters and spectators about both the process and the content: *how* they're performing and *what* images they're showing us as the audience (in this case drafts of illustrations for an imagined new edition of the book).

Because the young people were working in small groups with other teachers I only did a little of what I would normally do in the classroom: go round to each group and facilitate collaboration as necessary to focus on a goal, embody possible ideas, or choose an image to show. Whereas small group learning happens mostly in the preparation of work to show, whole group learning can also happen during the presentation.

BRIAN:	OK, everybody, can you look over here at another draft illustration for the book.
BRIAN (to performers):	Dominic and Mara, who's in your draft illustration?
DOMINIC:	Simon and that old woman, the hag.
BRIAN (to performers):	Thanks. Can you get ready to step into the illustration and hold it still for us just like the other groups? But again, don't look at us, look into the imagined event. I'll count 3-2-1 and you step into the world of *Brave Margaret* and hold still as if you are in the drawing. Ready? 3-2-1. Freeze. [They hold still.]
BRIAN:	Can someone read the words on their title?
JANE:	Hag of Sorceries.
BRIAN:	What do you think is happening?
JANE:	She's giving him the ring. [Dominic nods.]
BRIAN:	Sorry. I know you were agreeing with what he said but it's best not to move, unless you think Simon would move. Then we can just see the drawing and not you. OK?
DOMINIC:	OK
BRIAN:	Can you step back into the illustration? 3-2-1. Freeze. [They hold still.]
BRIAN:	What do you notice about those people? How might they be feeling about what's happening?
PETER:	Dominic looks kind of not sure.
BRIAN:	You mean *Simon* looks unsure, right?
PETER:	Yea. Simon's not sure.
BRIAN:	I wonder why he might be unsure?

JOSH:	If the ring fits he'll be fighting that giant. Could be dangerous!
BRIAN:	How dangerous?
JOSH (laughing):	He might go Bye-bye!
BRIAN (laughing):	Yes. He might end up as a pile of bones. OK. Thanks, Dominic and Mara. You can relax now. Who's next?

My facilitation had a dual purpose in relation to both the performers and the observers: make the brief sharing feel emotionally safe by supporting the performers in showing the image they had prepared, and focusing spectators on making meaning about the imagined event (not the actual event) by interpreting the created image.

Especially with adolescents, I try to ensure that students are performing to present meaningful images for the group to interpret, not to impress (or diminish) their peers, nor to make fun of the content. I model when necessary, or have students model. I remind people that they are looking at a moment from an imagined event, and I set a tone that is serious (though it may also be humorous), in a brief presentation that must be authentic within the world of the narrative.

As with short periods of dramatic play, dramatic performances may be informal and brief, lasting for only a few moments. Short, focused preparation and sharing minimizes potential feelings of being exposed.

If I know or suspect that students have had emotionally unsettling experiences with role-play or simulation (e.g. being graded on a talk as an historical or literary character or having participated in a simulation like "Blue Eyes/Brown Eyes") I make it clear that being 'dramatic' does *not* equate with acting out stories, being forced to pretend, performing superficial skits, or feeling exposed in front of peers. On the contrary, I want young people to feel free to *choose* to share their ideas via dramatic performance. That's one reason why I would never say early on (as I did as a young teacher): "OK, get into groups and act out this scene for us." Rather, as I did with this group within the first few minutes, I say something like this: "I want you to be able to choose what we do. So, I'll never ask you to do something you don't feel comfortable doing. You can always sit out or let me know if you have a concern. OK?"

The whole group, or small groups, of students with my assistance may create and/or show still or moving images, and they may speak words from a text, to represent events in any narrative. When people are ready and able to do so, I can make the task gradually more demanding:

- bring still images to life for 5–10 seconds
- speak in the voice of a character using a few words from the text
- interact as if they are the characters

Dramatic performances extend the possibilities of performative learning. Ideas that might have remained unshared may be made visible for others. Those watching and listening can interpret and evaluate visual representations of people, places, and encounters in a story (and not the people themselves). Of course, the performers can also interpret their own process of representation.

A performance always has two social positions: those performing an image of a narrative event by showing and telling and the spectators who interpret events by watching, listening, and reflecting on performed images.

Young people can interpret the performance as a 'performance.' It is important that students know whether the focus of reflection is on the content or the process. The latter becomes important over time for students (and you) for learning *how* to use these new tools with less and less need for teacher direction. However, the task requires sensitivity and negotiation so that students are supportive and positive of one another's work, otherwise performers will feel emotionally unsafe and may not want to repeat the experience.

Reflective Learning

As Dewey (1938) stresses, intellectual growth comes through reflection on experience: reflection "is the heart of intellectual organization and of the disciplined mind" and allows us to "understand the *significance* of what we see, hear, and touch" (pp. 87, 68). Rodgers (2002) summarizes Dewey:

> Reflection is a meaning-making process that moves a learner from one experience into the next with deeper understanding of its relationship with and connection to other experiences and ideas.
>
> (p. 845)

Reflecting is the inverse of doing as we step back from an experience or performance. When we experience our focus is on the present moment but when we reflect we focus on making connections among past experiences authoring meaning that we may also connect with current and future imagined experiences.

Reflective dialogue on events in narratives (factual, fictional, biographical, staged, narrated, etc.) can give us the distance and sense of "outsidedness" that Bakhtin (1986) argues is needed for authoring meaning. "In order to understand, it is immensely important to be *located outside* the object of his or her creative understanding in time, in space, in culture" (p. 7). This is because in everyday life "I" usually don't know why I'm acting until I stop and think about "me." All forms of narrative (from movies to Facebook to memories) hold the past still for us, so that we can get outside of and thereby make sense of it. The arts are especially effective at creating objects to reflect upon. When those objects are arti-facts that I make (like a drawing, writing, or a tableau) they both hold still and record my thinking in an image allowing me to get "outside" of it and reflect on it to make meaning.

Over time, we learn through accumulated experiences. But reflective dialogue about factual or fictional experience allows us to speed up, slow down, choose, refocus, direct, critique, and at times resist what we're learning. As teachers we're not destined to teach like other teachers, although we may admire their approaches. Everything is changing, but reflection is a prerequisite for *intentional* change. We know from teacher education research (c.f. Zeichner, 1999) that we can improve our teach-ing practices best when we have the opportunity to reflect and dialogue in supportive professional groups. I started to become a better teacher when I began to reflect honestly on my practices and experiences in the classroom with trusted colleagues. Only in reflection (especially on video tapes of my own teaching) could I even recognize some of the habits I had developed early on as a teacher that I wanted to change, for example, talking and telling more than watching and listening.

In the classroom, as we introduce new tasks, and use dialogue to position students and focus their attention, we can mediate a shift for students among experiential, performative, and reflective modes (as well as, as I note below, inquiry modes). For example, with the middle level students, in preparation for creating tableaux I provided photocopied pages from *Brave Margaret* and asked small groups to dialogue about a paragraph that they had chosen, focused by an inquiry question that I posed: what illustration might have been drawn for the book to accom-pany the passage? In Photograph 1.21 students and teachers are shown in reflective dialogue making meaning about the narrative as they con-nect their understanding of illustrations from past experience of books with the current task of socially imagining and creating an image to accompany the words they are reading at that moment.

Tasks like reading, writing, drawing, or making tableaux, are all inherently active and reflective tasks. Additionally, young people can shift into reflective mode any time they watch or listen, especially when witnessing performance.

Dorothy Heathcote (1978/1984) stressed the importance of actively teaching for reflection in relation to experiential, performative, and inquiry learning: "If you cannot increase the reflective power in people you might as well not teach, because reflection is the only thing that in the long run changes anybody" (p. 104).

Teacher Performance for Student Reflection

As teachers we are frequently in a performative mode. We can perform to support and encourage young people to participate collaboratively in tasks,

Photograph 1.21 Reflective Dialogue.

as I did in my dramatic performance with *Jack and Jill*. I pretended to swim, to be a fish, and then to be Jack. In the *Brave Margaret* work, I-as-the-giant encountered the three who fed me words to say. Any performance models and sets both tone and expectations: I'm doing what the students are being asked to do and showing them a standard of what's possible.

At other times we want students to reflect about what we are saying to them—for example, when we introduce the rules for a game, give information, or provide directions. One issue we face as teachers is that we are often unaware whether students actually know what we're asking of them. A 'yes' said in response to asking 'Do you understand?' or a perfunctory 'OK?' doesn't necessarily equate with understanding.

Rather than just *telling* students something, we can be more performative by also *showing*. We can always do this when demonstrating any new task, as I did when I was introducing The Trading Game and Cross the Circle. Showing while telling is a much more effective way to share the way to do something. Showing can also convey more meaning than words alone, as when I pretended to swim or when I 'bravely' held up a sword. As high school teacher Becky Searls puts it:

> There are so many times in teaching when it seems like we have to use so many words just to express an idea that could have been acted

out in seconds and been completely clear to everyone. Although sometimes it's good to engage in whole-class discussion for the express purpose of encouraging students to be clear, concise, and articulate, often I think we do students a disservice when we continue to have roundabout conversations that result in at best cloudy understanding where an active or dramatic approach could result in deeper comprehension and shared meaning-making.

Additionally, we can ask people collectively to *show* their comprehension so that we can better assess whether or not they need clarification—for example, by asking for a student volunteer to demonstrate what everyone is about to do or by using a game like Cross the Circle where everyone's understanding is immediately visible. Even more simply, I often ask young people to "**step forward**" (or "**stand up**" if they are sitting down) 'when you know what you're going to do' (or 'say,' depending on the task). I can then ask anyone who does not move if there is a problem or confusion or as a group we can help them come up with an idea.

Hotseating Teacher-in-Role

Students engage in dramatic reflection when they participate in dialogue about an event in the real-and-imagined world. The versatile dramatic strategy of teacher-in-role is a very effective way to quickly position students in a dramatic reflective mode. It is also an effective way to encourage students to step into an imagined world. Provided they have a positive relationship, most students love seeing their teacher pretend to be someone else.

Dorothy Heathcote (1984), who invented the strategy, notes that when you use a role you gain:

- a person for the class to respond to.
- a life-style that comes into the room.
- a holding device that lures interest.
- Something to inquire into, which acts as a focus.
- a specific example of emotional/intelligent life and attitudes to challenge.
- a pressure exactly where you want it.

(p. 205)

Justin-as-Jack provided exactly the "pressure" I wanted the children to "respond to." A person who had broken his crown "lured," "held," and "focused" their interest and gave them something to "inquire into" as they tried to help him.

Whereas the preschool children did not move into "challenging" the "life-style" or "attitudes" of Jack or his family, they could have. In contrast, the middle level students did have a chance to challenge the giant when, soon after students shared their tableaux, Mary Kate, one of the teachers in the class, briefly took on the role of the giant using the **Hotseating** variation of the teacher-in-role strategy. The young people could ask the teacher-in-role any questions they wanted.

After sharing their tableaux, as the group discussed what choices Simon had, David looked quizzical as others were advocating attacking the Castle at White Doon. When I asked him what he was thinking, he said he was wondering what had happened to all the warriors who had previously fought the giant. Rather than just telling him, I asked him if he would like to speak to one of the characters in the story and ask his question. When he said that he wanted to talk to the giant, Mary Kate volunteered to briefly step into the imagined world.

If I had been teaching alone I could have done what Mary Kate is shown doing in Photograph 1.22. First, I still would have asked what I did in this case. Then I would have stepped in briefly to talk with the students as the giant, and then stepped out to talk with them as their teacher.

Though Mary Kate-as-the-giant took up a giant-like physical posture for only a few moments, she became a powerful "lure" for a new whole group task as she "represented an attitude" in an image very different

Photograph 1.22 Hotseating Teacher-as-the-Giant.

from anything else in the room. She engaged in a brief dramatic dialogue
with David (as himself, and not as any character from the story).

BRIAN: OK everyone, if you look over here, Mary Kate is going to
represent the giant for us standing outside the Black Castle at
White Doon. We'll be able to ask the giant questions if we
want. David, do you have a question ready?

DAVID: Yes.

BRIAN: OK. Mary Kate, when you're ready can you-as-the-giant step
into the world of *Brave Margaret* for us.
[She does.]

BRIAN: Now, we're safe from the giant because we're outside the world
of *Brave Margaret*, looking in. It's like we're able to talk to one of
our illustrations. Here's the giant with the Black Castle behind
him. He's standing here at a place called White Doon where he
fought all those warriors who'd come before to try to get the lands
of the old woman back. What do you notice about the giant?

PETER: Pretty scary.
[Students laugh.]

BRIAN: David, did you want to ask your question?

DAVID: What happened to the other warriors who came to fight you?

MARY KATE (with a gleeful snarl and a laugh): I killed them all in battle.
[There was silence for a moment. No one asked another question.]

BRIAN: OK. Thanks, Mary Kate, you can relax.

BRIAN: So, do you believe the giant?

TINA: He might be boasting.

TRISHA: He might not.

BRIAN: You know, I was wondering about the name of place where
the giant was standing outside the castle. I noticed earlier
some of you having a look at the model we made before you
came in (indicating the **model** shown in Photograph 1.23 that
was on the floor behind Mary Kate). Can you have a look at
it now? Did any of you notice in the text there's a reference
by the giant to "the field of bones"? I'd not thought of it
before, but I was just wondering why that place might have
been called "White Doon"? Why white?

DAVID: Maybe it was white because of dead warriors' bones.

BRIAN: What do you think? Possible? Probable?
[No apparent response from the students.]

BRIAN: Anybody else you'd like to talk to?

STUDENT: What about one of those warriors?

BRIAN: Hey, we could talk to the spirits of dead warriors if you like.
What do you think?
[There is a general nod of agreement from the students.]

BRIAN: OK, let's do that then.

Photograph 1.23 Model of Black Castle at White Doon.

Learning to step into the imagined world as if I was someone else with the whole class watching was challenging for me as a young teacher. Dramatic playing with young children was much easier, as I had learned a lot about the experience by pretending with the three-year-old son of a friend. Dramatic performance to promote student reflection was harder.

For Mary Kate it was important that she was clear about her purpose:

> I wanted to help David believe that he was somewhere else, that he was talking to a giant.

At the same time, she was apprehensive:

> I was concerned about laughter from the boy and others about my performance, afraid that the performance wouldn't be believable, wouldn't help us enter into the story world, and that the students might laugh and be distracted rather than encouraged to join in.

Focusing on the task, the person she was answering, and physicalizing the role all helped her create and present an appropriately aggressive image and attitude of the giant.

> I didn't have much time to plan a response, so I changed my body into what I felt a menacing giant would look like and the words just came out when I answered David.

I learned to feel more at ease with stepping into a dramatic performance provided that I had planned what I might do (I still often practice when I'm alone in the car) and that I had already participated with the students in previous active and dramatic tasks. Mary Kate had a similar experience:

> We had prepared before the class arrived by reading, discussing, and planning what might happen. But changes always happen when the children and their responses are added to the mix. I remember just letting go and becoming a part of the story. I was no longer just a teacher, but an active participant, thinking and working together with the children to bring this story alive. Then, when I stepped in as the giant I remember imagining what the giant would say.

Significantly, Mary Kate was simultaneously aware of herself as teacher and as the role. She was Mary Kate-as-the-giant. I think of it as similar to using a puppet. Just as I decide how the puppet moves and what it says, similarly I am in charge of the movements and language of the role both because of how I want to address the students and in response to what the young people say and do. And just as I lift up a puppet and put it down again, I step 'into' a narrative world to represent a character but at any moment I can step 'out' and return to the world of the classroom. In doing so I am using dramatic performance to mediate reflective dialogue that can shift back-and-forth from active to dramatic learning.

Dramatic Dialogic Inquiry

Dramatic dialogic inquiry, or dramatic inquiry, is my term for the fourth dramatic mode that unites and extends dialogue in the other modes of dramatic playing, dramatic performance, and dramatic reflection (as well as in the active learning modes). We develop understanding across time through sequenced inquiry-based tasks. Dramatic inquiry is inquiry learning extended by social imagination.

John Dewey viewed an inquiry approach as at the core of teaching and learning. He argues that, "To maintain the state of doubt and to carry on systematic and protracted inquiry – these are the essentials of thinking" (1997/1910, p. 13). For Dewey, experience and reflection should always be moving toward inquiry which as Rodgers (2002) stresses is a "rigorous, systematic, and disciplined way of thinking" which is "the thread that makes continuity of learning possible, and ensures the [growth and] progress of the individual, and ultimately of society." Rodgers further stresses that inquiry is best used not as an individual pursuit, but "needs to happen in community, in interaction with others" (p. 845). And as Cochran-Smith and Lytle (2009) stress, inquiry is at root a *stance* toward collaborative learning in context about the world (rather than a methodology used to research a topic). Inquiry is "perspectival and conceptual— a world view, a critical habit of mind, a dynamic and fluid way of knowing and being in the world" (p. 121).

In other words, as people dialogue, become curious, and explore questions *over time* about their relationship to events and one another, they engage in inquiry. Inquiry is central to substantive thinking and understanding social relationships.

In order to be able to think in depth about how to help Jack, it was essential that we as a community had a stance of *not* knowing what to do so that we could systematically try out possibilities as we played around with ways of using medical tools to help him. Justin-as-Jack helped sustain an inquiry stance so that the children could discover and begin to refine ways in which they *might* care for him, by engaging in more protracted conversations, as if they were tending a sick person. Similarly, with the middle level students, uncertainty about the wisdom of fighting a dangerous giant was the thread of continuity that sustained learning for over an hour. Once the young people were engaged I could begin to try to make their inquiries more rigorous and more disciplined, for example by insisting that the tableaux be presented and observed with care and attention to meaning.

The importance of extended inquiry for learning is broadly accepted in education from early childhood through college. Learning in the classrooms of educators who are committed to the Reggio Emilia approach revolves around collaborative long-term inquiry projects, that are "open-ended spirals," as well as short-term tasks, all of which involve "joint exploration among children and adults who together open topics for speculation and discussion" (Edwards et al., 1998, p. 5). Access to a wide range of materials and supportive relationships with adults promotes use of "the hundred languages of children" as children explore ideas and express themselves, often working in small groups, using words, movement, drawing, painting, sculpture, collage, music, etc. (ibid., p. 3).

Gordon Wells (2000), who coined the term dialogic inquiry, shows in his classroom-based research how young people will begin to adopt an inquiry stance when their classroom experiences and dialogue generate "real questions" that are "taken over and owned by the students" engendering a "desire to understand" (p. 64). He stresses that inquiry must be dialogic and collaborative among young people and adults since "it is by attempting to make sense with and for others that we make sense for ourselves" (p. 58). Additionally, Wells insists that the focus of young people should primarily be on "making not learning," on knowing as a verb rather than knowledge as a thing (p. 64). As he notes, "Learning is an outcome that occurs because the making requires the student to extend his or her understanding in action—whether the artifact constructed is a material object, an explanatory demonstration, or a theoretical formulation" (p. 64).

The preschool children were authoring understanding about medical care because they were intrigued by Jack's problem. Their dialogic inquiry began to move into a *dramatic* inquiry mode when it was as if they were taking charge of Jack's treatment. The children's dramatic playing and dramatic reflection as well as their responses to adult dramatic performances had created shared experiences and ideas that could have been recorded, referenced, and pursued later if the medical inquiry had continued. The middle level students collaboratively created moving images and tableaux, and engaged in dialogue with teachers as well as peers, all focused by an inquiry question written on the board that they began to answer: what does it mean to be 'brave'? As themselves, and as if they were warriors, they inquired about the wisdom of fighting the giant. All students were focused on their inquiries in imagined worlds not on decontextualized learning.

In an hour-long session, inquiry cannot develop into extended explorations of topics or texts. Choosing to follow one path of inquiry always leaves others unexplored. For example, though we only briefly touched on gender as a theme, the *Brave Margaret* story raises critical questions about cultural assumptions in relation to women that we could have explored if we had had more time. After her betrothed has fought the giant and been killed, the female title character discovers that the ring fits her finger: she could be the "champion" foretold in the words above the fire. Should she fight? When working with other groups, it's been interesting to listen to girls and boys explaining in what ways Margaret is brave, heroic, and a champion. A girl once said that Margaret had to convince herself before anyone else that she was able to fight a giant.

Over time, as Wells (1999) puts it, dialogic inquiry can lead to "both the enhanced understanding of the problem situation gained by the participants ... and the representation of the understanding that is produced" (p. 67). Though I can't know to what degree the middle level students' understanding was enhanced, it was clear from the reflective writing of Hui Fen, a graduate student in the Foreign and Second Language Education program, that she had transformed her thematic understanding during the *Brave Margaret* session.

After the students had expressed a desire to talk with the spirits of the dead warriors I asked the university students to show us the moment of their death (a dramatic action I could also have asked the young people to do if the adults had not been present). Everyone seemed to enjoy seeing them fall over, which they did several times, with suggestions, and a few demonstrations, from the young people about how to make the deaths more realistic! They wanted screams and staggering falls. The joking mood was soon contrasted with a more somber one. I asked the university students to lie down and close their eyes as if they had been killed in battle with the giant.

Through *narrating actions* I mediated moving the university students into dramatic performance while shifting the young people into a dramatic reflective mode.

> When people came to the field of bones they saw the earth but also what looked like white stones. But they were not stones. They were bones. The bones of the warriors who had fought the giant and been killed lay in that field. It was said that if you walked there at night, were respectful of the dead, and listened carefully, you could hear the spirits of warriors say why they came to fight the giant, why they risked their lives, and were killed.

I paused at this moment to shift back into the world of the classroom for two reasons. First, to agree with all the participants about what was going to happen so that they would feel physically and emotionally safe as we continued. Second, to give instructions to the adults.

> OK, so what I'd like those of you who are standing to do is go stand now by one of the people lying down. Can you spread out as much as possible so that everyone lying down has a person standing with them. Can those people lying down please listen. Can you think of why the warrior you are representing might have come to fight the giant and risk their lives. And in a moment the living people who are standing near you are going to bend down to listen to your whispers. They're not going to touch you or ask you questions. They'll just be listening and wondering if you were brave. Any questions before we begin?

Writing later, Hui Fen remembered how she began to think more about 'bravery' as she imagined she was the spirit of one of the dead warriors who had been killed by the giant, as shown in Photograph 1.24.

> I had not imagined the perspective of the other warriors who had fought the giant until I lay down, pretended to be the spirit of a

Photograph 1.24 Talking with the Spirits of Dead Warriors.

warrior, and responded to what Dr. Edmiston said. I imagined why
the warrior would have been willing to fight with the giant. When the
students bent over to listen I said, "My neighbor promises me that he
will give me a big fortune if I beat the giant." I know it was obvious
that I was a greedy person and far from brave. [The student who had
listened interpreted her words as meaning the warrior was not brave.]
But I also have a voice of myself at that time. If I fought for a promise, was it brave? And what if people judge others' behavior according to external deeds instead of exploring intrinsic motivation/
thoughts? These are moral questions with many aspects that could be
discussed with students.

Conclusion: Dialogue Can Transform
Classroom Community Life

Active and dramatic approaches to teaching and learning can begin to
transform the life and social practices of any classroom community as well
as the agency of the participants. In that week-long class I taught in June
2011, my teaching, and the teachers' learning, was active, and often dramatic, as we engaged in dialogic inquiry focused by this question: how

and why might you use active and dramatic approaches to teaching in your preschool-college classrooms? Table 1.1 represents a summary of the active and dramatic learning modes (shown diagrammatically in Figure 1.3) explored during the course and in this chapter.

By the end of a week of practical experiences and collaborative analysis, participants found Table 1.1 a useful resource as they developed rationales for using active and dramatic approaches in their own educational settings. In Photograph 1.25 participants are shown using the strategy of *Interview a Partner* on the last day of class. Becky Searls, a high school Spanish teacher, and Kylee Fleshman, a preschool teacher, are using the interview as a tool to explore possible answers to the inquiry question that focused dialogue in our final session: how would you justify your use of active and dramatic approaches to school administrators? Working in pairs, students imagined possible challenging professional events. For example, Becky and Kylee are considering how to justify to an administrator, sitting in his office, why young children had been standing on a table and if the teacher was in compliance with the school's safety policy.

Teachers took turns speaking and responding first as if they were the teacher in the scenario, and then, after trading seats, from the perspective of the administrator. In dialogue they explored collaboratively how to explain both why young people need to be able to move and why they need to imagine they are characters in stories. They explained the importance of embodying Jack and Jill (from the nursery rhyme) climbing a hill to "fetch a pail of water" and how, since adults were participating with and monitoring the children's activities, the children's safety was no more of an issue than at any other time.

As part of our extended conversation about how to present a compelling argument, participants momentarily performed for each other some of the mental images that they carried with them of children learning through active uses of imagination (shown in Photograph 1.26).

They did so, as shown in Photograph 1.27, as we reflected on how to reference such examples in talking with others who might not appreciate the significance of these ways to transform teaching and learning.

As the teachers dramatized ways to explain the value of active and dramatic teaching and learning, they referenced, connected with, and reflected on their own experiences during the week both with peers and with young people. Participants later wrote reflections about what they had learned, which also served as an assessment of their achievement. For instance, Becky realized the significance of changing her students' physical experience of space so that she could be more physically active in her high school classroom:

> My biggest goal is to increase the active, physical movement of my students in class. I truly believe that in making this one change, I will

Table 1.1 Active and Dramatic Learning Modes

Active learning mode	Active learning social practices	Dramatic learning mode	Dramatic learning social practices	Dramatic action	Key teacher language
Experiential	Experiencing with others	Dramatic playing	Experiencing with social imagination	Stepping into imagined spaces to embody and experience as if we are in a narrative event ... and stepping out	"Let's step in ... step out" "What are you doing?" "How are you feeling?"
Performative	Showing and telling about images	Dramatic performance	Showing and telling about an event as teacher-in-role and/or as students-in-role	Choosing selectively to show/tell us as if we/they are in an event	"Can you show us ... and tell us" "What image are you showing us?"
Reflective	Watching and listening to reflect and interpret	Dramatic reflection	Reflecting and interpreting an event as dramatic spectators or spect-actors	Watching and listening to others, to reflect and interpret as if they/we are in an event	"Can you look over here ... what do you notice?" "What would you like to know now?"
Dialogic inquiry	Dialogue to inquire over time into the meaning of a topic/text	Dramatic inquiry	Dialogic inquiry over time into the meaning of a topic/text through dramatic playing, dramatic performance, and/or dramatic reflection	Dialoguing and inquiring into a topic/text as if we are various other people	"What are you wondering about?" "I was wondering ..." "What did we/you learn from that?" "What do we (not) understand now?" "What might we do now?" Who would you like to meet now?

Photograph 1.25 Interviewing in Role.

Photograph 1.26 Showing Mental Images.

Photograph 1.27 Reflecting on Mental Images.

be motivated to change all sorts of other aspects of my teaching as well, and move closer to the type of teacher I always dreamed I would be.

In the learning community we created that week each teacher had begun a journey of transformation in their stance toward teaching and learning and in their sense of agency to change their practice. I too am on that journey, which as Dorothy Heathcote (1972/1984) stresses, requires "patience and commitment." What we do in the classroom is less important than our goal since when we know where we are headed we can always reflect on and learn from what actually happens as we explore with young people. Heathcote's vision describes the community of teachers I aspire to belong to and to which I come closer with every group I am privileged to work with.

Teachers ... who bring all of themselves to school and demand that their classes do the same; who can actually change their modes of work to suit the needs of their classes at the time so that learning is kept meaningful, who like to get on with the people they teach ... who are unafraid to make relationships with classes, who are unafraid to admit that they do not know, who never stop seeking to learn more about the dynamics of teaching.

(p. 40)

Getting started with active and dramatic approaches

- Some teachers I know try out a new approach 5–10 minutes before lunchtime or toward the end of a period so that it feels a task is more contained and is easy to pause. They can immediately reflect and plan what might come next.
- When I incorporated informal assessment into my teaching I could begin a dialogue with students about our process as well as their content learning. I felt more confident about moving forward. I now routinely ask questions like these: How do you think that worked? Is this way of working helping us learn? What could we do the same or differently next time to make it work even better for everyone? Answers to such questions led me to consider in more depth how to build a community of learners.

Notes

1 I refer to the dramatic approach to teaching and learning that I develop in this book as dramatic pedagogy. There are many other terms for educational uses of drama. Heathcote and others used these and more: drama in education, educational drama, classroom drama, and drama as education. For the most comprehensive analytical overview of the history, philosophy, terminology, and diversity of practice in classroom drama see the writings of Gavin Bolton, especially his 1999 book. Cecily O'Neill (1995) introduced the term 'process drama' that has become widespread. More recently the term 'applied theatre' has become popular. My intention in using the term 'dramatic pedagogy' in addition to the related terms 'dramatic teaching' and 'dramatic learning' is to highlight the interrelationship between teaching, learning, and an underlying theoretical framework in any educational uses of drama.

2 Dorothy Heathcote's collected writings on education and drama, edited by Liz Johnson and Cecily O'Neill, were published in 1984. To draw attention to the time, extent, and diversity of her publication record I always additionally cite her writing by its original date of publication if this is different from its date of collection.

3 I use the terms dramatic play, dramatic playing, and pretend play interchangeably. In this book I do not use the other widely used term, sociodramatic play.

4 Inquiry is implicit, and sometimes explicit, in much dramatic pedagogy. Dorothy Heathcote's work was always centered by inquiry.

Chapter 2

Build Community

> Our classrooms ought to be nurturing and thoughtful and just all at
> once; they ought to pulsate with multiple conceptions of what it means
> to be human and alive. They ought to resound with the voices of artic-
> ulate young people in dialogues always incomplete because there is
> always more to be discovered and more to be said. We must want our
> students to achieve friendship as each one stirs to wide-awakeness, to
> imaginative action, and to renewed consciousness of possibility.
>
> (Greene, 1995, p. 43)

I begin every university class in dialogue. I ask the group, "What sort of
community do you want us to create?" The words that people write
down in response on the roll of paper I lay out may be different, but the
meanings we make in the ensuing conversation are invariably very similar: people want to feel emotionally and physically safe, be equally
respected, have fun, not feel embarrassed, be heard, and together learn
things that are useful in our lives. No one ever says, "Why build community?" or asks, "What do you mean by community?" From our experiences in families, schools, and by participating in team sports and other
shared leisure activities we have all come to know the value of living and
learning with others and what people *do* to make it feel good (and sometimes not so good) to spend extended periods of time together in a group.

After ten minutes of getting-to-know-you games and tasks through
which people become more aware of the productive diversity within any
group, participants have started to become a "collaborative learning
community": in the words of Mary Kalantzis and Bill Cope (2008) they
"regard themselves as a knowledge-producing community [where] the
learners come to understand themselves as makers of knowledge, who
connect it with their own experience and who explore applications for
that knowledge in the 'real' or 'outside' world" (p. 211).

For me, building community is not an option. What is optional is
the *quality* of the community I build with people. Every task affirms (or

undermines) ways of being together (or being apart from one another) and working together that become 'normal' social practices for us.

I most often turn next to fiction as I initiate some active and dramatic tasks. The scenarios in John Burningham's *Would You Rather ...* (1978) present engaging choices that I have used with groups of all ages. For example, "Would you rather be squeezed by a snake, sat on by a rhinoceros, or swallowed by a fish?" Each event can lead to brief dramatic encounters as I facilitate the group working together as if they are elsewhere, to deal with imagined problems they have created such as, how do we untangle a person from a snake without getting bitten or (like the students in my June 2011 class shown in Photograph 2.1) communicate with someone trapped inside a giant fish? The book, and inevitably any dramatization, allows us to reflect on "multiple conceptions of what it means to be human and alive" (p. 43) that Maxine Greene (1995), the philosopher of education I quoted above, believes must be our focus in building community. In 5–10 minutes, filled with laughter and social imaginative actions, we experience the interrelationship between individual choices, collective consequences, and collaborative responses.

Photograph 2.1 Working Collaboratively.

The conversation about community continues as stories are told in which inevitably a strong sense of common agreement on goals is discovered. People add phrases like these: feel accepted, imagine the unusual without being laughed at, be able to take risks without feeling judged, develop trust, ask questions, be honest, discuss problems, and be able to go to the bathroom when we need to! When I ask teachers how they think their students would answer the same question, 'What sort of community do you want us to create?', I have never had anyone say that young people they teach, or have taught, would say anything substantially different than they had. That's hardly surprising since kids are people, adults were once children, and everyone desires to experience community.

Although the reality of schooling is unfortunately quite different from what I desire, nevertheless I can strive, in my own classroom, toward creating a *transformative* community, which M. Scott Peck describes as

> a group of individuals who have learned how to *communicate* honestly with each other whose *relationships* go deeper than their masks of composure, and who have developed some significant *commitment* to rejoice together, mourn together, and to delight in each other, and make the conditions of others our own.
>
> (As cited in hooks, 2003, p. 196, italics added)

Any classroom may be established on assumptions that it is a place where students are treated as individuals. Though each person in any group must take primary responsibility for their own learning, if I establish my classroom as only valuing *individual* experience and understanding then I will have robbed the students of what can only be learned when groups work *collectively and collaboratively*.

Have you ever valued any of these shared experiences?

- Playing a game and cheering because of our success.
- Singing a group song and adding harmony.
- Remembering how we felt diminished when a person is absent or when our pet has died.
- Telling or showing a cumulative story and laughing in sync with half-a-dozen other people.
- Writing down spoken reflections, revising together, and relishing the gathered silence after reading a class poem the second time through.
- Having a group hug (see Photograph 2.2).

Classroom collaborative tasks, like those listed above, build a history of positive community experiences in which people may delight in each other's company, know what it feels like to make something together,

Photograph 2.2 A First Grade Group Hug.

and begin to build honest relationships grounded in moments of authenticity. When people feel that their thoughtful suggestions have mattered and that tasks have accommodated their needs, they are more likely to feel accepted and nurtured.

Every classroom activity is both social and academic. For instance, how we work in relationship with others affects what we learn, and vice versa. All community tasks will be richer when experiences are created and adapted over time by an evolving diverse group of people with overlapping and intersecting relationships and interests who are learning how to build on one another's different strengths as well as how to acknowledge and accommodate to one another's differences.

In all community activities 'we' experience together, and can reflect to make meaning 'for us'. At the same time, each person is an individual 'I' who makes meaning 'for me' about shared experiences.

Building community can transform learning in two interrelated fundamental ways: collective experiences are qualitatively different from individual ones; and each of us can learn collaboratively in ways that we cannot learn alone.

Learning and Being Together in a Community

Community can only be built when people come together wanting to *be* together. Being with others is connected with, but different from, understanding something together. Everyone desires both. However, people in groups who *have* to be in the same place (like in schools) cannot even begin to become a community unless they feel safe and respected enough to want to collaborate in some activities with shared objectives they care about. The people in any *growing* community share implicit intersecting long-term goals of desiring to be with everyone in the group and wanting to learn together. Herbert Kohl has a simple but transformative vision that echoes the collaborative, experiential, performative, reflective, and inquiry approaches outlined in Chapter 1:

> I want students to explore learning through doing but also through reflection and hard study. I want them to learn hard skills in soft ways. Most of all, I want my students, wherever I teach, to feel part of a compassionate learning community where they are honored as individuals, where they respect each other and love learning itself.
>
> (Kohl, 1998, p. 18)

To build a community *intentionally* grounded in shared values, people must choose to be a community. Further, they have to agree to 'hang in there' together even when 'we' encounter problems. That includes the teacher. Put another way, people must *identify* their *selves* with the social life of a group sufficiently that each is an active *agent* in the ongoing creation of the community though social participation in shared activities. As Holland and her colleagues (1998) argue, people with agency are "authoring" (using Bakhtin's term) a community that is a "world" with its own implicit rules, social practices, and cultural norms.

Every group that wants to *grow intentionally* as a community (rather than just change) must inquire. As a group leader, it's part of my role at times to focus everyone, including my self, on dialogic inquiry centered by an essential social question like this: *how* do *we* build the sort of community *we* want? Not doing so can undermine the positive nature of any community.

How to Build Community

> Community is a question of what might contribute to the pursuit of shared goals: what ways of being together, of affirming mutuality, of reaching toward some common world.
>
> (Greene, 1995, p. 39)

Maxine Greene is emphatic that we build community when we pursue shared goals in tasks that reach toward "some common world." It is not enough to just be together; people must mutually affirm one another in dialogue as they consider who and what might contribute to a shared goal that reaches to a world beyond their individual selves.

The arts can provide pathways for transformative collaborative common pursuits. People are actively learning through the arts in ways that include bringing the fictional and factual worlds of literature to life through dramatic learning. Examples in this book illustrate how, as Maxine Greene (1995) stresses, "the arts offer opportunities for perspective, for perceiving alternative ways of transcending and of being in the world, for refusing the automatism that overwhelms choice" (Greene, 1995, p. 143).

Tracey Bigler-McCarthy, a primary teacher at Indianola Informal K-8 School, an alternative public school located in central Columbus, Ohio, has been working at building communities with children aged five to nine from socioeconomically, ethnic, and racially diverse families for over twenty years. How do they build community? Tracey has a deceptively simple answer:

> There's no magic. You just live together all year; you can't build community in a day-and-a-half. Make things together and keep on working out how to get along with one another.

My understanding of teaching and learning, and in particular of community building and the arts in education, has been deeply shaped by conversations I have had with Tracey over the past two decades in and out of her classroom. Her brilliant teaching has been the subject of several academic studies, most notably by Sipe (2008). In her classroom people are always building a common world. Step inside and you'll see children and adults engaged in authentic conversations as they collaborate on substantive tasks that may involve painting or pretending or solving math problems. All tasks are part of bigger projects with shared outcomes they are committed to achieving in which real-world concerns dovetail with imaginative explorations. One year, six-year-olds rescued pilots who'd crashed in the Amazon as part of their study of rainforests. Another year, seven- to eight-year-olds learned about caring for homeless people they both imagined and met in real life at a shelter.

In 2008–09 she and the children made art, raised money, and sent urgently needed materials to the Maulana School for 1,600 AIDS orphans in Zimbabwe. The goal of her critical inquiry was to help K-1 students imagine their part in creating a different future for African children and for their selves. Their work was focused by questions designed to extend the imaginative reach of these young children from the world of their classroom, via the worlds of informational and imaginative literature, to a community literally half a world away: "How can we build community?" and "How will our community include the people in the Maulana School?"

To bring this common world to life in actuality and in imagination students employed a range of mediating tools that often involved collaboration with visiting adults and older students in the school, such as researching the Shona culture; dramatizing moments from the lives of people in southern Africa and comparing them with the children's lives in central Ohio; sending letters and drawings to Zimbabwe and replying to those sent in response; learning to sculpt with a renowned Zimbabwean artist Gedion Nyanhongo; and interviewing the administrator of the Sahwira charity they were helping. They also planned a fund-raising exhibit at the local art museum where they displayed and sold paintings and sculptures. The creation of a sixteen-panel mural became a whole school project that culminated in a dedication at a celebratory dramatized dance performance attended by local politicians, artists, and educators. One panel is shown in Photograph 2.3. The mural was attached to a container shipped to Zimbabwe filled with books (donated by Ohio State) as well as clothes, educational, and personal supplies for children and young adults.

The H in the mural is from the name of the charity (Sahwira) but when I see the hands of diverse people crossing cultures and turning the world I am reminded of bell hooks' *Pedagogy of Hope*: "a place that is

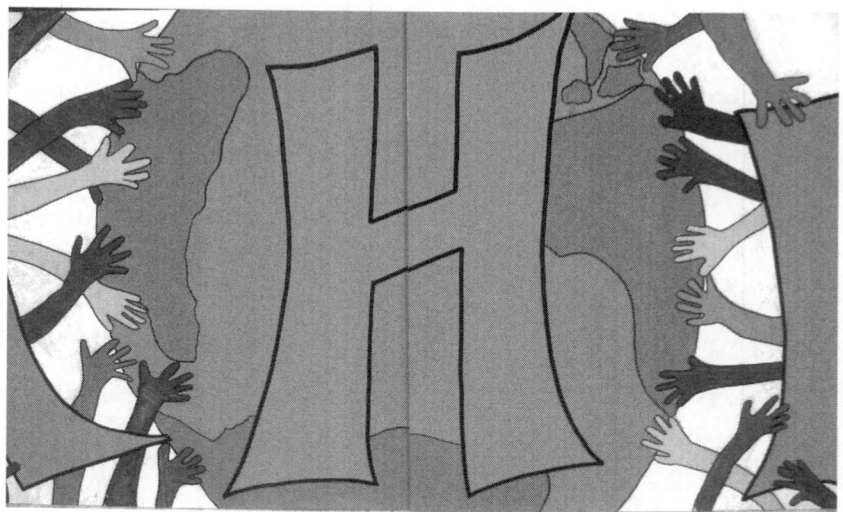

Photograph 2.3 Liberating Mutuality.

life-sustaining and mind-expanding, a place of liberating mutuality where teacher and students together work in partnership" (2003, p. xv). In Tracey's words:

> If we develop awareness, engage in meaningful dialogue and experiences which they and we care about, and negotiate a plan to work together as a community, children will realize and embrace the power to make change. When given this opportunity they easily engage not only in social activism but also in meaningful social and academic learning: caring and tenderness, questioning and reflection, exploration, and finally culmination of the learning process through celebration.

The arts were central but not in any rarefied or privileged sense. For Tracey, the visual arts enfold her use of the dramatic and narrative-making arts and, like Cecelia Traugh (1986), she regards educating in and through the arts as providing a holistic approach to teaching, learning, and life:

> Teaching and learning come to be about meaning, and the tasks of teaching become more open-ended: holding the vision of the whole, of what could be ... finding the relationships and discovering the wholeness in seemingly disconnected pieces [in] a classroom so that its individual members and what they are about and its unity of purpose are both included.
>
> (p. 110)

The mural was researched and created across K-8 classrooms but what could have been disconnected pieces made by individuals had wholeness because it was created with a unity of purpose and outcome.

In Tracey's classroom people dialogue not only about narratives, ideas, and skills but also about dialogue itself; they learn, and teach one another, about how to use language, listen, and take turns all as part of learning to build relationships. Part of their reflective learning is coming to know more about *how well* (and not so well) they work together in addition to being honest about how they work through challenges (or don't). Tracey acknowledges after two decades in the classroom that negotiating with so many children to help them commit to learning to be better listeners who can adapt and forgive one another, and their selves, can at times be exhausting for her. She knows that there is no alternative.

> We can't build a community without learning how to build! You wouldn't expect to build a home without learning how to use your building tools. Building community is similar. The classroom is like another home for many of the children—a home that we have to continue to build every day.

As teachers, we have academic responsibilities for every group. However, as people we are also members of our particular classroom community. Just as she expects the children to do, Tracey often tells the children how she's feeling. If she's delighted or cranky they'll know it and they've learned to accommodate.

> I've had to learn I'm part of the community too. Giving to the group means I have to give to myself as well. I have to be clear and explicit about caring for and including everyone, and that goes for me as well. I tell the kids when I'm feeling frustrated or tired. That builds more trust.

Agreeing on and establishing clear classroom expectations, routines, and limits are essential if we want a community to develop. These help navigate what is inevitably an ongoing challenge for us as teachers: how do we balance our needs and desires with those of individual young people and of the group as a whole?

Tracey always works with the children in the first few weeks of the year to synthesize in a chart the shared understanding arising from their ongoing polyphonic conversations about community. Like the adults I work with, her children want what Maxine Greene (1995) advocates: a space that is "nurturing and thoughtful and just all at once" (p. 43). The chart, which may later be amended, is used as a guide for action, reflection, and inquiry throughout the year. In September 2008 the five- to six-year-old students agreed on the shared meaning of community shown in Photograph 2.4.

Community only exists when people desire to be together. The more history people have of working collaboratively on short-term tasks and more lengthy projects to create meaningful outcomes the group is proud of, the more resilient their community and the more accommodating individual people will be of one another.

Over time young people and their teachers have collective experiences and performances that in reflections accumulate as 'our shared history.' Referencing and making meaning about that shared history is crucial for the group to be able to create ongoing new understanding about how to better build community.

Make Core Values Visible With the Whole Group

Knowing that we agree the classroom should be a respectful, physically and emotionally safe space where there will be 'no put-downs,' and where everyone's ideas are equally valid, allows people to take risks, make mis-takes, and learn with and from each other. Four core values

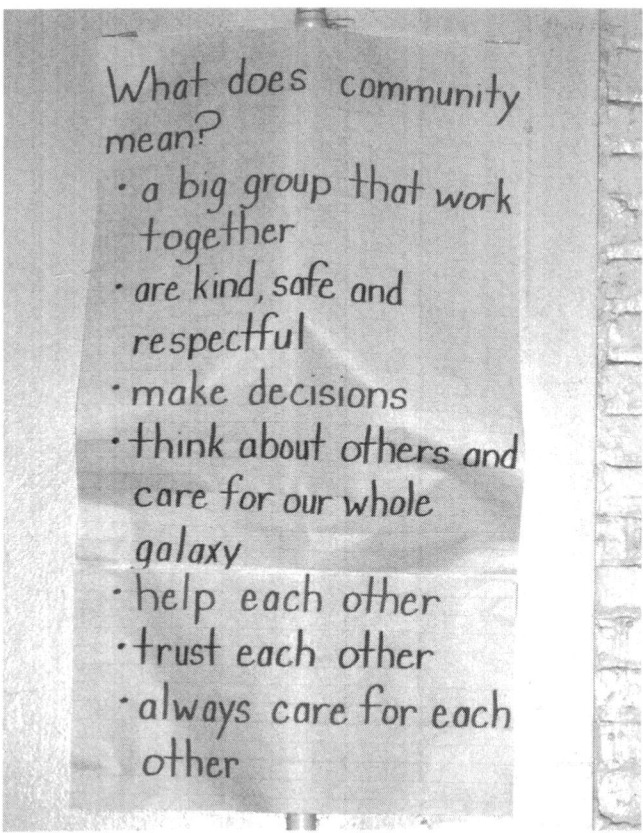

Photograph 2.4 What Does Community Mean?

could be placed on the walls of any classroom where I teach as social guarantees to all people who enter about the quality of our dialogue and the community that I will work to build. This is a space where:

- We feel physically and emotionally **safe.**
- We are **respectful** of everyone and their possessions.
- We treat others' ideas as of **equal** value.
- We learn from our **mis-takes** as well as our **successes.**

The circles in the Chapter 1 figures represent an *ideal* community where everyone feels safe, gives and receives respect, and all are treated as having an equal voice. In a circle no one is 'in front' of anyone else including the teacher. As a teacher I must provide direction and information, organize tasks, lead negotiations, and take executive decisions. But treating people's *ideas* as of equal value builds a more non-hierarchical community of equals rather than a group where the opinions or ideologies of some dominate the meaning-making.

In conversations, games, and other whole group activities, I want everyone to experience from our first interactions what it feels like to create together, reflect collectively, and inquire collaboratively into how *we* may make tasks more successful for all of us.

I intend to accept what people bring in the door. I affirm positive deeds and when there are negative comments or actions I name my values and seek agreement that though all voices are equally valued, everyone deserves respect and must feel safe in what is always a shared space. I make it clear that learning from and not repeating a mistake is what's most important. As people go off elsewhere, they are hopefully changed in knowing more about how to build a valued community.

I view students working in small groups, pairs, or as individuals as always in relation to whole group work. I mediate bringing people together, moving into smaller groups, and back to be together again where we can share and reflect collectively.

Pragmatically, working with the whole group I can read group dynamics, more easily provide clarification, gather ideas, and respond to individual concerns quickly, all within the context of group needs. In contrast, requiring students to work in small group 'teacher-less spaces' is much more socially demanding on young people: they have to provide for themselves the sort of direction that a teacher can supply as needed before they may have learned to do so with peers. At first, I only ask people to work in pairs or groups for a short time on focused tasks to generate ideas that may then be shared with the whole group; working collaboratively for longer periods of time requires that some students are able to be leaders.

Whole-group collaborative *decisions* that grow out of dialogue make visible how any group functions, those who tend to dominate or accommodate, and some individual needs and abilities. Dorothy Heathcote (1971/1984) argues that, "Group decision-taking is not easy but there is nothing quite so revealing of either the needs or the resources of any community" (p. 66). Early on, decisions, and reflections on 'how we collaborated', can be in response to questions that should be easily agreed, such as the following:

- Can we form a circle?
- Would you like to play a game?
- Can we walk around the room without touching anyone else?
- Can we agree to follow the rules of the game/classroom expectations?

More demanding polyphonic decisions that are responsive to different views in the group, such as negotiating among competing expectations on outcomes, can only be taken once some group trust and shared understanding has been established through whole-group collaborative tasks with shared goals.

Photograph 2.5 was taken in Megan Ballinger's freshman high school classroom in March 2012 when she was in her third year teaching in a high poverty Columbus urban high school. Though there may seem to be little that is remarkable about the photograph, it shows a stark comparison with how these fourteen-year-olds had participated six weeks previously when they had started the semester with her. At the time of the photograph only one person is absent, everyone in the room is sitting in a circle, they are listening to one another when they talk, and they are following Megan's lead as she introduces a text to read. In January, absenteeism was high, just sitting in a circle was resisted, respectful dialogue was not a norm, and many students resisted reading.

Megan had reorganized her physical space from the previous year so that now there were moveable chairs and tables at the edge, rather than chairs with wing arms crowding out the room. She could begin classes with chairs in a circle to play collaborative games like 'The Sun Shines'

Photograph 2.5 Whole-Group Collaborative Talk.

(see page 89) that remained a favorite. From sitting in a circle, they could move to crossing the circle, moving round the room, agreeing on expectations (posted on the wall, and visible above her head), sitting at tables to read or write with partners, dramatically perform events, and interpret collaboratively. All the while, Megan was listening to the young people, being patient, trying out different approaches, and just being there for the kids. The actual circle, through daily collaborative tasks, was gradually transformed into a predictable metaphorical circle of trust.

As trust begins to be established, I draw more attention to learning from our mis-takes as well as our successes. Learning from success can happen whenever we celebrate and reflect on why it was we were able to do what we did. However, groups, as well as individuals, not only need to know what they are good at, they also need to know how to improve by learning from mistakes.

I often use the spelling 'mis-take' rather than 'mistake' to highlight the idea that something we, or others, judge as an error most often just didn't quite 'fit' in the social context. Social mis-takes usually mean that in a different situation the same words or deeds could have been appropriate, just not here-and-now. As with a digital photograph we don't like, we can always do a 're-take.' Though it may take time, people can learn to be more generous in their initial interpretations of others' actions realizing that what they thought was intentional could be just another social mis-take.

With young children I will ask, "Can you try that again? Let's do a re-wind." For example, I've done this when people have run into one another. After acknowledging regret by saying "sorry," I ask children to literally move back to where they started and proceed. Young children tend to forgive and move on more quickly than those who are older. Reframing an individual's actions socially can help. In both Tracey's and Megan's classroom I have observed them use words that mean, 'It's OK to mess-up, I make mis-takes all the time. We have to forgive ourselves and one another and then move on to try again.'

Academic mis-takes are usually an error in skill or located in ignorance. Cheering to celebrate 'mess-ups' in skills when playing games is a public acknowledgement that mis-takes are 'normal' when we are learning to do anything new. Rather than expecting people to already know conceptual or informational knowledge, working through inquiry turns ignorance on its head: now not knowing is a virtue provided people know it's a norm that 'no honest question is a dumb question.'

The Language of Collaboration

Our values are apparent in the language we use. Using the language of collaboration with a group builds a lexicon of words and phrases as verbal tools that over time I may use to name actions that can become normative and thus affect the type of community we build. Peter Johnston (2004) summarizes a library of books on language and learning when he says, "Language creates realities and invites identities" (p. 9). The language and related experiences of working collaboratively invites participants to view their selves as part of a community.

Using "we" and "us" as much as possible rather than "I/you" conveys a sense of classroom life as an ongoing shared collaborative endeavor and frames experience as shared: *we* are working together to create meaning for *us*. Thus, rather than say, "I want you to get up and walk around," I begin to move and say, "Let's move around the room." I've seen children remind peers (and adults) to adjust their language choice and thus their relationship to a task: "The markers are ours, not yours, so we have to share."

Because participants must *choose* to work collaboratively, intend to enter imagined spaces, and accept agreed expectations, I give students as much choice as possible and use the language of choice. Thus, rather than give directives like "Get into pairs," I indicate respectful requests with language such as, "Please find a partner." Questions like "Can you find a partner?" may better reveal who tends to be left out. Our language can always invoke prior agreements, for example, "Remember that we agreed to work with people we don't usually work with, so can you find someone new and sit down facing each other."

Additionally, when I position a difficulty as "our problem" rather than "your problem," as well as celebrating achievements as "our" accomplishments, I am promoting an overall framing of community life as one of ongoing collaborative work in which we grapple with the inevitable challenges of working together while also honoring the rewards.

My Stance Shapes Classroom Community Values

There is much we cannot change about schooling but all teachers can draw on their core values, made visible in the words displayed in classroom expectations and in the language they use to address students, to adopt an intentional stance that makes their values visible in deeds and dialogue.

My stance affects what I expect from people, and from my self, my assumptions, and how I respond. My stance shapes my pedagogical practice and the emerging values of our community. Not only do I strive to respect all children, treat them as equals, and expect them to take risks and make mis-takes in spaces that feel safe to them, I have also cultivated what Herbert Kohl (1998) calls "the discipline of hope: the refusal to accept limits on what your students can learn or on what you, as a teacher, can do to facilitate learning" (p. 10). When I am hopeful I am changed in how I interpret what happens in classrooms and how I respond, plan, and dialogue.

Megan, as I noted above, has embraced the struggle to create a more hopeful, egalitarian classroom community. She stresses the need to accept students as they are, yet she also works with students to create the sort of community they desire while being realistic about the unavoidable challenges (Enciso et al., 2011).

> In our classroom the kids have a chance to create an alternative type of community. Their perception of their home community is pretty negative: drugs, crack addicts on the corner; everyone has experienced the death of someone close to them. Almost all of the kids come from single-parent-, or no-parent, homes and they talk about their friends as their family. Whether it's because their moms are working long-hours or maybe strung out on drugs most kids are being raised by siblings or grandparents. Getting them to care for others beyond their friends is my biggest obstacle. Collaborative games and drama activities have been key in the past two years for learning about including everyone in the community. But a community has to be built from one class session to the next.

In a never-ending string of conversations students begin to learn to own their behaviors and their choices. One week into the 2011–12 school year Megan was reflecting on how she was trying to help her students recognize that they all have to be active and intentional to create community:

> Like last year, the students in each of my three classes say the same thing: they want a respectful, safe classroom community. I respond, 'Can you *do* respect? Can you *show us* what it looks like?' Right now many of them are watching to see if they can be honest with me. Many of them have siblings or friends who had me last year and that helps. I've written down and put up the expectations we've come up with. I say we all need to agree to them, and *do* them. I ask them to call me out if I'm not following our rules. No cell phone use applies to me too. So does apologizing when I make a mistake. I want them to know that we all make mistakes. I'm a big fan of being fallible! Most important, I want them to know that building relationships based on mutual respect is key; that we are all equal in this classroom. But if I want them to respect and trust me then I have to show that we all matter, that I respect, and trust them, that I genuinely care about all of them, will listen to them, and want to help them if I can.

Ensemble Tasks Build a Collaborative Community

If collaborating with others in tasks are the steps of community building then participation in ensemble tasks is the dance of classroom collaboration.

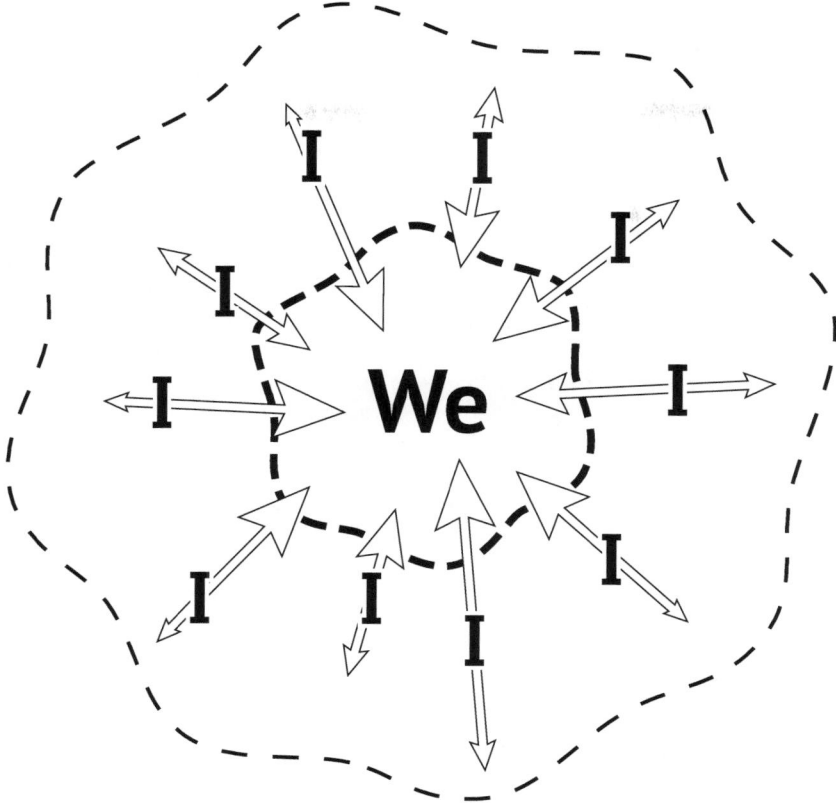

Figure 2.1   Community Tensions Between Acting as Individuals and as a Group.

Ensemble tasks build a strong collaborative community as people learn to trust one another, take risks, and create understanding together.

People have to *choose* to act as a group; they must want to collaborate to achieve something they value. Figure 2.1 illustrates the ongoing tension in any community between actions by individual 'I's' to create (or undermine) a sense of a collective 'we' (represented by the inner dotted wavy line). The stronger the sense of cohesion, of working collaboratively and collectively across tasks as a 'we,' the more a group can be regarded as working together as an ensemble. Whereas the figures in Chapter 1 represent an ideal classroom space, Figure 2.1 represents the 'permeable' nature of an actual classroom culture open both to productive ideas and to distractions from beyond the school (the outer wavy line). The inner wavy line represents the ensemble sense of working collaboratively as a 'we' rather than as a collection of individual 'I's.'

Whereas each person in a classroom community may or may not participate in some community tasks, ensemble tasks include everyone. Michael Boyd, the artistic director of the Royal Shakespeare Company (RSC), is speaking of the cast of a play working as an ensemble to perform. If he had said "perform or play" he could be speaking of using the learning modes I introduced in Chapter 1:

> We operate as an ensemble; a group who learn from each other, and a group that gets stronger as we get to know and trust one another. You cannot perform a play without relying on each other.
> (Royal Shakespeare Company, 2010, p. 8)

Geoffrey Streatfeild, an RSC actor, explains the social value and learning potential of working as an ensemble over time. He's talking about working on the floor of a rehearsal room. However, he could be describing (at their best moments) Tracey's and Megan's active, safe, respectful classroom community of equals where young people are able to move around, work on their feet as well as at a desk, and learn from one another:

> Our ever-growing trust enables us to experiment, improvise and rework on the floor with an astonishing freedom and confidence. This ensemble is a secure environment without ever being a comfort zone. All of us are continually challenging ourselves and being inspired by those around us to reach new levels in all aspects of our work.
> (Quoted in Neelands, 2009, p. 183)

Whatever the age of the people I work with, after one or two sessions they will have experienced beginning to work and learn together as an ensemble. Though the groups don't stage and perform plays they do begin to trust one another, author understanding collaboratively, and hopefully inspire as well as challenge peers via active and dramatic tasks that present and explore the possible meanings of texts and topics.

Core Dimensions of Ensemble Tasks

To work as an ensemble, participants must choose to participate in the same time and space, led by one or more group members who everyone agrees will take on a leadership role, using appropriate tools, in collaborative meaningful tasks with shared goals that the group cares about.

Jonothan Neelands (2009), the internationally known drama educator and scholar who has worked extensively with the RSC, has described working as an ensemble as a model of democratic "living together in the world" (p. 184). Stressing that creating an ensemble requires "the art of togetherness" he usefully lists the following as key common characteristics of ensemble-based learning as he has observed the process in rehearsal rooms and drama classrooms:

> the uncrowning of the power of the teacher/director; a mutual respect among the players; a shared commitment to truth; a sense of the intrinsic value of theatre making [or dramatic pedagogy]; a shared absorption in the intrinsic process of dialogic and social meaning-making.
>
> (Neelands, 2010, p. 139)

In Table 2.1 I present my similar conceptualization of the core dimensions of ensemble tasks that build community. As noted above, I regard mutual respect, along with safety and equality, as broad community values. The table is structured as answers to the widely used '5 Ws and an H' questions along with examples from Chapter 1 (*Jack and Jill*; *Brave Margaret*; and the adults' work on the final day of the class) as well as examples and advice on playing ensemble games.

The wider the availability of *collaborative* tools the more varied the possibilities are for engaging everyone in making meaning in tasks with shared goals shifting among a variety of active and dramatic learning modes; at times people may use different mediating tools to achieve the same goal as they play, perform, reflect, and inquire. For example, the preschool children could sing, and use pails, blocks, band-aids, bandages, and stethoscopes to dialogue, imagine, create, encounter, and inquire into how they might resolve problems in the world of *Jack and Jill*; as some talked with Justin-as-Jack others investigated how to use medical supplies.

The preschool children joyfully participated in collaborative experiences of going up the hill and helping Jack, culminating in a dramatized singing of the *Jack and Jill* rhyme shown in Photograph 2.6. Their trust is evident as they sit with adults they'd just met ninety minutes previously.

Megan Ballinger's high school students shown in Photograph 2.7 are all involved. For five ninety-minute sessions the students have had a shared goal: exploring events in a factual story, *The Other Wes Moore* (Moore, 2011), the first book that, to Megan's knowledge, these young people have asked to take home. Their inquiry question, written on the wall is this: Should Wes Moore be eligible for parole? He was convicted of murder a decade ago and has been in prison ever since. The students had been collectively shifting among dramatic performances and reflections on the narrative event when Wes's mother discovers drugs hidden under his mattress. Six weeks into the semester the students are fairly comfortable using the tools of creating a scene with chairs and tables as well as brief tableaux that may move or speak. The students could make

Table 2.1 Core Dimensions of Ensemble Tasks

Core dimensions	Examples from Chapter 1	Examples and advice on playing ensemble games
WHAT are we actually going to *do*? **Dialogue** in **collaborative words/deeds** using active and/or dramatic learning modes	Singing together; pretending together; playing cross the circle; creating a shared list of how to justify this work to administrators	Whatever collaborative game(s) you choose to play initially keep them simple, enjoyable, and non-competitive
WHY are we doing this? **Shared** longer-term **goals** (or shorter-term objectives) we care about	Finding out how to help someone get better; working out how best to defeat an enemy; inquiring into how to build community and how to use active and dramatic approaches in the classroom	Games have clear, achievable, intrinsic shared goals; if the young people like a game then they care about the goal; achieving a curriculum objective is less important initially
WHEN is this happening? *Choose* to engage at the **same time**	Preschool children getting up to pretend together; middle level students stepping forward to raise their arms; adults finding partners	Games are structured play that you do together for enjoyment—the young people have to enjoy and want to play; informal repetitions of pretend actions, especially with young children, have a 'game-like' feel, e.g. repeatedly falling down together and giggling, hiding and finding, or chasing and catching
WHERE are we doing this? **Shared bounded space**	Anywhere in the room except near tables; anywhere in the circle; on chairs	Games need bounded space: a circle, lines on the floor, chairs to show somewhere 'safe', the whole room except … e.g. under tables
WHO is taking the lead? **Distributed leadership** among teachers and, at times, young people	Peer director for group creating still image; teacher; other adults	You need to lead the game. When volunteers' ideas are used you make it clear that others will be able to lead
HOW might we do this? Multiple appropriate **collaborative tools**	All done together: talking, moving, listening, watching, singing, drawing, using objects (e.g. chairs, pails, band-aids), meeting adult-in-role	Moving in space relative to others, talking briefly to lots of people, and listening are essential tools to introduce initially

Photograph 2.6 Singing Together.

Photograph 2.7 A Task with a Shared Goal.

meaning, as the photograph indicates, through the mediating tools of dialogue, standing, moving-as-if-a-character, reading text, moving in the space-as-if-in-Wes'-bedroom, use a bag-as-box-for-drugs and a table-as-bed, ask questions, refer to their lives out of school, and laugh.

Out of sight, there are two girls sitting out working independently, with Megan's knowledge. I don't know the reasons but she did. Aaron, the boy sitting in the corner, is watching and listening. Five minutes later he is on his feet dramatically engaged. Crystal, the girl standing, had returned to school that day after a suspension. She has paused in the middle of performing as Wes' mother. Marquis, the boy leaning back, is a leader in the class who, just before the photograph was taken, had been in the role of Wes.

As people choose to participate in ensemble tasks with common goals and relate to each other they achieve what is not possible when working alone. In dramatic learning, young people in groups author understanding as they create and reflect on *shared* experiences of fictional or factual worlds.

Collaboration in an ensemble goes beyond that of the well-known acronym TEAM: 'together each achieves more.' Collaboration is not synonymous with cooperation when one person helps another to complete his or her individualized task, though the former includes the latter. As Keith Sawyer (2007) in *Group Genius* confirmed in his analysis of dramatic and musical ensembles, working collaboratively people are smarter in the sense of being more creative and innovatively accomplish more than the sum of each individual's achievement.

Figure 2.1 illustrates how working as an ensemble requires that people shift from framing their selves only as individual 'I's' separated from an experience of the 'groupness' of the group, to positioning their selves, additionally, as a collaborative 'we.' The double-headed arrows suggest how each person feels pulled 'out' at the same time as they feel pulled 'in' to collaborating with others. The more commitment people have to a common goal the more engaged they are they likely to feel in a collaborative task.

The potential for working as an ensemble is being undercut whenever the perceived task feels less interesting or appealing to individuals than any of the potential distractions (for example, noises outside the room, actual or perceived negative comments by peers, memories of recent events, or expectations about what will happen later). For some, real life may be undermining their ability to participate (for example, an argument in the hallway, a sick parent at home, or a late night).

People feel pulled *in* to working as an ensemble when they experience a felt shared *need* to work collaboratively, as the high school students were with Megan. Weeks before such socially demanding work, the students had collaboratively played ensemble games.

Ensemble Games

Initially, collaborative tasks in a group unused to working together may be very brief. Playing collaborative games in circles are powerful community-building tasks that can be used very productively early on and throughout the year. Games can be adapted to introduce themes, characters, or situations from whatever narrative a teacher is intending to explore. A great advantage of games is that once a group knows a game, everyone knows what to do, including me! Those who might baulk at a more open-ended task may feel safe in bounded and predictable tasks like games. Below I list games that I've played with many groups of young people of school age. I've added examples of how to use games with *Macbeth* (explored in Chapter 4).

Collaborative Games Played in a Circle

The Sun Shines On All Those Who ...

This game establishes commonality, mixes up who sits with whom, and requires brief movement from a circle of chairs. The leader, who has no chair, initiates by completing the title, e.g. "The sun shines on all those who like ice cream." All who agree find a new seat. The person left in the middle continues the game by completing the phrase. Another name for the game is **The Big Wind Blows On All Those Who ...** A variation is that the person in the middle can tell a brief relevant story. You can reference generic events, relationships, or actions that are also in the world of the text or topic you are about to, or are already, studying. For example, with *Macbeth*, "The sun shines on all those who have been a leader ... have held a dagger ... who knows someone who walks in their sleep." Another variation is to alternate with 'darker' statements that complete "The moon shines on all those who ..." know someone who's been in a war. **Cross the Circle** is a dramatic playing variation where people cross "as if you are ..." e.g. briefly moving as a character in an event from a narrative.

Social Atom

This game shows commonality and difference. Questions are asked in a similar way to 'The Sun Shines.' However, people move closer to the center of the circle the more they agree. Questions can relate to narratives, e.g. "Who thinks Macbeth is a good leader?"

Zip, Zap, Zop

Standing in a circle, this game establishes brief eye contact and generates energy and communal laughter. The words are said in order: one participant begins by saying the word Zip and passing energy, accompanied by sliding one hand on top of another, to point at someone else in the circle who now says Zap. You could play the game in two circles if necessary or use people's names early on in the year. The words and movement can be changed to key words from a text (for example, soldier, friend, traitor from *Macbeth*) and/or appropriate movements (for example, pointing a sword as a soldier.

Red Ball, Yellow Ball

This game builds on the previous one. It requires more focused listening, concentration, the use of names, and the practice of saying 'thank you.' An imaginary red ball is introduced by the teacher. The ball is only 'passed' after calling a name and establishing eye contact: "John, red ball." The person who 'catches' the ball thanks the 'thrower' and continues by passing it to another person in the circle: "Thanks, Mary. Peter, red ball." Once the red ball is being passed smoothly a yellow ball is introduced. More balls or objects may be introduced that could be significant in a text being studied—for example, with *Macbeth*, a dagger, a crown, and a letter.

Count to Ten

This game focuses energy and develops group listening skills and a feeling of gathered stillness. The object of the game is to count to ten. There is no eye contact among participants who may lie down. If two people speak at once we have to begin again at one. As a variation, significant words from a text can be spelled out letter-by-letter, for example M-A-C-B-E-T-H.

Building Community Takes Time and Commitment

Building community takes time and commitment. I cannot build a community alone: the young people have to become committed to working with me (and vice versa). The more we work as a productive ensemble, the more we establish a collaborative supportive community.

A classroom community must have established rituals and trusted procedures that students can help lead. Responsive Classroom publications are filled with ideas and strategies for building community by integrating social and academic learning. As young people take on more shared responsibility for daily classroom life, with the teacher they create a social and cultural classroom context for the students to take on more individual responsibility for their own learning (www.responsiveclassroom.org). These ideas can be applied in any classroom. Paula Denton and Roxann Kriete (2000) in *The First Six Weeks of School* lay out how to establish routines for "morning meeting," ideas for songs and greetings, suggestions for how to handle transitions within and between classrooms, and a process for drawing on young people's "hopes and dreams" to create shared classroom expectations and a vision for the classroom community.

Denton and Kriete believe that, "The ideal classroom [learning] moments reflect freedoms, choices, and responsibilities which are the result of students' ability to govern themselves—to draw upon individual self-controls that will enable the whole group to function smoothly" (p. 3).

Of course, no real group of students ever does run 'smoothly' all the time. Communities are made up of people; they are not well-oiled machines. Lorraine Gaughenbaugh[1] reflected in March 2011 on the shared journey in her third-grade classroom of students, aged eight to nine, becoming more self-managing and self-regulating (her teaching is described in Chapter 4). Lorraine's suburban classroom had nearly half of the children classified as economically disadvantaged, with six students who were English Language Learners. She talked not only of the significance for community building of playing collaborative games from the first day of school but also of how people's collaborative learning affected their subsequent individual action:

> The students probably think we are just playing games, but it is more purposeful than that. We are learning to work collaboratively, share ideas and work towards a common goal. Collaborative play was not easy at the beginning of the year. I've had students who were upset or angry when a game did not seem to go their way. We had discussions on how games are played and that there are no losers. We discussed how the choices we make if things don't go your way are your choices. Now, six months into the year, their participation shows how much the children have moved from being often self-centered to thinking and acting more as a community.

Leadership in the Classroom Community

I once worked under a principal who believed that students' respect for male teachers pivoted on the wearing of ties. He would not have understood Robert Greenleaf's (1977) belief that "the only authority deserving one's allegiance is that which is freely and knowingly granted by the led to the leader in response to, and in proportion to, the clearly evident servant stature of the leader" (p. 10). Servant leaders are people who "care for both persons and institutions and who are determined to make their caring count" (p. 330). Though they "act on what they believe," servant leaders are also "constantly examining the assumptions they live by. Thus, their leadership by example sustains trust" (pp. 329–330).

Put another way, we must earn the respect and trust of our students by primarily acting and being there for them both as individuals and as members of our classroom community. Further, dialogue with young people must at times focus on how any one person's actions, including those of the teacher leader, affect and are affected by our shared values made visible in classroom community expectations and our actions. As Neelands (2009) puts it, as an ensemble leader "there is a distribution of the power of the teacher in favour of a more democratic and demanding autonomy" (p. 184).

Engaging in active or dramatic tasks may feel risky, especially in high school. Photograph 2.8 is significant because it illustrates Marquis in a leadership role changing the mood of the classroom as he brings vitality to the room and meaning to a text while creating a space where it feels safer for others to do the same. He was the boy who most often took on a very visible leadership role in Megan's classroom. At the moment the photograph was taken, five minutes into the session (when the next three photographs were also taken), for about ten seconds Marquis walked across the room as if he were a confident Wes Moore on the street. His *walking-as-a-character* action was transformative. It was pivotal in encouraging others to participate and collaboratively create the event when the robbery took place in which, it was alleged, Wes Moore participated.

Photograph 2.8 Walking-as-a-Character.

In Photograph 2.8 Marquis has the text extract in his hand that they have just read. The boy behind him in the photograph remained seated throughout the session, watching but not volunteering ideas. But ten minutes later, when Photographs 2.9 and 2.10 were taken, as Megan directed and students *narrated actions*, nearly all students were actively dramatizing the event.

What would not have been apparent to any visitor on that day was the fact that two months previously Marquis had been one of the most disruptive students in the class. However, toward the end of January, when Megan began to use more dramatic approaches, he had begun to realize that in their classroom he could move and talk provided he did so in a way that was appropriate for any character in any text they were reading. As Megan's actions repeatedly demonstrated her stance of respect and equality, and as she led tasks that were consistently emotionally safe for everyone, Marquis transformed his stance and thus how he framed the classroom and his position relative to Megan, his peers, and the content. Almost overnight he moved from being oppositional to being an advocate for participating in tasks that were active and dramatic. Though he

Photograph 2.9 Small Group Dramatic Performance.

Photograph 2.10 Megan Directs When Needed.

would still lose focus, and could blurt out what was in his mind, or get 'off task,' he would be apologetic when Megan, or his peers, called him on acting inappropriately.

Megan began to create the trusting basis for relationships with all students so that they could choose to participate in tasks that granted her authority as leader. When people feel emotionally safe in a caring, inclusive community they are ready to take risks. As Bob Fecho (2011) stresses in *Teaching for the Students*, "the idea is not to create classrooms that are *free from risk*, but classrooms where it is *safe* to take risks" (p. 114). Students' readiness to take risks, make mis-takes, and thus test community are prerequisites for them taking on responsibility for their learning and moving into leadership roles.

Testing Community

For the French philosopher, Jacques Rancière, a community is always a "community of equals" (Ranciere, 2007, p. 87). Similarly, for Bakhtin, in polyphonic dialogue each person is a subject with a voice to be heard and answered. A child's ideas are no less important than an adult's.

For Rancière, the inevitable community tension between 'we' and 'I/you' is never resolved. Acting collaboratively in an ensemble as 'we' does not mean that individual 'I's' acting in relation to other 'you's' disappear. Rather, as Rancière stresses, the "members of a community are all equally capable of being an 'I', and it thus creates a new kind of 'Us', an aesthetic or dissensual community" (quoted in Davis, 2010, p. 156). Instead of seeking a consensus that ignores or minimizes disagreement, a dissensual community embraces the potential and power of difference and dissonance in both the possible meanings of a topic explored and in the process of engaging in tasks.

If we aspire to be a community of equals then the meaning and practices of community cannot be stable. Rather, what it means for *us* to be a community is different from any other community and our understanding is repeatedly tested in an ongoing struggle between any previous shared or implicit agreement based on our belief of what community looks like in action and new meaning that emerges through polyphonic dialogue revealing how we are actually working together in current tasks. Using Megan's phrase, we have to "do community" not just talk abstractly about it. For example, when I was a teacher of eight- and nine-year-old children in a classroom meeting at the beginning of one year we agreed that people should use the markers that they "needed." When Joanie had twenty markers, one of each color, on her desk, leaving others without any available, we had to meet again to reinterpret "my need" as always in relation to "our needs." She had to learn how one person's actions always have consequences for everyone in a community.

A community of equals is always "insubstantial" and "completely determined by the contingency and resolve of its enactment" (Rancière, 2007, p. 87). Community is never 'achieved' since people only experience "dialogic moments of community" when, for example, "a word out of place or an ill-judged assertion may open the door to a fresh testing of community ... in the juncture between the violence of a new beginning the invocation of something already said, something already inscribed" (ibid., p. 91).

In other words, in genuine dialogue the meaning of 'our community' is continually being performed and forged experientially and reflectively, in-the-moment. As young people participate in tasks they are both implicitly affirming their support for community norms while also sometimes testing them and extending their individual and shared understanding of what it means to collaborate.

Community is tested when people work in small groups. Without direct leadership by the teacher, students reveal how much they have learned to collaborate with peers. Lorraine provides an example.

For one task I assigned a group of three students to work together. Their goal was to dramatize two lines of text from *A Midsummer Night's Dream* that we had been working on. The groups had to collaborate, decide how to act out these lines and how to incorporate the words, and make sure that everyone was included. One potentially challenging group of three had Tara (who is very domineering, often has anger issues, feels she doesn't have many friends, and many find it difficult to work with her), a boy who is very active and has difficulty staying on task, and a rather shy girl who exhibits very little self-confidence. Amazingly this group collaborated really well and performed their interpretation of the lines of text. Afterwards, Tara told me that they had worked well together and that she had enjoyed it. When I asked if she would have chosen to work with them she admitted that she wouldn't have. However they did work as a group again subsequently.

Rancière stresses that it's moments of dissension that test community: whether or not one person's question will be heard or how another person's reaction will be judged by peers or teacher. As Rancière notes, and as teachers we all know, such testing moments may become heated. How people handle those tests affects the *quality* of community actually built, rather than any ideal community we might wish for. Lorraine's example continues.

That same week another student, Kim, showed her generosity to the group. One boy didn't have a part in a little performance we were putting together. Kim offered him the part she was assigned. However, this boy had already tried that part and wanted to play a different role. So, Kim found someone to take her part so that this boy could switch roles. She generously made sure everyone was content and had a part to play in the group. Another activity had students sharing roles to perform a short scene from *Midsummer Night's Dream*. One boy, who struggles with reading and doesn't always make good behavior choices, stepped into the role of Egeus, the angry father. He performed it superbly with his facial expressions and the use of his whole body to interpret this character. He was admired and appreciated by the class. He heard positive comments, where before, he had mostly heard negative remarks from his peers.

The generosity that Lorraine describes is one significant dimension of a more complex understanding of community building.

Complexity in Community Building

Whereas Figure 2.1 represents an ideal ensemble, Figure 2.2 is a more complex image of collaborative action in a group that is on its way to

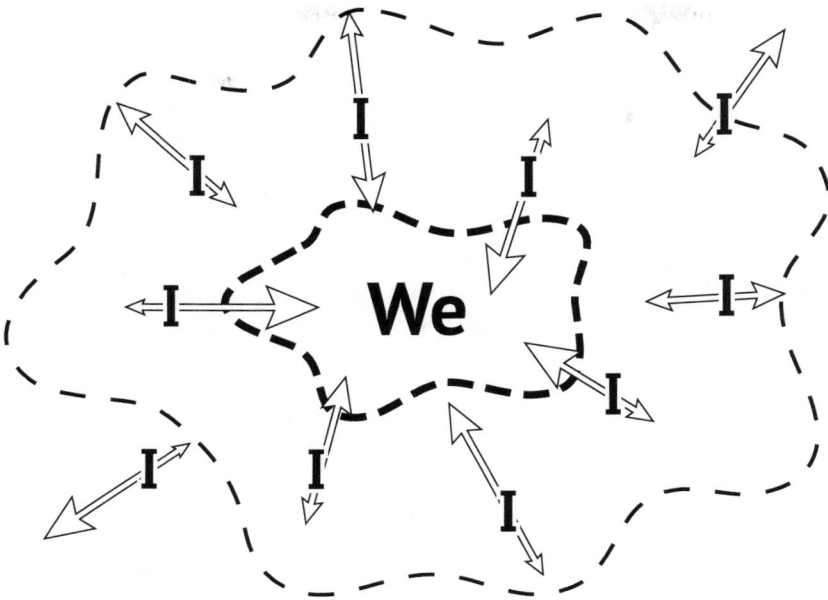

Figure 2.2 People Choose to Act as a Group.

working more often as an ensemble. Despite the inevitable experiences of dissonance in any community, people have to *choose* to act as a group; they must want to work together to achieve something they value and as necessary work through difficulties in collaborating. Figure 2.2 illustrates the ongoing tension in any community between actions by individual 'I's' to create (or undermine) a sense of a collective 'we' (represented by the inner dotted wavy line).

In collaborative tasks some people will feel more at the center while others will feel more on the edge. Ideally, across time everyone not only feels but also knows that they are valued for what they bring to the group in the various tasks of community living.

When people participate and engage in collaborative community-oriented tasks each feels, and generates, a pull 'into' a shared action stronger than feelings pulling them 'out' of the task, and perhaps the classroom (represented by the double-headed arrows). I find Bakhtin's (1981) concept of centripetal and centrifugal forces pulling in opposite directions useful for recognizing that collaborative tasks both demand energy from, and create energy with, everyone in the group in order to have a shared sense of coherence to counter-balance potential feelings of disarray.

When people commit to achieving common goals in sequences of tasks over time the stronger their sense of 'we are in this together' as they return to the classroom each day. Cumulatively they become more engaged with the ongoing academic project alongside the community-building project of learning to live together. Yet, especially early on in the life of every community, some students may barely have their minds in the room, or may not be physically present (represented by the arrow outside the outer dotted line).

People engaged in collaborative tasks have what I think of as a 'we are acting for us' stance toward the group. In other words, actions, goals, intended outcomes, and the language that sustains and interprets tasks, are understood by everyone to have a collective meaning greater than how any one individual understands their role or position. Within collective activities people's individual or small group tasks contribute to the overall purpose. For example, in Tracey's classroom different people designed, sketched, painted, wrote about, assembled, and then mounted the mural on the truck. And the mural was only one outcome in a multi-faceted complex project involving hundreds of people overall. The same 'nested' principle applies every year in Tracey's classroom from day one in daily tasks as well as in relation to any extensive project: one task is always understood in relation to sequences of tasks that are collectively harnessing individual energy to build 'our' community as we explore topics collaboratively.

Being Generous to the Group

As the teacher-leader I must plan and initiate projects whatever their size. I must be generous enough to keep on giving to the group with an 'I am acting for us' stance. Rather than act for myself, I bring ideas, materials, texts, and tools to a group in tasks that open up different learning modes for students to achieve goals 'we' care about. At its heart, being generous is an act of love. Though I want students to take on generous leadership roles as well, I must take the lead in establishing a stance of generosity.

Caring for Others

When people are 'on the edge' of the group, for whatever reason, as teacher-leaders we must care for them as individuals. Caring is rooted in the principle of equality. Every human being needs care at different times and children are no different. I stand *with* people because I care enough to listen non-judgmentally to discover what individuals need. And I try to provide that need if possible in relation to the needs of others in the community, including my own. I want everyone in the group to know that my intention is always 'I am acting for you.' I want to be students' equal in dialogue and their ally in life. I do not want to be positioned as the enemy. Despite the struggle, I want to support people who feel on the edge of the classroom so that they feel able to move back in to participate in some way.

Including Everyone

Sometimes a person is on the margins having felt excluded from activities in or out of the room. Or it may be that they have an idea that has not been heard. In either case they may need my advocacy on their behalf so that they can be heard, or my support to assist them to participate more fully. This is inclusion: acting with the group to accommodate individual needs or ideas that had not been included. Making tasks more likely to be inclusive is another way to approach inclusion, which is rooted in equality of intelligence: if everyone is considered to have an equal voice when the group makes decisions then everyone deserves to be heard. However, inclusion goes further than equality. Attention to equity requires that I believe each person should feel that when 'we are acting for you' we are ready to change our actions based in an awareness of your individual experience, knowledge, or need that connects you with life beyond our group.

Teaching and Community Building

Having grown up in the divided and increasingly violent society of Northern Ireland in the 1950s and 1960s I intuitively knew much about what I did *not* want to experience in a community: **inequality,**[2] segregation, discrimination, and abuse of privilege resulting in the **inequitable** distribution of public resources (for example, housing). The schools I attended were academically rigorous but socially echoed the wider cultural norms of **exclusion** at the root of wider division, hierarchies, oppression, mistrust, and sometimes fear. After my first few years of schooling, I experienced all-male classrooms through high school in communities largely devoid of an ethic of **care.**

Dewey (1938) would have characterized much of my schooling and community experiences as "mis-educative" since they were often "arresting or distorting the growth of further experiences" (p. 25). Yet, my reflections and inquiry into those experiences have been "educative" because they've been "directed towards the ends of growth and development" (p. 25). In other words, like anyone else, I can learn from my own and other people's mis-takes and successes.

Though the two secondary schools in England where I had my first jobs as a teacher were not divided along religious lines, as school communities they were only marginally more **caring, inclusive, equal,** or **equitable.** Some teachers were open to sharing ideas about innovative practice though many talked *at* students in classrooms that were physically and philosophically closed. There were tales in one staff room of the 'good old days' when corporal punishment was allowed. Testing had been used to categorize and 'stream' children while the voices of the 'less able' were mostly ignored or diminished.

Table 2.2 The Language of Community Building

Dimensions of community building	Examples of classroom expectations/rules	Key teacher language	Examples
COLLABORATING "We are acting to make meaning for us"	Be respectful; be responsible	"We ... for us" "agree" "Yes, and ..."	"Can we agree to ...?" "What does that mean for us?" "Yes, and what else could we do?"
BEING GENEROUS "I am acting for us"	Share as much as possible; take risks; thank people	"share" "add on" "let go" "thank you"	"Does anyone have another idea to add on for us to consider?" "How could you help us?" "Thanks for sharing those ideas." "Can you let go of that idea for now?"
CARING those ideas "I am acting for you"	Be safe; be kind; be honest	"How are you feeling?"	"Can you give us a thumbs up/down/ across response?" "Does anyone have a concern or a reservation?" "How can we/I help you?"
INCLUDING "We are acting for you"	Include and don't exclude others; no put downs; let others help you	"Who have we not heard from?" "Please" "How do you think X is feeling?"	"Has anyone not had a chance to speak?" "Did you hear what [name] just said?"

In stark contrast, a decade after I first entered the classroom full-time, as an elementary teacher for two years in Ohio, I was fortunate to be welcomed into a school community with an 'informal' (i.e. child-initiated project-based) philosophy where I grew exponentially as a teacher. Highland Park Elementary in Grove City had multi-age classrooms, minimal testing, frequent sharing within and among classes, a norm of mutual teacher support, and a practice of communal **care** and **inclusion** of all children who were very visible in the open-plan building. It was a norm in the school that children's voices counted as **equal** to adults; they would frequently be quoted in staff meetings and consulted about decisions.

In my first year there was a girl who hid under a table in my classroom for her first two days snapping at people like a dog. When asked, colleagues were ready with helpful advice but no one demonized her. Previously I had first glimpses of what a school community, with my self in a leadership role, might feel like during my six years as an English teacher in England. All involved dramatic art. Working with young people who often challenged me, as a young teacher I struggled with issues that other novices did: control, student participation, and selecting content. At that time I didn't realize they were aspects of foundational questions: What tasks engage students in learning? Why do students choose to participate? What is an adult's role? Two ensemble examples stand out, as I look back, one fleeting, one prolonged.

In my first year of teaching I had the sense to follow my intuition, charter a bus, and take my challenging class of fourteen-year-olds to London to see Ian McKellen and Judi Dench in *Macbeth*. This was an act of **generosity** since I did all the arrangements and covered some of the incidental costs. From a pedagogy viewpoint, more importantly the trip was a bold act of **inclusion** on my part. The experience of taking the students to the theatre changed the dynamic of our relationships without demanding any change on their part, except cooperation on the trip. Just 'hanging out' with students meant I could get to know them better. Though I didn't actually do much except listen I expect some felt I **cared** enough to chat with them about life outside school. In terms of the academic curriculum, by extending the 'classroom' to include a bus trip to the theatre, the play narrative and Elizabethan language came alive for the students who were now eager to talk in depth with me, and with one another, about murder, monarchs, and war. If only I had known what to do next!

The school theatrical productions that I later directed as Head of Drama gave me a clue. As Eileen Landay and Kurt Wootton (2012) discovered in their meticulous analysis of classroom staged performances within the ArtsLiteracy Project at Brown University I too came to recognize that, "When students feel they are in a supportive community they are willing to focus, work hard, and take risks" (p. 19).

I found that young people of all ages will be diligent, learn to **collaborate** with people they don't know or may not previously have liked very much, and participate over time in demanding tasks in order to explore and dramatize a narrative if it has characters and situations with whom they identify and **care** about. And they will take direction from an adult when they want to achieve a shared goal important to them, their friends, and/or the families who will come to applaud and cheer their achievements.

I **included** anyone in the cast or crew who remained committed to the rehearsal schedule. Additionally, I won an **equity** argument with administrators that those few students who had been excluded from other activities because of minor infractions should not be removed from the production.

My most successful performance text was improvised from a nineteenth-century history of the area of Bristol where Kingsfield School was located, which had been researched by an amateur historian; many historical characters shared names with families in the local community whose children attended the school. The places where fairs, robberies, and trials had happened were still identifiable on the map. We created an ensemble that I led, but where every voice counted **equally** as we improvised text and made performance choices. For three nights, to packed houses, nearly 100 young people aged 11–18 dramatized and staged some of the comedy and tragedy in the lives of the members of an infamous ensemble, The Cock Road Gang.

When I first saw *Three Looms Waiting* (Heathcote, Smedley, & Eyre, 1972), a BBC film about the pedagogy of Dorothy Heathcote, I was captivated and intrigued by her use of drama in ordinary classrooms. How could she work one day with young offenders and the next day with 'mentally disabled' adults and children yet have everyone so active and deeply engaged? How was she able to use drama so that people would have conversations about life-and-death issues? Could I learn to teach like that?

Community Building is Possible With Any Group

Aged nearly thirty, I first experienced a transformational educational community when I was one of sixteen people from the UK, the US, Australia, and New Zealand who spent a year together at Newcastle University on Dorothy Heathcote's drama in education master's course. Unlike most college courses, Dorothy's ran full-time and all-day. Alongside her we planned, reflected on, and wrote about our dramatic pedagogy. If she was in town, Dorothy was with us either in seminars or in schools. At the beginning of our course, we began to build a community among ourselves that soon extended to **include** unconventional students when we taught for a week in Earl's House hospital and school for adults and children diagnosed with cognitive disabilities. There we met a few of the adult 'patients' I had seen on the BBC film. One was John, whom the nurses told us had been eagerly awaiting Dorothy's annual return visit. He greeted her with joy as she beamed at him.

At the end of the week John showed his anger. More accurately I believe he enjoyed experiencing and playing with feeling righteous anger. At one dramatic moment he commanded the other adult residents, those who sat in armchairs and wheelchairs as well as those who had risen to stand with him, to hide a baby blanket bundled up as if round an infant.

In apparent distress Dorothy had just given him the blanket as she pointed at me. As if I was King Herod, with a regal-looking shawl round my shoulders, I stood nearby waving my grandfather's blackthorn stick. In a gruff voice and with a sneer I had practiced that morning, I looked around as I asked, "Where are the babies?" Holding the bundle, John hid behind one of the residents who moved to block me. Then Dorothy brought my colleagues to life as the musical and dancing procession that minutes earlier had captivated the residents. In our narrative this was the entourage of the brightly attired 'Three Queens' following the Magi, their husbands. John turned to the procession, pointed at me, and shouted defiantly, "Don't help him. He wants the babies!" As the music and movement ceased other residents made sympathetic noises and gestures. As Herod, I slunk off. When Dorothy indicated that the percussion music could resume, many of the residents smiled making sounds as they joined in the celebration. We ended the session eating a snack while we all sang and then hummed *Star of Wonder* that many residents remembered. As we left, a woman whom I had seen every day rocking back and forth apparently in her own world, looked up, struggled to wave her hand, and carefully mouthed the word, "Goodbye."

I doubt that John, or any of the less mobile residents, knew that, in imagination, we had collectively stepped into the world of the Biblical story of the Massacre of the Innocents. However, John had again experienced taking a leadership role with his peers, alongside Dorothy, me, and other visiting teachers, as we had collaboratively created a valuable outcome: an emotionally powerful dramatic encounter from a narrative that transformed their lives for a few hours.

As visitors we had been teaching, but not telling. We had brought **inclusive** energy, experientially appealing images using the arts of music, movement, story, and drama to awaken the interest of people whose lives were often monotonous. And we had dialogued with people who had limited verbal language abilities. The adults from our course accepted and extended John's energy, ideas, and capacity, as well as those of the others who had become engaged. Some sat with 'patients' and **cared** for some of their individual needs such as helping them move or shake a percussion instrument. Dorothy continually modeled her stance of **equity** since people participated on their terms not ours. All were given multiple opportunities to engage but were not forced to do so. All were socially positioned as part of the community we were creating. John, and the other residents, chose to work with Dorothy, their fellow residents, and us visitors: collectively we used verbal, musical, visual, physical, and dramatic mediating tools to actively and dramatically imagine a cluster of events with the shared goals of experiencing the struggle to protect an innocent child from a violent man and then celebrate our success.

Equality in a Community

Over a few hours each day for one week, working as an ensemble we had begun to establish a community based on **equality**. Though Dorothy led the session, each person in the room could bring their intelligence to each task. There was no hierarchy of competence based on age, or whether or not we had teaching degrees, or who was resident in the hospital. We were people on a shared journey of exploration.

In an article about her work with people identified as cognitively disabled, Heathcote (1978a/1984) is emphatic that, like all people, "they be recognized fully as individuals with rights [including] the power to affect a situation, and to respond in a growing complexity of ways to that situation" (p. 153).

I need to make it clear that, especially early on that week, I experienced real difficulties working equally with cognitively disabled people and **including** them fully as "individuals with rights." I had to wrestle with my own cognitive 'disability.' I experienced two challenges as I compared my difficulties with Dorothy's success: I had to learn to foreground their abilities rather than their disabilities, and recognize that old ways of controlling situations would likely not work. The challenges eased once I had realized that rather than rely on *words* to tell people what to do, the 'patients' could be enticed into engagement primarily by *showing* them a *narrative event* to engage with in a *task*, like join the musical procession and stop the hateful man with a stick. Our dramatic performances were tied to their participation in active experiential tasks that could become dramatic play for them. Challenges could also become opportunities when, rather than resist what they did because it was unexpected, I was tactically able to work *with* the energy and interest that they made apparent in their reactions. I've carried these realizations with me into classrooms ever since.

Dorothy had initially enticed the residents to engage and had then collaboratively harnessed their energy by **including** their ideas and actions, as she worked to create a significant dramatic experience collectively experienced by everyone present. Her aims were not short-term or merely functional but rather emotionally charged goals that could unite everyone: she sought to "try to reach below the task levels of a confrontation or problem to the sense of the mythological or universal aspects of living with people" (p. 152). She argues that, as with very young children, though people with cognitive impairments may not always behave in ways that are commonly socially acceptable, this does not mean that able-bodied people cannot relate to them while working together collaboratively to achieve outcomes that go beyond everyday experiences: everyone should know what it feels like to protect a child, defy a hateful man, and celebrate success.

Like Rancière, Heathcote always began with a presupposition of equality as she worked toward creating a community of equals. Her practice was democratic, verified the equality of all voices, and was "political" in the sense that "people who appear to be unequal are declared to be equal ... the equality of any speaking being with any other speaking being" (Davis, 2010, p. 79).

Heathcote connected dramatizing events with building community. She stresses that, "dramatic activity, of whatever kind, can be said to provide us with metaphors to our real lives, which in turn allow us to reflect about life's experiences [and] the affairs of people" (ibid., p. 149). Throughout that year I continued to experience, reflect, and inquire into the life-changing potential of ensemble learning and by year's end like others on the course I had taken a quantum leap in my understanding of pedagogy that I presented in my end-of-year dissertation and examinations. I had also achieved humbling insights as I reflected on my previous classroom teaching: so often I had not treated young people as equals. I was more concerned with controlling students and imposing my ideas than with listening to them, forming working relationships, and collaboratively exploring topics through dialogue.

The lives of everyone in our course community were, using Scott Peck's criteria noted above, significantly transformed. Over the year we communicated honestly about all aspects of education, most of us were very committed to joyful and sometimes heated gatherings, we learned from one another, and many formed lasting relationships. Soon I moved to the US, began studying for my doctorate at Ohio State, and had a vision for active, dramatic, ensemble community learning that has informed my theoretical and practical education ever since.

In reflections on my experience of that year's events, and inquiry into countless others in classrooms since then, I have explored the significance of using active and dramatic pedagogies with people of any age, experience, and ability and shared some of my developing understanding in print. I have also come to know how working with students as an ensemble supports me in learning to be a better teacher, significantly extends what can be achieved in a collaborative community over working with young people largely as individuals, and opens up transformative possibilities for making a difference in people's lives inside and outside a classroom's walls.

Being Generous For Our Community

We couldn't be teachers if we weren't generous, continually giving to the classroom community. M.J. Ryan (2000), in her book *The Giving Heart: Unlocking the Transformative Power of Generosity in Your Life*, argues that we are generous "when we give our knowledge, our awareness, our

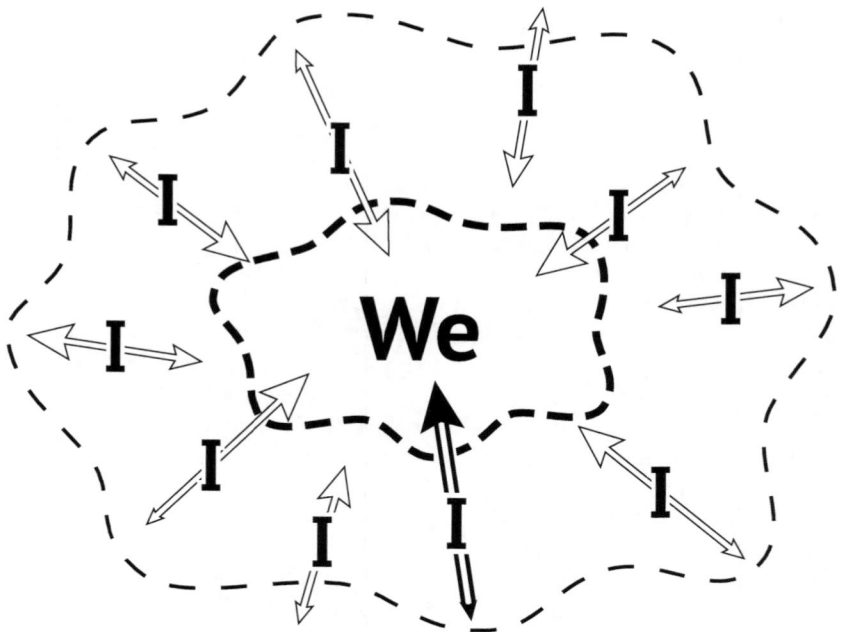

Figure 2.3 Being Generous.

empathy, or our silence" (p. 6). She stresses that giving is also about letting go: "letting go of grudges, hurts, and concepts of ourselves and the
world that stand in the way of our connection to others" (ibid., p. 6).

As teachers we are continually modeling generosity when we create or
bring resources, texts, and tools to a group as well as when we share
what we know and are aware of about the world. Every teacher I know
brings ideas, questions, and humanity to enrich the lives of young people,
illustrated by the black arrow in Figure 2.3.

Think of all the information you've every passed on to students, or
the life suggestions you've ever made, for example, about how to
create positive social relationships, or how you've cared for students
empathetically. I cannot have authentic conversations with children
without the gift of silence as well as of words so that I can actually hear,
pay attention to, and respond to what they may be saying (or not saying).
If I didn't let go of hurts I couldn't go on teaching from year to year. And
if I hadn't transformed prior apparently stable ideas about what I thought
good teaching was (in dialogue with brilliant teachers like Dorothy
Heathcote and Cecily O'Neill) I would never have continued to grow as
a teacher.

Generosity in a community is visible when people share. I want all young people to discover the secret that it feels good to share our things, ideas, or energy with others. William Kittredge (2000) concludes his book, *The Nature of Generosity*, arguing that, "We would profit by learning to think of progress as a movement toward sharing, rather than accumulating, and to consider our values in terms of our willingness to give" (p. 261). For giving to be generous it has to be "freely given altruism, which is to say it involves no discernible feedback except for increased self-regard. We feel better about ourselves" (p. 33).

When I introduce new tasks, that some may find daunting, there are inevitably people who are generous enough to step forward, volunteer, and demonstrate. Heathcote (1971/1984) notes that, "The first leaders are often those who have language confidence though not necessarily the most ability" (p. 94). I try to remember that I should always acknowledge their generosity, by saying for example, "Thanks for helping us out" or "Thanks for volunteering first."

Only when people feel included by the group are they likely to offer substantive suggestions or ideas to share. The most outgoing positive students are the ones most likely to step forward at first. However, our ongoing generosity as teachers over time is essential for creating spaces that feel inviting for *all* students to share their ideas and gifts, including those on the margins of collaboration. Everyone needs to know that, at different times, we are all teachers as well as learners.

A stance of generosity includes being generous in our interpretations of others' actions. As a guest teacher in classrooms, I never want to know those considered the 'difficult' or 'smart' kids. Though I need to know about any agreements that must be followed (e.g. being able to take a time out), rather than being tempted to psychologize or pathologize children or to impose prior behavioral expectations on them, I desire to start from a presupposition of equality. I plan to look for, and acknowledge, what each person actually brings (or does not bring) to our collaborative tasks: when they volunteer, what they actually do, how they work together, and how they include and care for others.

Continuing to engage with students with a stance of equality can be difficult when I encounter students who have very challenging home lives that affect their behavior in school. Yet, I must agree with Alfie Kohn who argues that kids from "loveless sometimes brutal places" need our "unconditional support, encouragement, and love" (Brand, 1995, p. 16). When I am positive in my positioning of young people, I show I am ready to give my time and my expertise, and assume the best in them. As I address them, in a sense I am 'calling forth their best selves' with a voice that comes from my best self. Megan agrees.

I am giving and giving when we begin the year. I come to school early and leave late. I try to plan activities that will be interesting to the kids. I listen to them. I talk with them. I laugh with them. I believe in them and say I think they can do better. But as much as I am generous at the beginning they soon give it back. And by the end of last year we were all level. They're giving to each other—working together, helping each other out, giving people a break. And they were staying in school.

A colleague once admonished me when she said, "You're too positive. You always talk about how great everything is." Her dominant approach to leadership was to control, segment tasks, and find fault in other people's behavior. She, wrongly, thought that because at first I look holistically for what is working in situations and support what's best in people's contributions that I don't also see obstacles and challenges. What I've discovered over the years is that being as positive as possible with all people in dialogue most often seems to bring out the best in me and in them in response.

Caring for Individuals

When I seek to collaborate with people, I do so from what Nel Noddings (1984) calls "an ethic of care." If young people are to begin, and continue, to commit to collaborative tasks, each person should *feel* heard, accepted, respected, and valued by teachers and their peers as whole people. My actions must show that I accept people for who they are in-the-moment. That does not mean I automatically support what they are doing. Noddings (1984) stresses that when one person cares for another he or she first acts receptively to feel *with* the other person in their particular situation. When we care we empathize with a person as we dialogue rather than conduct a detached rational analysis.

> Caring involves stepping out of one's personal frame of reference into the other's. When we care, we consider the other's point of view, his [or her] objective needs, and what he [or she] expects of us. Our attention, our mental engrossment, is on the cared-for, not on ourselves. Our reasons for acting, then, have to do both with the other's [needs], wants and desires, and with the objective elements of his [or her] problematic situation.
>
> (p. 24)

In other words, when I really care for the people in a classroom, I plan to observe and listen to them in order to empathize with their needs and feelings, pay attention to their suggestions, and consider amending tasks accordingly; I do not ignore, minimize, or dismiss concerns that become apparent to me. When I know more about how they feel I can respond from a position that as much as possible accommodates my perception of their emotional needs. Equally, wanting young people to empathize with one another I position them accordingly. Megan provides a high school example:

> Today I talked with two young women who had had a verbal fight over a boy. I realized there was a problem I had to address when a girl was crying in class. I took her outside the door to talk and it soon was clear that another girl was involved. I asked if she'd be OK with me asking the other girl out as well. She was fine with that. We heard her side. Then the first girl told her story. It was pretty clear that they had just misunderstood each other. Once they had heard the other's point of view, accepted that they'd both been mistaken, the tension was pretty much gone. It only took a few minutes but it was so important to deal with it there and then. I've had times in the past when I didn't address a problem and the problem built and built with people not talking or even getting violent with one another. And of course, everyone else in the group was watching to see what would happen.

Figure 2.4 provides an image of a caring teacher, like Megan, who literally and emotionally is ready to stand beside any student when they need to feel heard, accepted, and cared for. At the same time she points back into the community ready to dialogue about how to return.

Caring for people contrasts with a Behaviorist approach to cooperation that can easily settle for minimal tolerance of others: as long as kids behave and get the task done attention to the state of their relationships with others is minimized. However, as Alfie Kohn argues, learning in a community is "not only cooperative learning but helping kids feel part of a safe environment where they feel free to ask for help, in which they come to care for one another, as opposed to having to be manipulated to share or not be mean" (quoted in Brand, 1995, p. 16).

Caring helps people feel safe, heard, and honored. Personal issues should be handled by talking with individuals, peer problems dealt with by the people involved, and only group issues should be brought to the whole group. I have to be ready to have brief or, if necessary, extended caring conversations with people individually, in small groups, or with the whole group.

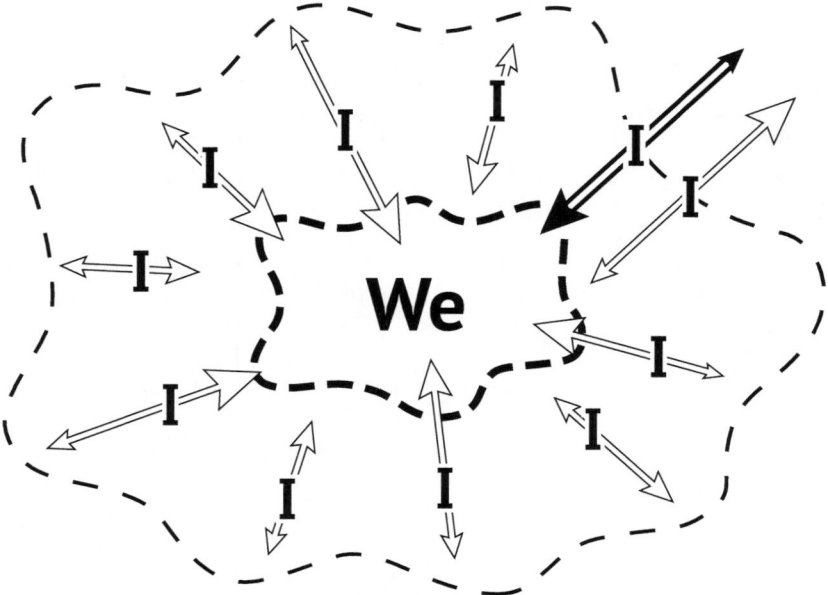

Figure 2.4 Caring for Individuals.

Some core questions that I have found can initiate caring conversations are as follows (with some language changed depending on the age of the young people):

- What do you feel you need right now?
- What would you like to do, e.g. to be alone?
- Do you want to talk?
- Is there anything else you would like me to do, e.g. give you a hug?
- … or us, as a class, to do, e.g. hear what you had to say?
- Is there something you wanted to say but couldn't say earlier?

It's my responsibility as a teacher to care for *all* the people in a group. When students are enthusiastic and positive in their responses to tasks, merely participating accommodates their feelings. More challenging is when students are silent, ambivalent, or resistant. And if they feel that their emotional needs are being ignored or if they have come to feel undervalued in the group then their inclusion in the classroom community will begin to be undermined. To develop some cohesion with a group of people in collective resistance requires strong servant leadership.

Caring Enough to Have Real Conversations with a Group

Jill Sampson is an experienced Columbus City Schools teacher who works with students placed in special education. In October 2011 after four weeks of school she was still struggling to establish a safe respectful community. Despite having agreed on ground rules, played collaborative games, introduced engaging content, and shifted from small group work to working mostly whole group, many of her twelve students were abusing practices like going to the bathroom and they were still putting down their peers. As Jill notes, "I had relationships with them as individuals, but it was like as a group they treated me as the enemy."

Jill believes in having caring "real conversations" with a group that's being dysfunctional in order to confront behavior, point out possible long-term consequences, and work toward them taking on more responsibility for their actions. However, she stresses that such conversations will only be successful if teacher and individual students have already built up some mutual respect and trust in collaborative tasks.

Jill decided to devote an entire fifty-minute period to a serious honest conversation. She showed the students the district's form suspension letter that they were on course to receiving the following year in high school. She made it clear that she cared for them, that she wanted them to succeed in school, but also that there were limits to the practices she was prepared to tolerate. She stressed that unless they worked *with* her to change their anti-social habits she was very limited in how much she could help them succeed.

During this serious conversation students accepted that they had choices about how they behaved and they all agreed to change. She shared responsibility for change with the students in two ways. First, they agreed to make group decisions about individual requests that would affect the group, for example whether or not people should be allowed to go to the bathroom. Second, she met one-on-one with students whom others looked up to as leaders and asked for their help. Within two to three days, students were staying in the room and Jill felt the group shift significantly toward being more self-directed and cohesive. In Heathcote's (1978b/1984) terms Jill is an "excellent" teacher.

> I must be able to see my pupils as they really are. I mustn't discourage them—I must accept them ... I must see what they are in the process of becoming ... I must have the ability to see the world through my students, and not my students through [the world]. This ability can give a teacher a new perception, a renewal of energy and teaching style; there is a sort of regeneration when suddenly a class shows you a whole new way of looking at something.

(p. 18)

Rather than give up on a class that had challenged her so unexpectedly despite all her generosity toward the group and care of individuals,

Jill continued to care enough to accept reality, show students two possible futures, and in honest dialogue risk accepting their response. Having done so, Jill not only created an unanticipated deeper understanding of how to build community but because of how they collectively answered her she felt renewed in her goal to build community with them through working as an ensemble.

In contrast to eager young children, older students like those in Jill's or Megan's classrooms that have had little experience collaborating in classrooms may be ambivalent about working together. After talking with Jill and Megan, some of our suggestions for possible ways to offset initial resistance with older students are listed below.

Anticipating Resistance

1. Introduce tasks that other teachers have used successfully with similar aged students.
2. Modify tasks by following 'The Goldilocks Rule': not too hard, not too easy, but just right for the group. The more you know about your group the easier this is to do. Once you've played whatever game you use, or completed another task, you can always increase/decrease demand on the students and/or ask them for suggestions.
3. Ask if anyone already knows or likes the task. If influential students do, peers are more likely to participate. Share leadership, if at all possible, for example by asking for a demonstration.
4. Ask for one or more volunteers to model the proposed task with you. Work with those who are already eager to participate so that everyone can see what's on offer. Additionally, answer any clarifying questions people have.
5. Stop if you notice reluctance to participate. Discomfort beyond mild resistance has to be acknowledged and addressed or it may easily begin to undermine community trust if people begin to feel emotionally unsure or unsafe. Initially this is especially the case with popular students whose negativity would likely influence others. Often it is obvious if someone is uncomfortable when, for example, they sit out, complain about another student's actions, or are reluctant to join in. Don't make them continue.
6. Because you set the tone, be positive, enthusiastic, and encouraging. Students pick up your tone and will often go along with a task. If you can have people laughing *with* you early on you've begun to establish the idea that the work will be enjoyable. And if you reflect on what they liked, and why, you can promise to do more like that.

Finding Solutions Without Excluding Students

Remaining positive and caring with students can be difficult if young people become highly oppositional or even violent during an activity. What do I do when, despite all my attempts to reach out with engaging tasks, some seem to find it hard to care about their peers in a respectful way or may even exclude themselves? Heathcote (1978b/1984) has some advice about how to remain an authentic teacher in-the-moment: "I must also have the ability not to be lessened by my students, to withstand them, to use my own eyes sometimes and be myself ... refuse to give back what the pupils give you, especially if they are being uncooperative" (p. 19). But how can we do this in practice?

Geoff James is a behavior support teacher who practices a "solution focused approach" developed from a therapeutic practice. Whereas others have proposed teaching techniques (e.g. Metcalf, 2003), James (2005; 2012) has theorized and devised a pedagogy for working with students, including those who are at high risk of exclusion from school and who are categorized as having severe emotional and behavior difficulties. An "SF approach" (solution focused approach) begins with the assumption that every one can discover how they are:

- resourceful in the present;
- competent and successful in the past;
- hopeful for the future; capable of desiring to improve the present and future situation.

Rather than focus on the causes of any students' 'problems,' which are always elusive, or on students' competing views of an event that led to disruption, using the SF approach James imagines with students what their world would be like *without* the problem. This dialogic inquiry approach seeks to find solutions often dialoguing one-on-one *with* young people by building on their recognition of their past successes in similar situations to help them be more successful in future participation. James' stance toward each individual student is to "respect his emotional needs, hoping to start to make changes happen, to help him achieve his dream" (2005, p. 2).

At its simplest this approach is a 'seeing the glass half full rather than half empty' approach. But our stance is pivotal: how we 'see' students affects how we interpret their actions as well as what we say and do in response. James (2012) insists, "I treat the child as doing their best *even when it seems like they are not.* I see a child's apparent non-cooperation as the best cooperating they can do in this moment. I approach the young person with an inquiring mind intending to set out on a joint inquiry toward a solution."

To be 'successful' as James summarizes on his website, "you look for what's already working and respect the [student] as being expert about her or himself. When the particular solution is happening in a 'good enough' way, the [student] can move on as a more resourceful and resilient solution-finder without needing [you]." He adds as a gloss, "I'm not reading what they are doing as resistance. I want the child to express their view of the world, to talk about what's already working, and what they might do a bit more of to get them to their preferred future."

At the same time James is emphatic, "I must shift myself away from noticing deficits toward promoting and describing strengths." He cautions against a technical approach to SF work because, "If my words say 'I see the best in you' or 'I'll give you the benefit of the doubt' but my values say 'I know you're a failure' then I will be the one failing the student."

An SF approach with a group avoids making personal comments or trying to find out 'the truth,' for example, "Why did you do that?" or "Do you have a problem?" Instead, the teacher asks non-judgmental questions focused on opening up inquiry about possible solutions. For example, "What's your best hope for this now? Does anyone have a suggestion for how we might do this differently so that it works better for everyone?" When a question leads to a future-oriented discussion, community has been tested yet strengthened.

Being solution focused also provides a systematic approach to working cooperatively with an individual young person who might be getting close to agreed boundaries. If possible, James advises to talk with young people before they blow up. But even if they do explode, the approach is to find a time to talk calmly outside the classroom.

Remembering and building on positive images of past success is different from focusing on problems. We can ask students, for example, "How were you able to keep calm" (*not* "How were you able not to lose your temper that time?") or "How would you feel if you kept calm?" (*not* "How would you feel if you didn't get angry every time someone said something you disliked?"). Finding past exceptions are the building blocks of future success: "When was a time you didn't lose your temper and you kept calm? How did you manage to do that?" Then students can be helped to imagine a successful future, e.g. "Suppose we were all working together in a good way. What might you be doing then? How would you be working if we were all collaborating?"

When they can focus on possible solutions students may be released in imagination into transforming situations: "Instead of shouting out, what could you do instead? What could you do a bit more of what already works for you? What would you like to get from this class? What might be happening that might help you achieve that goal?" For James, it is a key goal that "a person develops a secure image of the self as a resourceful *agent* for change so that they may live in a way that expresses that desire for a hopeful future."

In SF pedagogy James sees his role mostly as an adult offering experience when needed and as a coach enabling students to recognize and build on their resources, describe their best hope of the future, and devise the small positive steps that will move them in that direction. We can assist, support, and include students as they take those steps in the classroom to participate in the successful ways already envisioned.

Including Everyone

Kliewer (1995) argues that, "Inclusion is a way of looking at the world that enacts the fundamental meaning of education for all children: full participation, full membership, valued citizenship" (p. 320). I came to understand more of the transformational implications of Kliewer's Disabilities Studies perspective when I worked with five seven-year-old children who were legally blind or had visual impairments in Mitch Randolph's second-grade classroom (Edmiston, 2007).

Nel Noddings (1991) stresses that we must be open to what children need in-the-moment rather than assume in advance. Working with 'disabled' children brought her words into sharp relief and extended my understanding of the need to enter any dialogue open and ready to respond however I am actually addressed: "Guided by an ethic of care, we cannot decide a priori, on the basis of principles alone, what to do or how to respond to the need of others. We must enter dialogue to [try to] find out" (p. 160).

Photograph 2.11 shows me communicating with the children as if we are astronauts on a mission to the planet Mars in the midst of a fantastical story we invented collaboratively centered on whether or not to trust 'aliens.' I used my ability to *see* and watch not to make meaning apart from the children, but rather to guide my tactical decisions about how to make meaning *with* them. I let them guide me to places in the room and often shut my eyes. We dialogued not only with words but also by touching hands to make mutual hand movements of the spacecraft landing, feeling a clay model of Mars, laughing together, and making a myriad of sounds ranging from Mission Control beeping to the sound of alien bugs.

Reflecting on the work made it clear to me, as Figure 2.5 illustrates, that inclusion means teachers must be prepared to modify tasks to accommodate to the needs of particular individuals on their terms. Who 'we' are must extend to include who you are and in doing so this can enrich the communication and experiences for all.

I must take the lead modeling inclusion. In conversations with groups, I may propose, negotiate, and on occasions insist, on changes to tasks so that people may feel more included. Some examples from my teaching:

• Asking adults to kneel so that heads are at the same height as young children's.

Photograph 2.11 Inclusive Dialogue.

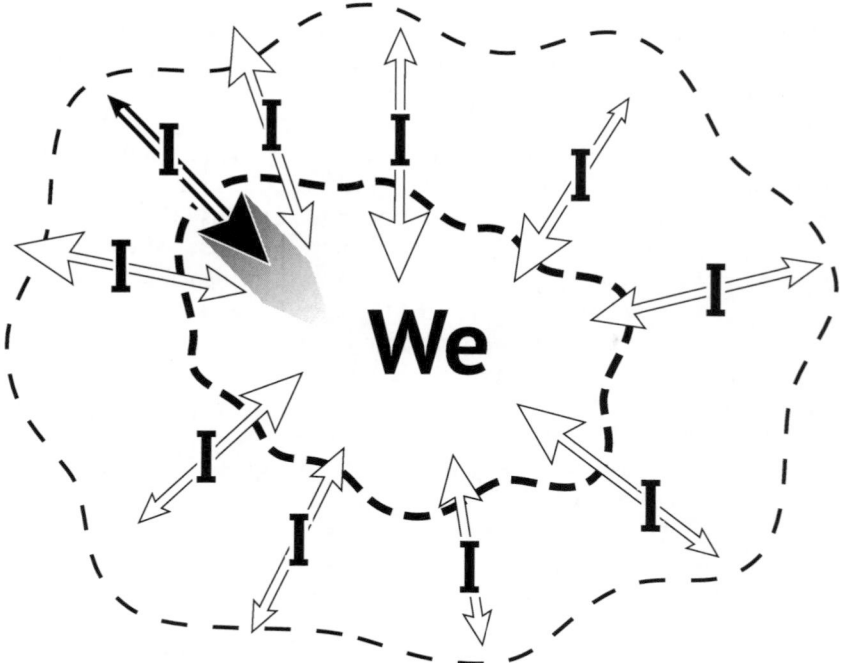

Figure 2.5 Teacher Includes Everyone.

- Moving more than sitting to accommodate a person diagnosed with ADHD.
- Allowing people to draw about the topic during a discussion.
- Creating space for a usually invisible and silent first-grade boy to share his idea about using a helicopter; the flight was then enacted by many of the children with the boy as the pilot.
- Publicly asking a clique of four first-grade girls in the same class how the group might help them with their hotel design. Then insisting that they listen and respond to suggestions: they incorporated a fountain and included the proposer.

One way that Megan demonstrates her inclusivity is by paying attention to the changing context.

> I want them to know that there are no absolutes. I can't have a rule like, 'You will not use these words.' I want them to know that language use always depends on context. So, it can be OK for them to use cuss words in writing, provided the words are needed for the meaning. But cuss words are not OK in classroom conversations. I tell them, 'You need to know about context for the rest of your life.' With me, everything is always up for negotiation, including the rules. But that doesn't mean they can argue with other teachers—there are different rules in different contexts. Early on last year we decided on a 'no cell phones or MP3 players' rule. Kids agreed that they caused a lot of distractions. But later in the year some kids said they could concentrate better on individual writing when they listened to music. I agreed, provided no one else could hear the music. We changed the rule.

Alfie Kohn (2005) believes that there is an urgency to promote "unconditional teaching" in schools. "Teaching the whole child requires that one accepts students for who they are rather than for what they do," or don't do (p. 20). He argues that we should include every young person based on *their* experiences, abilities, and gifts rather than value students for how they have shown their worth based on the classes they are in or their achievement on standardized tests. And that should be the case, especially when they mess up or don't achieve as much as we had hoped. "If some children matter to us more than others then all children are valued only conditionally ... every student gets the message that our acceptance is never a sure thing" (p. 20). Megan agrees:

> I want kids to know that in our classroom everyone matters. Nobody's voice will be excluded and we need to include everybody. Everyone in our community is on an equal playing field. It's easy to *say* that everyone matters but when we play games and engage in

other collaborative ensemble tasks those *show* that everybody does matter. I know that kids believe that when they trust me enough to share personal information they want me to know. Last week a girl told me she's had a miscarriage. She wanted to explain that she had not been upset with me but had been feeling really down.

Unconditional teacher acceptance has both social and academic consequences for students. Kohn (2005) summarizes significant research (Makri-Botsari, 2001):

> Students who felt unconditionally accepted by their teachers were more likely to be interested in learning and to enjoy challenging academic tasks, instead of just doing school work because they had to and preferring easier assignments at which they knew they would succeed.
>
> (p. 21)

Adapting Tasks to Be More Inclusive

Another way to think of inclusion is as dialogue in order to adapt tasks or environments to create spaces where people are less likely to feel excluded. Over time, how I set up tasks can promote or undermine a sense of inclusion. Table 2.3 provides examples.

Sometimes people's feelings of discomfort are not apparent. It's important to be aware of those so that I may try to avoid them expanding into self-imposed exclusion. One way to demonstrate my intention to be inclusive is to use informal assessment.

Table 2.3 Inclusive Tasks

Potentially excluding tasks	Likely inclusive tasks	Possible negotiations
Competitive games can leave people feeling that they are 'losers'	Play mostly collaborative games	Talk with the whole group about how to make a game feel more inclusive
Unchallenged put-down comments about a person's contributions destroy trust	Agree on, and ask the group to monitor respectfully for, a 'no put-downs' classroom expectation	Talk with someone who makes 'put-down' comments to try to discover any history between the people that needs to be addressed
Predictable small groups can create cliques	Intentionally mix up groupings in short-term tasks, so that a norm of everyone working with anyone is established, and cliques are less likely to form in the classroom	Negotiate with a small group about including another person

> ## Using Informal Assessment as an Inclusive Community Building Tool
>
> Some people may make their reluctance apparent by not participating. A way to assess, acknowledge, and quickly respond to possible discomfort, is to establish a practice of asking people for informal feedback:
>
> - Can you put your thumbs up/down/across to show how you are feeling right now?
> - On a scale of 1 to 10, how are you enjoying what we're doing?
>
> Concerns that surface may be able to be addressed immediately:
>
> - Can you tell us/me what the problem is? Is there anything I or we can do to help?
> - I can understand if you're reluctant to take part. I can promise I won't make you do anything you don't want to do.
> - Can we talk about this issue later when we've finished the game?
> - Do you want to watch first and then join in when you're ready?
> - Do you have a suggestion for how we might change the game/task to make it more fun for everyone or do you know a different game that we might all like to do?

Ensemble Practices Include All Students

Especially with older students, often I have no idea if people are feeling excluded despite my attempts to address concerns. When I repeatedly use ensemble tasks I establish a practice that is continually inviting participation by all students and creating space for students to include one another.

Early in this chapter I commented on the fact that Aaron, the boy sitting in the corner in Photograph 2.7, was watching and listening but that five minutes later he was eagerly on his feet actively engaged in a dramatic encounter (see Photograph 2.9). When I first observed in the classroom I had noticed that Aaron had only marginally talked with others in the group Megan had asked him to join and he had opted out of the presentation. Yet, at the moment shown in Photograph 2.12 Aaron had stepped in when Marquis asked for someone to show how during the robbery people in the store had raised their hands when a gun was pointed at them. Aaron was clearly ready to respond to a request to participate.

What I did not know was that Megan and I (as a visitor to the classroom for five sessions) later came to believe Aaron had been excluding himself from tasks because his peers had never personally invited him to

Photograph 2.12 A Student Includes Himself.

participate in a task (Edmiston, 2012). As she had put it in our first post-session reflection, "He wants to join in but I think he just can't bring himself to do it." Only later did we question that inference. On the surface Megan assumed that he was choosing to sit out and watch, especially as he frequently resisted academic work. Others would also sit out or resist but they would 'hang out' with peers. Aaron frequently parked himself in the corner to watch what was happening and make side comments.

Photograph 2.13 was taken just over two weeks after the previous ones. Aaron has just rolled his chair in order to chat with some of the other students for a few minutes, having just completed a writing assignment on the computer you can see on the table. The significance of a moment of comradely exchange that I had never previously observed could easily have been overlooked.

Aaron was the only student who identified as White in an all-Black classroom. Paradoxically, working as an ensemble to deal with wider cultural racialized issues seemed to have had a significant effect on Aaron's relationship with others in the classroom.

Two weeks prior to taking the previous photograph, when I had not been present Megan led a discussion on whether the fact that Wes Moore was Black could have influenced the jury at his trial. None but Marquis

Photograph 2.13 Inclusive Student Dialogue.

was vocal in saying that race was relevant. After Megan showed a video of the Rodney King beating on the twentieth anniversary of the Los Angeles riots she supported those students who wanted to dramatize the event. Later, she analyzed what happened and its significance for Aaron: "I now think that dramatizing the event was transformational for Aaron. For the first time his difference was noticed, it became valuable, and he was invited in as 'Aaron'" (as illustrated in Figure 2.6).

> Aaron came into the center of the group for the first time. We were talking about race and whether it might have something to do with Wes being in jail. Several of the boys wanted to talk about the video we'd seen. They said if Rodney King had been white and the cops black the outcome would have been different. They really wanted to dramatize the beating. Four boys stood up to be the cops and they turned to Aaron saying, 'You can be Rodney King because you're white.' Aaron literally jumped up and said 'OK, I'll do it.' I said, 'Remember we're just acting' because I knew it could get kind of violent and they said, 'Oh Ms. Ballinger we know, we're not going to

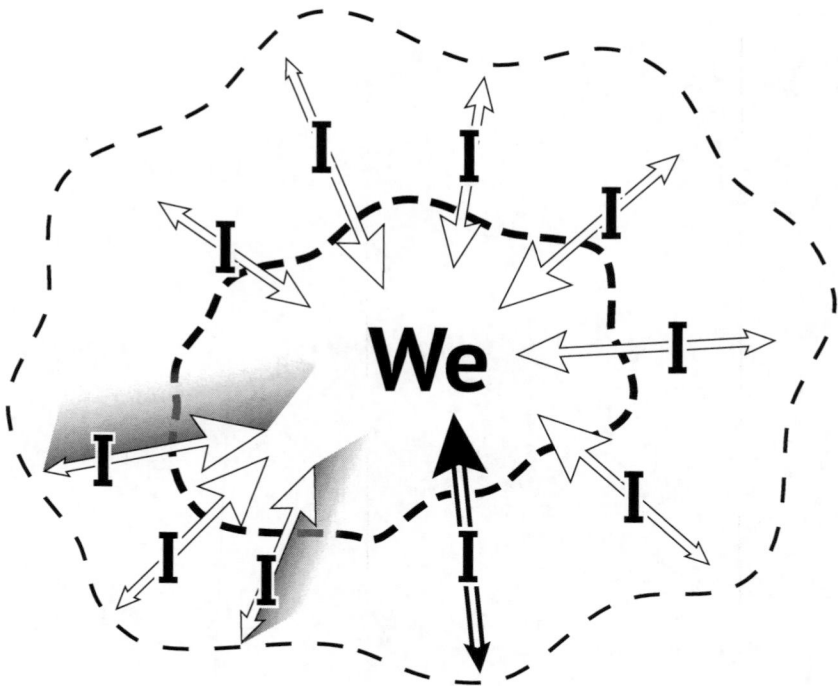

Figure 2.6 Students Including Peers.

hurt him.' Aaron kinda looked back at them and said 'I trust them ...
I think' and they dramatized the scene. Like on the video at the end
they pretended he was on the ground and they were like punching him
and kicking him. It was pretty intense. And John kinda helped him up
and Aaron shoved him a little and said 'You got me there' and John
said 'Oh I'm sorry man, I'm sorry.' They were fine. I realized that it
was kind of a playful thing like between friends. And then Justin, who
had been the person most convinced that Wes was 'obviously' guilty
was clearly rethinking. He turned to one of the others and said if Wes
had been white the outcome could have been different. It was great.

Megan illustrates what Shirley Brice Heath (2012) has stressed about
the value of arts participation in general for young people. In her thirty-
year ethnography she shows how young adolescents (who feel excluded at
school) felt included working as a theatre ensemble provided that "none
of the theatre directors expected them to reach consensus, come up with
pre-scripted answers, or debate one position or viewpoint in opposition to
another" (p. 37).

Megan never pressed students to agree on or debate viewpoints but rather they collaboratively explored inquiry questions through dramatic pedagogy in tasks open to everyone's participation. Additionally, over time she opened up inclusive dialogic spaces that invited participation by all.

Heath is clear about the benefits. Even "the shyest, most reluctant speakers joined in the group's deliberations" when they could, "set up hypothetical situations or [to] pose problems" (p. 37).

> It builds within adolescents a reservoir of strategies for managing anger, foreshadowing outcomes realistically, and avoiding circumstances likely to bring them into trouble.
>
> (n.p.)

Conclusion: Build a More Hopeful, Strong, Proud, Sensitive Community

> Through engaging the minds and imaginations of children, teachers can help children develop the strength, pride, and sensitivity they need to engage the world, and not to despair when things seem stacked against them. Even though hope is not sufficient to provide a good life or even guarantee survival, it is a necessity. However, to teach hope you yourself must be hopeful, must believe that all children have a right to learn and can indeed learn.
>
> (Kohl, 1998, pp. 9–10)

Community is really a verb. If we grow in our desire to be together as well as in our ability to work and play and dialogically learn from one another then we may deal with difficulties together, we will joyfully celebrate our successes, and we can learn more about how to live together. Building a classroom community affects people's identities and thus their sense of agency. As Holland (Holland et al., 1998) recognizes, in the collaborative playful imagined spaces of a community all participants, even those often on the edge, "develop new social competencies upon which adult life depends" where "even distant others may construe their lives" (p. 272).

Groups are dynamic and are always becoming new communities: our shared history is always remembered in a living present that presses forward into a new future. When people work as an ensemble to build community they learn to collaborate in tasks with shared goals and thus learn from and with their peers and teachers. However, classrooms are not artists' studios and young people cannot create a sustaining supportive ensemble in the way adult actors can: people come and go, testing hijacks the curriculum, and youngsters are kids who may one day blow up and walk out while the next day join in with enthusiasm.

Tracey, Megan, Jill, and Lorraine are all hopeful teachers who believe, with Herbert Kohl, that hope is a necessity for all people. As they build intentional inclusive caring classroom communities with a reach that extends beyond the walls of the school, they inspire me with their belief in their students and their commitment to extend the ability of all students as they devise tasks to entice, engage, stretch, and challenge their understanding. I wonder if I would have the resilience to resist despair that many of their students have, given the challenging realities and stresses in their lives. If I did I would want to thank my teacher for being a leader in building a community that developed (in Kohl's words cited above) more "strength, pride, and sensitivity."

Notes

1   Lorraine Gaughenbaugh and Megan Ballinger were two of the twenty teachers in the first of three cohorts of teachers in a professional development program, an education collaboration between The Ohio State University and the Royal Shakespeare Company. Jill Sampson was a member of the second cohort. Chris Ray was a pre-service teacher in the third cohort. In 2009–12, through university coursework I directed the professional development of these teachers who participated in a training program devised by the Royal Shakespeare Company's education department. I am deeply grateful to all thirty-six teachers in the project with whom I learned so much and who opened their classroom doors to me. I am especially indebted to the four teachers whose work I write about in this book: Lorraine, Megan, Jill, and Chris.

2   In this section I bold the key community-building terms I introduced in the previous section, as well as their opposites.

Chapter 3

Plan for a Journey of Exploration

As a young teacher I had a fantasy: find a perfect lesson plan, follow the plan, and I will be a better teacher. Like so many beginners, I thought of planning as scouring books, now it would be the internet, for other people's ideas and then writing down a fixed plan of activities to follow, like a recipe that does not change. Teaching was implementing the plan with enthusiasm: 'Come on, kids. This is going to be great fun.' But, of course, the people I met every day in my classroom were never the students I had thought about fleetingly and superficially the night before. I didn't realize that my dream of a 'holy grail' plan was more likely to become a nightmare in the classroom. Enthusiastic teaching didn't guarantee meaningful learning.

My focus had largely excluded the students. I was thinking about *my* needs, *my* plan, and *my* great ideas for what to do. Instead, I should have been struggling with the realities of how to have meaningful experiences and reflections *with* young people, about events that interested *them* as well as me. To do this I first needed to ask, what sense will learners make of this topic or activity? Then I could ask how might we make meaning together?

I (and the students) fared much better when I largely abandoned formal plans and responded to what the young people were interested in. I used tasks to introduce topics and texts because they were engaging, not just because they were listed on a plan. However, that approach made it difficult to follow the required curriculum and I had largely left myself out of the planning process.

Pam Bowell and Brian Heap (2001), in the most useful book on active and dramatic planning that I know, illuminate an alternative:

[Planning] focuses on developing a dramatic response to situations and materials from a range of perspectives. Participants take on roles that are required for the enquiry [i.e. inquiry], investigation, or exploration of the subject matter. The task of the teacher is to find ways to connect the pupils with the content and enable them to develop responses to it through active engagement and reflection.

(p. 7)

As I did in Chapter 1, they stress that learning is experiential engagement, performative (in social and dramatic roles), reflective, and (across tasks) inquiry into a topic from multiple viewpoints. Learning is active and may be dramatic. Planning possible tasks in advance means I can prepare for how I expect a group will respond, which may include acting as if they are people from a narrative. Answering their responses I begin to dialogue and to create understanding with them.

Reading what William Ayers (Ayers & Alexander-Tanner, 2010) has written resonates deeply with my own transformation as a teacher. In contrast with his beginning belief that a teacher should be "master and commander, in charge and in control," he recalls how as a young teacher of five- to six-year-old children he began to find joy in teaching when he came to see himself as "an explorer on a journey of discovery with my students, a voyage of discovery and surprise" (p. 2).

I now envision planning as preparing for dialogue on a shared journey of exploration. A plan is never the journey, just as a map is not the territory. My planning lays out intended and possible paths to follow. But when I have drifted into laying down a teaching route that young people *must* follow, in the classroom I invariably find I am headed into a storm! Planning is creating a map of learning possibilities that guides our shared explorations of events in a narrative world and our inquiries into deeper understanding through dialogue in sequenced tasks that potentially address as many viewpoints and interpretations as there are people in a group and characters in a narrative. For me, planning is always in relationship to teaching a particular group of young people about a topic that I already know interests them or that I can reasonably expect will engage them. Following my argument in Chapter 2 that the social cannot be separated from the academic, my planning must focus as much on building an inclusive collaborative classroom community as it does on content learning and teaching.

Planning for a Particular Group

Planning requires imagination. The better I know a group the easier it is to imagine working with them as I plan possible tasks. The more my planning can be guided by my understanding (or by that of their teacher) of how a particular group tends to work together, along with an awareness of people's prior knowledge, experiences, interests, and attitudes, the more likely it is that they will engage in tasks I plan.

I plan for success. I must have high expectations that will stretch students, be realistic and not set them up for failure while always recognizing that any knowledge I have of students is partial, incomplete, and limited by my experience. It's crucial that in planning I adopt a *positive* stance of assumed social and academic *competence*. There have been occasions when I've gone into teachers' classrooms not knowing which students were designated as 'gifted' or 'learning disabled' only to discover later that because of the engaging nature of the tasks people displayed unexpected competence.

My planning grows out of, and returns as much as possible to, a focus on building community and relationships: mine with the people in the group, theirs with each other, and everyone's with a topic. These are the sorts of questions that guide me before and/or when I meet a group:

- How well do they work *together* (as an ensemble)?
- What might *engage* them as a whole group?
- What are individuals *good* at (and not so good at)?
- Who may need *special accommodations* for inclusion?

A well-known way to begin is to introduce a KWL chart to discover what young people 'know' and 'want to know' about a topic before returning to the chart to record some of what they have 'learned' (Ogle, 1986). Some initial questions I use to ground what I call 'KWNIL planning' are these:

- What do the young people and I already *know* about the topic?
- What do the young people *want* to know more about? What are they interested in or curious about?
- What do I believe the young people *need* to know (socially as well as academically)?
- How can I restate answers to the first questions as possible *inquiry* questions?
- How might I assess *as* they are *learning* (as well as what they have *learned*)?

'Why' and 'how' questions are often the most useful inquiry questions. I used the following criteria to devise 'OIA' inquiry questions for the work on *Jack and Jill* (Why do people need water? How might we help Jack?) and *Brave Margaret* (How could we defeat the giant? Should we try?):

- *Open-ended* (with no obvious answer)
- *Interpretative/inferential* (rather than literal/factual)
- *Action* would be needed in response (rather than just analysis)

Uniting all of these questions is my core planning question:

- How will I plan for *dialogue* about our *actions* in collaborative sequenced *tasks* focused by inquiry questions that explore the meaning of *events* in a narrative text?

After first working with a group (for perhaps only five to ten minutes) further planning includes what I have learned (or believe I have learned) about their interests, prior knowledge (or lack of it), the meaning they've made (or been confused about), their skill level (and mine, or lack of it) in using active and dramatic pedagogies, and any questions that they (and I) have raised. Once I know more about the group I can better align their interests and needs with mine.

At its simplest, a planning map has a beginning collaborative task and a few choices of follow-up tasks aimed at exploring a narrative event to achieve an outcome valued by all participants. More complex planning maps are variations. In relation to planning I use the term 'goals' to include both long-term and complex aims, for example building background knowledge, and objectives that are more short-term and focused, for example learning specific vocabulary or achieving a state standard.

Though tasks will invariably have more than one purpose, in planning particular tasks I tend to foreground one purpose over others. Each section in this chapter is focused on planning tasks for a specific purpose.

Topic, Goals, Intended Outcomes, and Beginning Tasks

- What **topic** or **text** must I address and/or is likely to engage people?
- What **goals** and **intended outcomes** do I believe the students need to achieve?
- What **beginning collaborative tasks** could lure them into the narrative world?
- Which of these might we **negotiate**?

Curricular Topics

Planning must be focused by the curriculum—*what* we are going to learn about together over time. I extend Kieran Egan's (1989) championing of "imaginative intellectual activity" and his belief in curriculum as "good stories to be told" (p. 2) as I advocate for the active and dramatic exploration of significant narrative texts with young people that may also be entry points into important topics. At the same time, I agree with William

Pinar (2011) that curriculum is a verb not a noun, a "complicated conversation" with ideas, rather than a set of preset objectives used to evaluate only predetermined outcomes. I teach for learning that is both required and responsive to young people's interests, and my own. Taking account of my own interests is important because if I'm not excited or intrigued by the narratives I introduce it's unlikely the students will be.

I am not naïve about the increasing constraints on curriculum and pedagogy in an era of 'standards' to be 'delivered' via textbooks, and test preparation masquerading as teaching. As a guest teacher in schools I don't have to cope with the increasing surveillance of schooling and extended control of what happens in classrooms and I don't suggest that teachers should ignore school realities. However, I do ask this: whom do you want running your classroom? Is it the textbook publishers, the testing industry, district objectives, or you and the young people? And how important is it to choose and explore topics and texts (or parts of them) that are likely to engage students?

Given and Emergent Academic and Social Curricula

Topics may come from what I call the 'given' curriculum in the sense that there are narratives to explore and conversations to be had that, as teachers, we are committed to as givens. *How* we explore them is negotiable but not *that* we focus on them. The given curriculum can always be considered to have two dimensions: the academic and the social (Skiba & Peterson, 2003; Rimm-Kaufman et al., 2012).

As I focus on what I believe young people need to know about any topic (for example, because of state standards or because I think ideas are conceptually important) I also focus on what I believe they need to know more about in terms of 'us as a community of learners'. Because the cohesion of the classroom community is inseparable from academics, as much as possible I work with groups in ensemble tasks; my social goals include young people choosing to participate and taking on leadership roles in collaborative tasks with intended outcomes that *they* care about as much as I do.

In addition to the given curriculum there is always an 'emergent' curriculum, exemplified by the Reggio Emelia approach (Edwards et al., 1998), when I plan in response to the interests, concerns, knowledge, abilities, and questions of young people as a group that arise because of who they are outside and inside school. The emergent curriculum is in relation to any topic and how people actually work together as a group. As William Ayers (2010) puts it:

> The classroom should align to the child and the community, not the other way round; there must be a focus then on the quality of

children's lives and opportunities for imagination, expression, and experimentation in a safe and buoyant space.

(p. 8)

There is an inevitable tension between the given and the emergent facets of the curriculum but they need not be in opposition: a topic can be both fascinating and important to me as an educator and interesting to the young people. We don't have to choose between the academic or the social, the given or the emergent curriculum. As Anne Haas Dyson (1993) argues, when we see the curriculum as "permeable" we expect a dynamic interplay between students' social practices and knowledge in the "unofficial worlds" of peers and home and those of the "official world" of schooling. Both may be harnessed to achieve valued outcomes.

Meaning-making Goals and Task Outcomes

As I dialogue with students, given and emergent curricula inform not only the particular topic we explore, but also explicit or implicit agreement about specific goals (why we're doing this), as well as the events in a narrative we focus on, the tasks we engage with, and intended outcomes (what we want to achieve). Such conversations are likely to be more effective *after* people are engaged by a task or have achieved an outcome (like having enjoyed a game).

As Figure 3.1 summarizes, the curriculum can be regarded as given-and-emergent, social-and-academic brought to life in the classroom in meaning-making tasks focused by dialogue about narrative events and inquiry that may be dramatic. The horizontal arrows point in complementary meaning-making directions. The goal of learning, viewed as dialogically exploring inquiry questions about a topic, is balanced by the goal of building necessary background knowledge. Similarly, an intended outcome of making artifacts that show change in students' understanding is grounded in showing knowledge of established shared understanding. At the center of the classroom is dialogue, and over time, dialogic inquiry that may be dramatic, as children author understanding in the active and dramatic learning modes introduced in Chapter 1.

When Megan Rogers Frazier and I met in March 2012 to begin planning for three two-hour teaching sessions in her suburban central Ohio first-grade classroom, knowing the six- and seven-year-old children's shared interest in animals she was sure they would like to explore a story I suggested: *Amos and Boris* is William Steig's picture book about a mouse and a whale who become friends. She was right.

I knew that the story would address several of the academic and social curricular topics that Megan had identified. First, in the given literacy curriculum her learning objectives were reading for understanding and

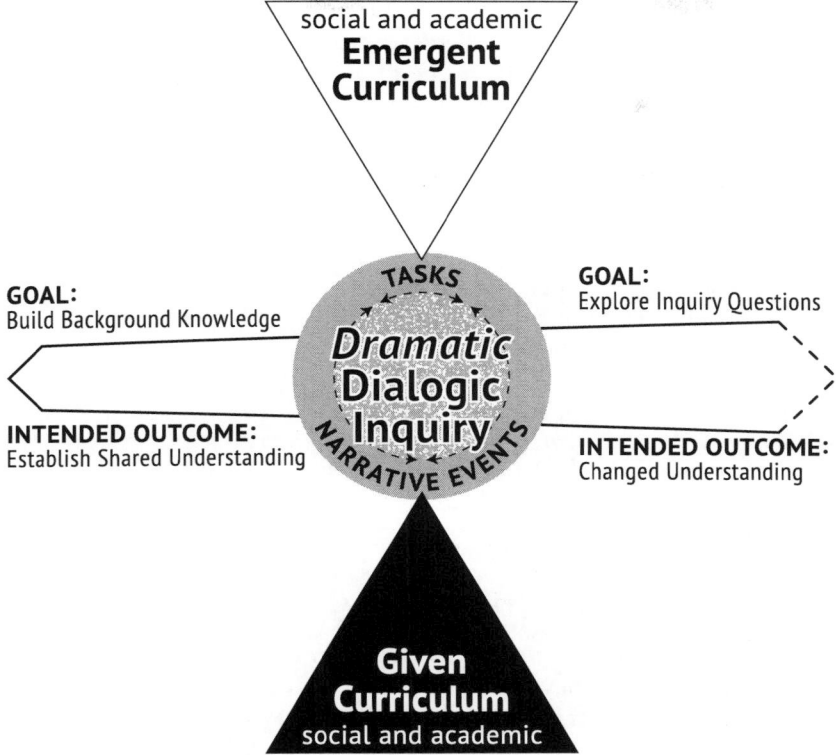

Figure 3.1 Planning Curricular Goals and Intended Outcomes.

sequencing events. The children knew the word 'sequence' and could parrot the phrase 'a story has a beginning, a middle, and an end'. However, as an outcome she wanted them to demonstrate that they understood *why* one narrative event might come before or after another. Her personal goal was to see how active and dramatic pedagogies could mediate building vocabulary and text comprehension, in particular how learners might infer meaning. Finally, as we were going to read a story about a whale, she was also interested in them learning some content knowledge about oceans and whale life. She added a writing outcome: all of the children, working in pairs, would write and illustrate a story. Those objectives were restated as academic inquiry questions: Why does one event in a story come after another? Why do characters act as they do? How do whales live?

In terms of the social curriculum, as with any group Megan noted that some children were friendlier toward some of their peers; her learning objective was for the class to think more deliberately about making friends with those considered different. She considered that the following would be essential social inquiry questions for these six- and seven-year old children, some of whom had been born in countries other than the United States: How do we make friends? What do friends do together? How do we make friends with those who seem to be very different from us? Applied to the story of *Amos and Boris*, addressing those questions would also support their comprehension and interpretation of a core theme in the narrative, friendship across difference. I interviewed Megan after she had read the final draft of this chapter. In italics in this chapter I've added some of her comments.

> *Rather than begin with standards as I used to I now begin with narrative texts. I work backwards from the events in stories to plan which objectives I can meet. Also, it's taken me a few years but now I plan for integration: I plan how a text, like* Amos and Boris, *can open up science and social studies as well as literature and language areas of the curriculum.*

Beginning Collaborative Tasks and Negotiations

Our beginning collaborative tasks had clear goals and intended outcomes. Using the journey metaphor, it was like having our destination visible ahead at a distance as we looked at the path immediately in front of us knowing that we could take a different path and still reach our goal.

Some negotiations with the children were embedded into beginning tasks. We wanted to make sure that the children were interested in exploring the narrative and thus the academic topic. As I introduced the book all would need to demonstrate actively their interest (or I would abandon the narrative and turn to my back-up text). At the same time, I wanted to dialogue with the children in order to begin to connect with them, especially those from overseas, in terms of the theme and social topic. I planned to share briefly how I too had once come to the United States from another country and had made friends with people from a different culture.

After gathering the children on the carpet, I drew attention to what for them would be my 'different' accent. I noted where I grew up and asked if anyone in the class also came from another country. Soon, someone had a globe in her hand that Megan produced. As they were trying to identify different countries I showed how I had traveled over an ocean and said how different I had found the United States from Britain. "Was it different for you?" Several heads nodded.

I said we had a story about a mouse who went on a journey by boat and who met a whale. Many seemed intrigued by how a mouse and a

Photograph 3.1 Sharing Illustrations.

whale could become friends especially when I showed some of the illustrations (see Photograph 3.1).

I had planned a choice between two follow-up whole-group dramatic playing tasks to dramatize events, hinted at in particular illustrations, which would introduce the characters. If it seemed the children wanted to move their bodies, we could move around the room as if they were swimming whales. Alternatively, if it seemed they wanted to sit for longer I had planned that they could talk with me-as-Amos and together we could imagine building his boat.

> *The children were used to having choice. I know how important it is to establish social patterns from the day they walk in so that as the year progresses the children know what to expect. Choice is key for engagement.*

They wanted to move. I showed several pictures of Boris, the whale, swimming and asked what they noticed he could float on the surface and dive. I stood, invited them to do so too, and asked if anyone could show us a whale swimming. Soon everyone was moving. When I stopped to reflect I asked if anyone knew how whales communicated. One boy said they sing. Assisting those who needed to be more deliberate about whether they were in the classroom world or a whale world,

Photograph 3.2 Pretending to Swim as Whales.

we practiced stepping into the imagined space as whales and out again to talk as ourselves. Stepping in again we made whale sounds. Once everyone could 'step in and out' I suggested they imagine swimming and then greeting one another (see Photograph 3.2) before 'swimming' back to the carpet and sitting down as themselves which all did with minimal fuss.

All were keen to continue. Within ten minutes we had implicitly agreed on (and did not need to negotiate) academic goals for the next sequence of tasks: reading and studying some the content of the book.

Later during that first session I introduced the inquiry questions, printed on pieces of paper, that Megan and I had come up with. Having waited until the children had already encountered Amos and Boris, knew of their unlikely meeting and friendship, and were hooked by the story, all agreed on the shared social curricular goal of exploring friendship including thinking about how to be friends with 'different' people. I shared what I had already noticed: they worked well together and were clearly very comfortable and friendly with one another. It was obvious that Megan had been exploring this aspect of the social curriculum from day one.

**A few things I remember about
NEGOTIATING with students:**

- I know what we could negotiate about. I talk with the young people before I plan a great deal.
- I give choices within and/or between tasks and as much as possible initially follow their lead. I ask what they like to do. I also let them know what I need to do.
- I try to listen and watch more than I talk (I have two ears and two eyes but only one mouth!). I observe for implicit interest and agreement.

Selecting a Narrative Event

- What narrative events are most likely to **hook** the young people and **engage** them?
- How does an event **align** with curriculum goals?

Every narrative is a sequence of events, narrated and implied. Using dramatic pedagogy with young people I can grapple with a theme, encounter characters, and begin to explore the landscape of a narrative by dramatizing an event.[1] Choosing which narrative event to explore and dramatize takes planning.

An Event as a Rupture or Crisis

A live event has two dimensions for Bakhtin, as I noted in Chapter 1: eventness (the dialogic meeting of more than one consciousness or perspective) and presentness (experienced here-and-now with multiple possible ways of responding). Listening to a monologue about abstractions is not an event. Dramatizing an encounter is a live event.

For pedagogical theorist Elizabeth Ellsworth (1997) events are "ruptures of continuity" in which "normal" life and the "status quo" is disturbed (p. 15). Similarly, the anthropologist Victor Turner (1974) argues that in the "crisis" situations of everyday social dramas there is a "breach" of norms requiring "redressive action" in which people attempt to resolve the crisis (or accept a schism) (pp. 37–41). In community terms, there is a tension between assumed shared norms and actions regarded by one or more individuals as disruptive (or in some cases, restorative).

An event is ...

a dialogic meeting of two or more consciousnesses ("eventness");

felt as tension

happening here-and-now with

multiple ways of responding ("presentness"):
an event is "a present filled with its own future."

When there is a rupture of continuity,

a crisis, or

a breach of norms

people feel a need to take redressive action

to reestablish what feels 'normal.'

In everyday classroom life we can't plan on having too many *actual* events since they disrupt the necessary routines and social practices of community learning and teaching. Of course, ruptures and crises arise naturally whenever people spend time together, and we can embrace them as unplanned learning opportunities within our life narratives.

Yet we can plan on engaging with highly disruptive events through curricular texts and topics: they are what make content interesting. The more we read about, view, and/or dramatize *narrative* events the more engaging the text. In this book, when I use the word 'event' I invariably mean an event in a narrative. Introducing dramatic pedagogy means a group can begin to engage actively in imagination with the ideas related to disruptions but without actually being disruptive in the classroom!

> *Kids who used to want to be silly usually like to pretend to be other people and now they can. And kids who are interested in mean characters often love to pretend to be them in our work.*

Experiencing the Dramatic Tension in Narrative Events

One reason why some events in narratives are more engaging than others is because of conflict between different characters' perspectives that, as readers, we feel as tension and that, as participants in a dramatization of the event, we feel as dramatic tension.

Engaging with events using dramatic pedagogy has similarities to experiencing dramatized events in the theatre where events are staged.

Actors and audiences are engaged by their experience of dramatic tension in a fictional rupture or crisis not simply because of conflict between people who may be arguing or fighting on stage or screen but rather because actors-as-characters and people in the audience experience conflicting perspectives between how things are and how it seems they ought to be 'normally.' Or to put it in terms of the future, between what we want to happen and what might happen that we would want to avoid/ embrace. Events are dramatic because, as the philosopher of art Susanne Langer (1953/1977) puts it, "only a present filled with its own future is really dramatic" (p. 306).

Similarly, as Gavin Bolton (1992) stresses, "the drama lies in the constraint" (p. 56). As he categorizes them, feelings of social, cultural, physical, psychological or procedural tension create reflective constraints on participants taking dramatic action. Feeling dramatic tension holds participants in an in-the-moment anticipation of future imagined action by characters— what Heathcote (1980/1984) calls "now and imminent time" (p. 161). This is so significant for learning because, provided they can move among modes and have access to mediating tools, participants will author meaning in dialogue about the narrative event both from 'inside' as well as from 'outside' the imagined world. The feeling of constraint for participants continues until there is some resolution of tension by some *dramatic action*, in relation to the real-and-imagined world, that alleviates the sense of crisis or rupture. At times, as Heathcote (1976/1984) puts it, especially with older students, alternatively they may be prepared to accept some "easement" in a complex problem situation rather than a more simplistic "solution" (p. 115).

On that first day in Megan's classroom, when the children discovered, as we read on, that Amos had fallen off his boat at night in the middle of the ocean I could tell from their faces that this felt like a crisis to them. All were keen for a few seconds to embody swimming like a mouse and then as if they were creatures in the ocean (including sharks!). The children anticipated a dangerous future for Amos if he could not find something to keep him afloat. We could have dwelled in Amos' crisis exploring how someone copes when they are alone and in danger. However, I read on. Meeting a friendly whale was a relief for the children who, as readers it seemed, had all projected in imagination into the event in briefly dramatizing it. Their engaging sense of dramatic tension in that event dissipated as I turned the page.

When they experience more than one perspective in, or on, the same event people experience dramatic tension between viewpoints. The children imagined from the viewpoints of both Amos and dangerous predators. In the work on *Brave Margaret*, the young people had imagined from the perspectives of both warriors *and* the giant. With the preschoolers we promoted dramatic tension through a third party consciousness concerned with the narrative event: physicians working professionally to restore order and normality so that Jack could leave his sick bed.

Sustained dramatic tension can support engagement in dramatic inquiry. With other groups I've explored multiple perspectives on an event that must be inferred (e.g. why did Jack break his head and not Jill?) and parental viewpoints on children's safety (e.g. why did the parents let their children go out alone?).

Dramatic Action

People experiencing the tension of a crisis in real life feel a desire to *act* in an attempt to restore order (whatever they consider 'order' to be). Similarly, in dramatic pedagogy students and teachers can take *dramatic* action.

Dramatic action is acting in deeds and/or words as if we are people in an imagined world. In dramatic playing people can act without consequences in the real world. In complex tense situations they may not know how to act though they may play out possible actions, which they can do from the alternative perspectives of different characters. Shifting into dramatic performance and reflection modes they may share and evaluate their real-and-imagined actions (and/or their ideas about how they might act) in dialogue with one another. Introducing dramatic inquiry focuses young people more on understanding events from different perspectives and exploring over time different possible ways of acting to restore order.

Just as in the everyday world, dramatic action has consequences for people in the narrative world—intended, and sometimes unintended, outcomes that may be ephemeral or lasting. For example, at the beginning of the story Amos unintentionally spent one night in the sea after he fell off his boat, whereas at the end of the story Boris returned alone to the sea for the rest of his life after Amos was cleverly able to rescue him from dying on a beach. Dramatic outcomes may always supplement any intended curricular outcomes to open up possibilities for further exploration.

ABCD Events

From an engagement viewpoint, the best narratives to read, and to dramatize, are those with events that *feel* dramatic to *the students*. If people don't feel moved by a rupture or crisis in the lives of the characters—if they don't care about them—then they're unlikely to be engaged for long. That's one reason why narrative texts, rather than lyrical poems or factual records, are more immediately engaging and why watered-down versions of stories in basal readers never have the potential of the original.

I summarize why participants in a group sense a shared desire to take dramatic action in response to feelings of dramatic tension in particular events by characterizing these as 'ABCD events.' The children in Megan's classroom must have felt 'hooked' when they experienced a **big problem**, that **all** of the children **cared** about and could experience and **dialogue** about from **diverse** perspectives: they wanted to **act** to restore order. Everyone wanted Amos to survive when he fell off his boat. Similarly, everyone wanted Amos and Boris to remain friends and wanted to get Boris back into the water when he became 'beached.'

A Narrative Event Contextualizes a Facet of a Curriculum Goal

Exploring a narrative event by dramatizing it contextualizes a facet of a curriculum goal in tasks experienced in the "now and imminent time" of a present situation filled with a sense of anticipated action in a real-and-imagined space. The academic and social goals identified above were contextualized by events in *Amos and Boris*. Similarly, with the preschool children an academic literacy goal of forming understanding about the nursery rhyme was achieved by saying the words while imagining we were inside the world of *Jack and Jill* experiencing and reflecting on the event from Jack's viewpoint. Social goals of more collaboration and learning more about caring for others were achieved in active and dramatic conversations as the children decided on actions to help someone with a "broken head".

Dramatizing stories can involve several ABCD events, but to begin with I must select and focus on one. Some stories only have a single event, like *Jack and Jill*: Jack (with Jill) went up the hill, fell down fracturing his head, and went to bed to mend.

Most written narratives have more than one event. One easy way to choose an event is simply to read a story and stop every time people feel that the characters' 'normal' lives are disrupted. That was how I introduced the first event in *Amos and Boris*. When Amos fell off his boat I could tell from the children's faces that they were thinking, "What will he do now!?"

> The kids know that we're always working with narrative events. They seek them out when they're looking at books and show them to me.

If teachers are in the midst of reading a story I suggest that they can always dialogue with the students about events they are interested in exploring and ask them why. Active strategies like 'The Trading Game,' 'Social Atom,' or 'Vote From Your Seat' (see page 242) can assist with choosing events.

Photograph 3.3 Pages on the Floor.

Identifying Events in the Whole Narrative

Another active non-dramatic approach to identifying captivating events is how Megan and I introduced the narrative as a whole at the end of the first session. With a short picture book I often copy the pictures along with as much text as I want to introduce. Or, as I did with *Brave Margaret*, I may hint at events by introducing names and key phrases from the text.

We laid out photocopied **pages on the floor** of most of the story but deliberately not in order (see Photograph 3.3). We intentionally omitted the final pages because those were to be introduced later (in terms of sequence they create a sort of 'postscript' in the narrative).

Megan had already put the children in pairs ('stronger' readers with 'weaker' readers in terms of their decoding ability). To encourage dialogue, I asked children to find a picture that interested them, share with the people near by, and to **stand up together** when they could say what they liked about it. This active strategy required the children to listen to each other, agree, and show they were ready to share. All became intrigued by events in the story.[2]

Sequencing Events

I asked the children to see if they could work out the sequence of some events. This provoked interesting exchanges within and between pairs. As children shared with one another, some read words while others read illustrations. Megan and I monitored and assisted whoever seemed to need help. As a whole group we had a conversation about the partial sequences groups identified. For example, one boy recognized the title page and placed it at the beginning. The children in Photograph 3.4 are agreeing that 'Amos making the boat' has to come before 'Amos sailing in the boat.' Then or later we could have focused on how every event, not just stories as a whole, has a beginning, a middle, and an ending. The first event begins with Amos, a mouse, on land wanting to go to sea; he builds a boat; and ends up launching it in the ocean.

Photograph 3.4 Agreeing on Sequence.

Once I had placed the pages in sequence, with the help of a few of the more eager children, everyone could see how the story unfolds (event by event): Amos constructs a boat to take him on a voyage of exploration. One night in the middle of the ocean Amos rolls off the boat. The next day he is fortunate to meet and be rescued by a whale, Boris.

Narrative Events and Themes

There were two particular events that could both be interpreted in relation to the topic of friendship, a core theme of the story. Both captivated the children. If we had not planned these in advance, or if we had chosen an event that did not interest the children, we could have just waited to see what *did* interest them. Additionally, I could always have paused in reading the book in order to plan overnight or during a recess.

The first crisis for their new friendship happens soon after Boris rescues Amos. When Boris 'sounds' (dives) and then surfaces, Amos is tossed in the air and falls into the water again: Amos, "crazy with rage," screams, and punches Boris. All the children seemed to identify with this scenario.

The second crisis occurs toward the end of the story when years later Boris is 'beached' in a hurricane. An illustration is shown in Photograph 3.5; we projected it on the smart board. Though Boris is fortunate that Amos happens to find him, as a tiny mouse, Amos cannot help. The event is not resolved until Amos is able to persuade some elephants to push Boris back into the water.

Goals

ABCD events likely to hook young people
All experience a need to **A**ct when they encounter a
Big problem in an event they
Care about and can experience from
Diverse perspectives and **D**ialogue about

Themes

Photograph 3.5 Illustration of Amos Finding Boris Beached.

A few things I remember about SELECTING EVENTS

- I often read a story and stop whenever the young people want to meet a character. Being hotseated briefly is the easiest way to enter a narrative event and being to explore its potential.
- If they, and I, aren't captivated by an ABCD event I find another.

Tasks Designed to Build Background Knowledge

- What tasks will likely build the **background knowledge** they need as a group for understanding the event?
- How much **teacher structure vs. student choice** does the group need?
- What material, physical, mental, and/or social **mediating tools** might we use with which **learning modes**?

When I plan substantive meaning-making tasks I may orient students more toward the acquisition of background knowledge or more toward developing changed or new understanding. Though my teaching can promote both at the same time, in this section I focus on the former and in the next section I additionally consider the latter. In both sections I describe how planning in advance influenced my teaching. Though I was also often 'planning on my feet', if I had been teaching in my own classroom I would have likely paused the work for more strategic planning to spread tasks over several days.

Building Background Knowledge When
Exploring Inquiry Questions

Figure 3.2 shows how the goal of acquiring background knowledge balances the goal of exploring an inquiry question. Dramatic dialogic inquiry is the *exploration* of a topic through dialogue about narrative events in sequenced tasks that may be dramatic. Building background knowledge is establishing shared understanding the group needs to know in order to engage in particular tasks. Using the map analogy, background knowledge of a topic is known existing terrain, or in other words 'old' knowledge that everyone needs to understand enough about in order to use or be aware of. An inquiry question is like a compass, or GPS, I can use with

Figure 3.2 Planning for Building Background Knowledge.

students to navigate our actual journey through the terrain where we will discover or create 'new' knowledge on the way. Intended outcomes are where we expect our actions to take us (though we may end up somewhere different) as well as what we make on the way: artifacts collectively are a record on the one hand of the acquisition of established, or agreed, understandings (old knowledge) while on the other hand, showing change in understanding as a result of the exploration of a topic (new knowledge).

Assessing the Need to Build Background Knowledge

Before I approach any narrative event with young people (or delve into it in any detail) I may first need to clarify factual information, share my own prior knowledge, or have students share theirs, as we collaboratively build background knowledge. At other times I pause in the exploration of an event to build background knowledge when it becomes apparent that the students don't know (or are confused about) something important. Additionally, as we engage and dialogue in a task the need for information, conceptual ideas, etc., will become apparent to me, and to the group, provided people listen to one another.

As the teacher I must identify academic content knowledge the students *need* to know if they are going to be able to make meaning about an event. This is key factual information, conceptual understanding, or particular ideas that the author of the story assumes readers already know or accept. I must also plan tasks in which people can make artifacts allowing them to author and demonstrate their understanding of established or agreed meaning that I believe is important for them to know. Though William Steig embeds a great deal of information in his picture book, he assumes that readers already know important knowledge about whales, for example how whales swim in the ocean, meet up in family pods, and could be beached in a hurricane, as well as the scientific knowledge that beached whales will die if they don't return to water. Additionally, he assumes we will accept that in his story whales and mice can communicate in English.

Structuring Tasks

When I was a young teacher I didn't realize that I could vary the amount of structure to set up any task. I tended to move between extremes of near total control (e.g. "No talking or moving. Just complete the worksheet") and largely open choice (e.g. "What would you like to do?"). I had the most difficulty in controlling behavior in small groups or other 'teacher-less spaces.'

Two things changed in my teaching stance. First, I shifted my attention more to the students when I came to understand that my purpose in controlling what students can do is to better mediate their learning by affecting material conditions and social relationships (not for instruction disconnected from their meaning-making). Second, I became more skilled at ways to vary the amount of structure I provide while always allowing students some choice so that they have agency as authors of meaning and are not passively receiving information.

To promote dialogue, rather than attempt to impose a fixed task structure, I create with the group a more dynamic "semi-structure." Sawyer (2007) shows how this is "not too rigid and not too loose" requiring a "subtle balance of planning, structure, and improvisation" (p. 29). Genuine dialogue is always, to an extent, improvised.

In every classroom task there is always a tension between the *structure* provided by the teacher and the *choices* that the students experience because of how they are positioned. As a localized aspect of curricular tensions this is a given-emergent tension represented by the two triangles in Figure 3.3, which is a close-up view of the previous figure. The meaning-making horizontal arrows have been diminished to foreground planning dialogue in a particular task in relation to a single event. Over sequences of tasks, the more students are able to take responsibility, work collaboratively, and improvise dialogue in pairs or small groups the less structure needs to come from the teacher for 'teacher-less tasks.' Conversely, when students need a lot of support to collaborate they need more teacher structure.

A group that has largely only been asked to work as individuals or where cliques have developed has to be taught to work more as an ensemble. That is primarily a social rather than a technical task, a longer-term cultural goal rather than a cognitive concern. Over time students can gradually take on more responsibility.

I ask the following reciprocal planning questions in planning every task:

• How much choice and responsibility can I expect of this group of students in this task?
• How much of a structure do they, and I, need?

I extend the use of the five W and one H questions I used in Chapter 2. In the hexagon in Figure 3.3 each question reveals a dimension of any task that affects the process of meaning-making. Though participation affects, and is affected by, the real-and-imagined world of an event I locate my planning of tasks mostly in the concrete physical reality of the classroom space since that grounds people's experiences.

> *I used to get frustrated when I had no exact structure to follow but I was expecting too much of the kids. Now I start with more structure and I watch for how kids handle a task. I ease up when I know they can control themselves and not be silly.*

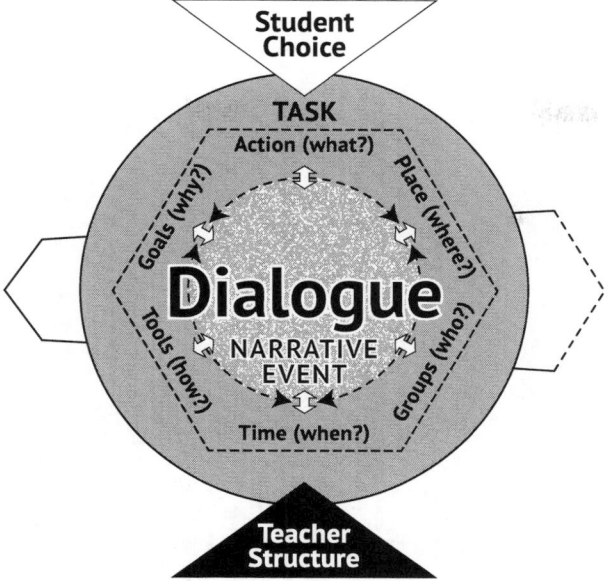

Figure 3.3 Planning a Task.

Table 3.1 shows planning for high/medium/low degrees of teacher structuring leaving open corresponding amounts of student choice.

All tasks are active in terms of making meaning. In general, the younger the children the more physically active they need to be and the less sitting and active listening they can handle. In dramatic learning modes participants take dramatic action. In every task (using mediating tools with others in a particular time and place to achieve a goal) people create artifacts in the sense that as they dialogue they always *make* something ranging from words to actions to still images to writing. Unlike, for example a crafted story, I think of a 'mini-artifact' as not made with a great deal of attention to detail. Yet every utterance and/or deed *shows* understanding (and may be informally assessed).

Every task has other dimensions of engagement. Though students will know my goals (e.g. inquiry questions may be written up) the goals that *they* have may feel much more engaging (e.g. to be able to move or draw or work with a friend). If possible, I take account of known student goals in planning and teaching. The time we spend on a task is a variable that I often tighten up; time limits usually focus attention. Likewise, limiting the place for tasks both allows me to monitor for safety and makes it easier to bring the group back together. I tend to use arbitrary groupings (e.g. **counting-off**) to encourage more social mixing or particular groupings (as Megan did for reading); this may disrupt

Table 3.1 Structuring for Student Choice

Task dimension	Core dimensions of ensemble tasks	High teacher structure/ low student choice	Medium teacher structure/ medium student choice	Low teacher structure/ high student choice
ACTION (what?)	**Dialogue in collaborative words/ deeds** using active and/ or dramatic learning modes **to create an artifact**	Students watch when I model with a volunteer; I check they understand directions; we begin; I stop if necessary to clarify or to redirect	I show/tell students the task. Ask students if they need any assistance	Students know the task already. They are self-directed; they could opt out or do the task later
GOAL (why?)	**Shared goals** (or objectives) we care about	There is a predetermined short-term objective. There is minimal clarification	I explain why we're doing the task and briefly answer questions	Groups already know the goal. We negotiate goals if necessary
TIME (when?)	Choose to engage at the **same time**	Very short time (e.g. one minute). I impose tight time limits. I begin the work together and give a countdown to finish	Not too long (e.g. 5–10 minutes). I ask if people need more time. I give reminders e.g. 3 minutes left	As much time as is necessary, e.g. extends over one or more sessions. Students can return to task, e.g. model-making
PLACE (where?)	Experienced both as a physical place and a **shared bounded space**	A familiar place (e.g. at desk, or on the carpet)	Specified place (e.g. "Please sit together on these chairs facing each other")	Anywhere in room (e.g. "Find a space")
GROUPS (who?)	**Distributed leadership** among teachers and, at times, young people	Teacher pre-selected; random selection (e.g. "Number off")	Limited choice (e.g. "Find a partner you've not worked with before")	Self-selected groups or fluid grouping, (e.g. "Share with one person and then another")
TOOLS (how?)	Multiple appropriate **collaborative tools**	Teacher selected; student choice of how to use (e.g. "Please use the musical instrument on your desk")	Limited choice (e.g. "Please pick up one instrument from those laid out on the floor")	Use any tools available (e.g. "If you want to make a soundscape come here; if you have another idea let me know")

engagement expectations. Because different tools extend potential meaning-making and engagement I try to increase the availability of possible mediating tools.

Planning to Use Tools

Across the three *Amos and Boris* sessions the mediating tools used included the following (dramatic strategies are in **bold italics**):

- talking with others;
- listening to parts of a story being read;
- holding, reading, and moving photocopied pages from a book;
- viewing pages from the book projected on a Smartboard;
- looking at and touching a globe;
- discussing a YouTube movie of whales swimming;
- ***hands-as-puppets*** (as Boris);
- ***hands-as-puppets*** (as Amos);
- moving, and talking, as if whales (in ***collective role***);
- moving, and talking, as if Amos (in ***collective role***);
- moving, and talking, as if elephants (***pairs dialogue-in-role***);
- writing down ideas about friendship;
- talking about those ideas;
- drawing on a whiteboard;
- making the sounds of a hurricane (***soundscaping***);
- moving as a whale or a mouse (in ***collective role***) in response to ***narrated action***;
- standing and moving on a continuum;
- moving to stand by an idea written on paper;
- ***hotseating teacher-in-role*** me-as-Boris;
- choral reading;
- a group hug.

Take away these tools, as well as the learning modes, chosen and used by the children, and their learning potential would have shrunk. The broad implication for planning is clear: be open to extending tasks using active and dramatic learning modes along with providing children with visual, aural, and material resources, all of which can be used as physical, mental, and social mediating tools to create artifacts that demonstrate understanding.

Increasing/Limiting Student Choice Across Tasks

Table 3.1 lists examples of high, medium, and low amounts of teacher structure with corresponding low, medium, and high amounts of student choice in relation to different task dimensions. Having assessed how well a group works within the structure of one task, in planning the next task I can either increase or decrease the social demands. The second column (adapted from Chapter 2) highlights the overarching social goal of engaging participants in ensemble tasks.

Given and Emergent Sources of Background Knowledge

The arcs in Figure 3.2 represent how background knowledge can come from given and emergent sources. As a teacher I am an important source of relevant knowledge already widely shared that I intend for the students to know and understand. However, students also know a great deal of prior knowledge. The increasing size of the arcs is meant to represent my planning decisions about how some information has to be established and understood by everyone (for example, that whales are mammals that swim) or ideas agreed to by all (for example, that in the story a whale and a mouse could communicate). At the same time, some information that individuals provide need not be shared or extended with the whole group (for example, different species of whales) and in dialogue some ideas may be interpreted differently (for example, why whales sing). Similarly, when people research in small groups everything they discover need not be brought to the whole group.

One of the easiest ways to share relevant prior knowledge is via brief analytical comments or discussion as we read: I may stop to explain something important or ask if the young people have questions. Some students may already know relevant information or ideas and can share with peers. I find quick sharing really useful, especially when I ask people first to turn to their neighbor to share prior knowledge or to gather up questions.

Longer sitting-down discussions can easily privilege the contributions of only a few and may become tedious. When the task is solely whole group talk, young children may easily ramble off topic, tell disconnected stories, or make random comments. I often make sharing tasks more active and more dialogic using games, like The Trading Game. Provided the students don't feel emotionally exposed in front of their peers, they will create and share 'mini-artifacts' (e.g. in response to 'Show us') that may demonstrate some understanding (or lack of it) to me, to others, and in reflection to themselves.

Some important knowledge is relatively easy to plan to share using active or dramatic strategies. When I met the children in the first session, we only sat still for five minutes as I read the opening pages, talked with them about the opening book illustrations, and identified Amos as a mouse and Boris as a whale. Using the globe was important as it introduced a visual representation of ocean and land; Ohio is landlocked and few of the children had been to the coast. Encouraging children to point to our state, and then to the blue area as everyone said the word 'ocean,' was a more active way to begin to connect some of their prior knowledge about oceans where whales live and the land where mice live. But practically, not all children could point or talk about the globe.

I asked if the children would like to imagine we were all whales. They were up on their feet in a trice when I said, "Let's swim round the room like whales in the ocean, and when we sit down on the carpet we'll be back in the classroom."

It was apparent through their movement (see Photograph 3.2) that most seemed to think whales swam like humans. It was clear that the children needed to build more background knowledge. In Figure 3.2 children's need to know is represented by the arrowheads that point back to the given/emergent curriculum. Megan had anticipated this in our planning and had a YouTube video of whales swimming ready to watch and use as a tool (see Photograph 3.6).

If you only use the drawings in a book, kids, without a lot of back-ground knowledge, can get stuck with an inadequate image. Whereas, when we use other media like video and pictures from the internet it

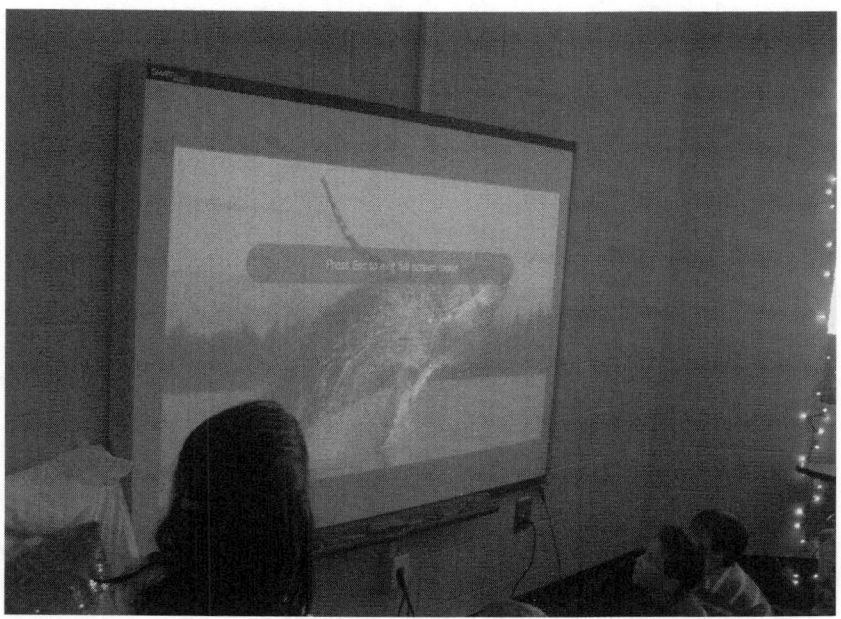

Photograph 3.6 YouTube Video.

extends kids, gets them excited, and gives us visual images to return to for more information and ideas.

Now, in imagination, everyone could see living whales swimming in the ocean and greeting one another. I introduced key vocabulary ("fin" and "flipper") and a key event in whales' lives referred to in the story (the gathering of a family 'pod'). In response to the movie and our brief analysis, as everyone again swam round the room in dramatic playing mode they-as-whales-swimming experientially embodied whatever meaning they had just made: as they moved their hands like fins, their rear-ends like tails, and made whale noises as they greeted each other as if in a gathering pod. As they did so I made a textual reference: this was the "meeting of whales" that Boris was anticipating and which he mentions to Amos (see Photograph 3.7). Though the task was oriented toward building *background* knowledge the children were also demonstrating in context some *change* in their understanding of whales.

Dramatic playing opens up meaning-making experientially for young people—they author their own understanding in actions that embody language and ideas. Yet, in contrast with an orientation toward more

Photograph 3.7 Dramatic Playing a Meeting of Whales.

Photograph 3.8 Whiteboard Drawing.

open-ended inquiry (as I analyze later), these ideas were presented as information only to be *clarified* in any reflective dialogue.

In order to understand how and why Boris had gone under the water when Amos was on his back (in the event I analyze in the next section), the children needed to know how whales "sound" and "breach" as well as swim like humans on the surface of the water. Rather than just tell them, I drew the following image on a moveable whiteboard to use as a tool (see Photograph 3.8).

Now the children could view and talk about the drawing, repeat the new words together, and in dramatic playing move *hands-as-puppets* as if they were whales, and again move their bodies briefly as if we were whales swimming, sounding, and breaching. We returned to the carpet where a few children shared more factual information. As individual children shared, experienced, and extended their prior knowledge experientially and reflectively they also collaboratively built background knowledge needed to understand the viewpoint of Boris in the event when Amos got so angry.

The following day, in preparation for introducing the beached whale event, I decided that the children needed to contrast how a whale swims in water with how a whale's movements are so limited when beached. Additionally, understanding how such a massive animal could end up on land during a hurricane was more background knowledge that I felt was

Photograph 3.9 Soundscaping.

best learned experientially through dramatic play. Finally, the tension in the urgency of the situation, which Steig assumes readers will infer, had to be recognized and experienced by the children.

After reading a short extract and looking at Steig's illustration, together we created a **soundscape** of a hurricane that I directed for volume (see Photograph 3.9). The children practiced making sounds using the floor, tables etc. As I raised my hands they worked together to make more noise and as I lowered my hands they made less: together they created the sounds of a hurricane coming, raging, and then departing.

Children could chose either to embody how Boris (in the ocean) or Amos (they decided he had hid in a hole on the beach) experienced the hurricane while those who wanted to continue making the soundscape did so; again I directed volume (as shown in Photograph 3.10). Since the class was in three groups and because I *narrated action*, how Boris was tossed around in the water and thrown up onto the beach while Amos hid, there was a dramatic performance dimension to the task.

I asked the children who had chosen to imagine they were whales in the hurricane briefly to embody Boris as I moved a beanie-baby mouse (used as a *puppet*) toward them addressing them as if I was Amos (as shown in Photograph 3.11): "Is that you, Boris? It's so good to see you again. But what are you doing here? Shouldn't you be in the water?"

Photograph 3.10 Narrating.

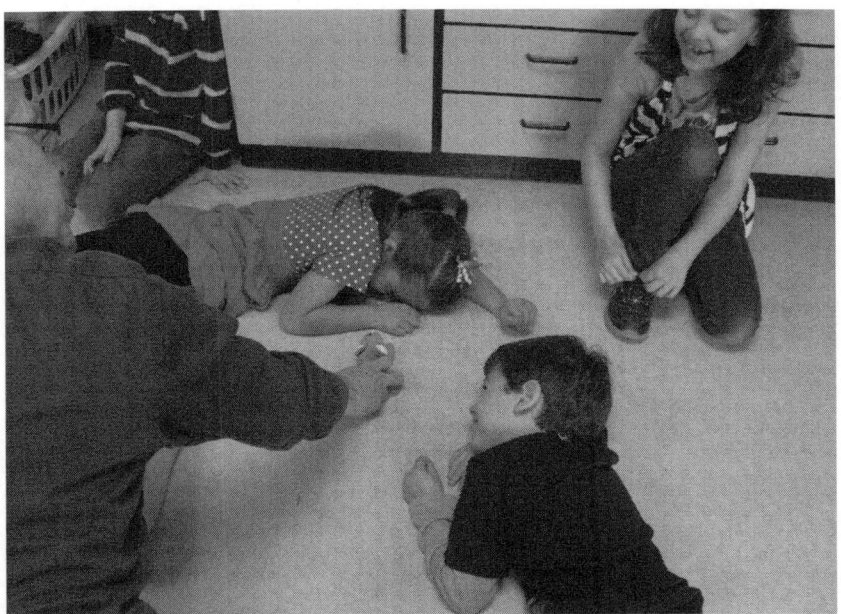

Photograph 3.11 Beanie Baby Mouse used as a Puppet.

Photograph 3.12 Hotseating Teacher-as-Boris.

From how the children were moving around it was clear that they did not realize how the whale would be unable to move. So, I decided to embody and represent Boris-as-beached-whale. I brought the children together at the carpet to *hotseat* me-as-Boris. Embodying and talking as if I was Boris (as shown in Photograph 3.12) I intended to clarify the problem from the whale's viewpoint and the action needed ("I'm drying out. I'm feeling weak. I must get back in the water. But I can't move.").

One boy asked, with a concerned voice, "Why don't you get back in the water?" Keeping my body very still I moved my hand saying, "See how I can't move my body with my flippers. I'm stuck. I don't want to die here. I wish you could help me, Amos, but you're so tiny." Another child responded, "We'll push you back in."

I stepped out of the world of *Amos and Boris* (as shown in Photograph 3.13) to talk with the children.

A reflective discussion seemed the best way to make sense of the event I had just begun to embody with them. Trying to help the children realize how impossible it would be for a mouse to move a whale, I asked if anyone knew how huge and heavy Boris was. One asked, "As big as you?" Agreeing with his response as much as possible, I said that a baby whale could be my size. I affirmed the response of one boy

Photograph 3.13 Stepping Out of the Imagined World.

who said Boris must be as big as a school bus while another suggested a truck.

Several of the children were interested in the relative weights of the 'light' Amos and the 'heavy' Boris. From an emergent academic curriculum viewpoint many children were clearly invested in studying the science of mass. They were intrigued by the weight of whales and elephants relative to school buses, trucks, and people. If Megan had wanted to she could have shifted to the *science* curriculum at this point. The children could have conducted discovery experiments using material tools such as objects of different relative weights and a water table to learn about science concepts.

Redirecting focus to the *social* curriculum I moved closer to the children, and then shifted back into the narrative event but now as if I were a mouse addressing other mice. Looking back at where I had just been lying, I asked, "What can we do as mice to help Boris get back in the water?" One of the boys suggested that we would have to find a heavy animal like an elephant to help. Almost immediately everyone agreed. To my knowledge he'd not seen Steig's illustration showing elephants pushing the whale. If the children had not come up with the idea of seeking out elephants, other powerful creatures, or humans I would have turned to the relevant pages in the book.

A few things I remember about
BUILDING BACKGROUND KNOWLEDGE

- I ask the young people what they want to know before I do a lot of preparation.
- I bring in and share intriguing images (video clips, photographs, drawings, etc.). I often use and reflect on images before introducing written text.
- At first I often share a few words on paper that everyone can see or have short pieces of information or single-page text extracts for pairs to read (rather than provide several pages for individuals).
- As much as possible I assess what they know (or are confused about) in action (that may be dramatic); in response, as I instruct or facilitate students' sharing (using active and/or dramatic learning modes) I can vary the amount of structure/student choice.

Tasks Designed to Develop Changed Understanding

- What tasks will likely develop **new** or **changed understanding** about events?
- How much **teacher structure vs. student choice** does the group need?
- What material, physical, mental, and/or social **mediating tools** might we use with which **learning modes**?

My core goal for any group is this: How will I plan for *dialogue* about our *actions* in collaborative sequenced *tasks* focused by inquiry questions (explicitly stated or implicit) that explore the meaning of *events* in a text? Events in a narrative contextualize facets of a curriculum topic. The intended outcome is for students to create artifacts demonstrating both shared understanding of relevant background knowledge other people already know about a topic and their new or changed understanding.

In the previous section I analyzed tasks oriented toward building background knowledge and students' demonstration of their understanding of old knowledge important to know in order to understand an event. We couldn't even have begun to comprehend the first meeting between Amos and Boris until we had shared and experienced some knowledge of how whales swim, the relative size of mice and whales, etc. Similarly, children's understanding of the 'crazy with rage' event created in the second session provided background knowledge for the 'beached whale' event in the third. Because the children had all embodied and demonstrated their understanding of a whale sounding I was then able to shift orientation toward authoring new knowledge. I focused the children on experiencing the conflicting perspectives of a whale and a mouse when Boris sounded with Amos on his back.

The shading on the horizontal arrows on Figure 3.4 represents a continuum of authoring understanding between, on the one hand, tasks oriented toward knowing the increasing solidity of relevant facts and ideas already accepted and shared by many ('old' knowledge) and, on the other hand, tasks oriented toward making more diverse meaning that is original to participants ('new' knowledge).

One sense in which people are *active* as they dialogue is when in a task they *act* intentionally in meaningful words and/or deeds to create

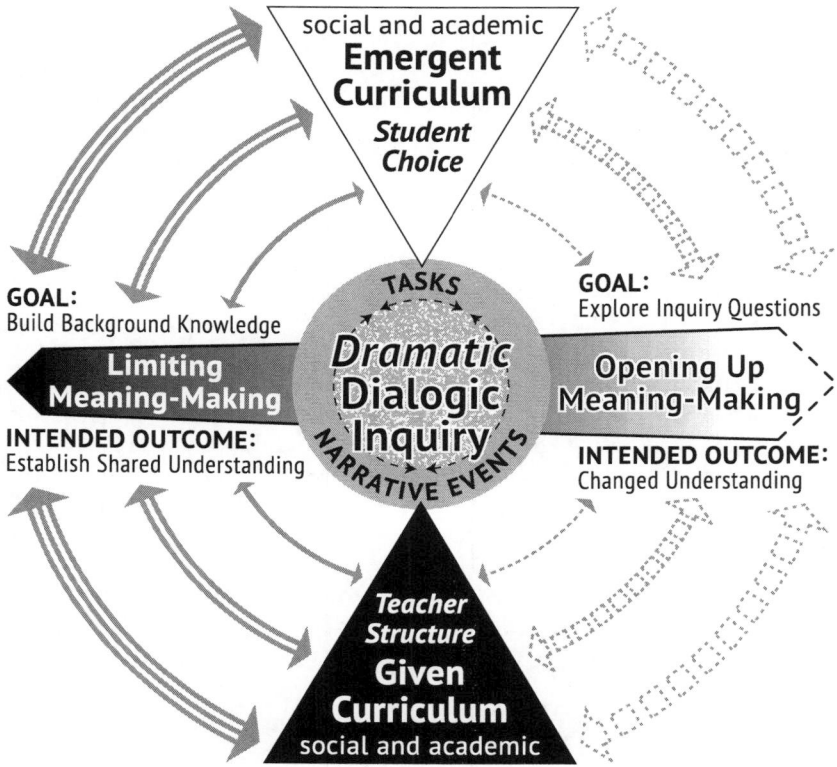

Figure 3.4 Planning for Meaning-Making.

artifacts ranging from selected words (e.g. to describe the feeling of being in a hurricane) or fleeting images (e.g. an embodiment) to more permanent records (e.g. writing and drawing). Some artifacts can be assessed as '*outcomes*' when they demonstrate learning in relation to a goal.

What their own and other people's actions and artifacts *mean* is a primary focus of dialogue since creating understanding (beyond mimicry, memory, and a purely behavioral response) must be an active, creative, contextualized meaning-making process, never a passive decontextualized response. As we dialogue, any artifact may be used as a *mediating tool* to make more meaning (and additional artifacts) and to develop understanding as part of an ongoing conversation. Young people may make and use their own artifacts (e.g. dictated words, a drawing, or using their hand as a puppet), or those produced commercially (e.g. illustrations in a book), or created by peers (e.g. a demonstration), or by a teacher (e.g. in role).

Academic Curriculum Goal: Comprehension and Inference

I began the second session by reading several pages from the beginning of the story about how Boris had rescued Amos in the middle of the ocean after he fell off his boat. My orientation was mostly toward authoring new meaning. I asked how they thought Amos must have felt and if they considered Amos and Boris friends. In reflection, the children seemed to agree with one boy who said Amos had made friends with Boris because he had helped him. Giving out half-page copies of the text, I asked the children to follow along with a partner, as I read the following edited extract (see Photograph 3.14):

> What a relief to be so safe, so secure again! Amos lay down in the sun, and being worn to a frazzle, he was soon asleep.
>
> Then all of a sudden he was in the water again, wide awake, spluttering and splashing about. Boris had sounded. He surfaced so quickly that Amos was sent somersaulting, tail over whiskers, high into the air.
>
> Hitting the water hurt. Crazy with rage, Amos screamed and punched at Boris ...

I asked them to consider how the animals might *stay* friends as I read the extract again but now incorporating **hands-as-puppets** dramatic playing so that the children could experience in an ensemble as if they were the characters.

Taking up Amos' perspective, I asked them to use their hands-as-Amos on me-as-Boris. I embodied the whale's actions and the children's hands embodied those of the mouse (Photograph 3.15). They loved lifting their hands up and bringing them down on the carpet as if they were Amos being hurt hitting the water.

Photograph 3.14 Following Along When Reading a Text Extract.

Photograph 3.15 Hands-as-Amos on Teacher-as-Boris.

Finally, using dramatic playing in pairs with one-as-Amos and the other-as-Boris I again read the passage as they embodied the actions of the characters.

Following these physically active movements we became quite still as we engaged in a brief reflective discussion about why Amos was so "crazy with rage." I made sure that everyone had a chance to speak and several people simply said that he was physically hurt. Several children nodded quietly when I asked if they had ever lashed out and hurt friends.

All of this dramatic playing had been to mediate their *comprehension* of this passage, viewed primarily as "sense-making" (Aukerman, 2008) or authoring understanding that is 'new' from the children's viewpoint. The children made sense of the key phrase "crazy with rage" contextualized by the children's real-and-imagined experience of the characters' actions and reactions in the event. Knowing our goal of *inference* in relation to Boris' perspective on Amos' action, I asked how they thought Boris probably felt about what Amos had done. The generic idea of "mad" was extended when some children used their bodies in brief dramatic performances to show the whole group ideas of what Boris *could* have done in response to Amos punching him. In doing so the meaning of "rage," a word that was new to the children, came to life. One girl showed how Boris could have hit Amos into the air because of his (using a synonym when I asked her to do so) "anger." Likewise, a boy said an "out of control" Boris could have killed Amos: he swung his fist to represent contact with a flipper.

Reading from the extract again, but now from the perspective of Boris, I stopped at the word "sounded." Again, we all used our hands but now as if all were whales. I reminded them of what we had done earlier in the session as I directed their attention to a drawing on the whiteboard. Previously, all had embodied whales diving ('sounding') and leaping ('breaching'), as part of whales' daily life. Amos had been hurt but it was now clear to them that Boris had not intended to hurt him. As one boy moved his hands up-and-down he said, "Whales sound and breach" but with a tone suggesting that's what whales do.

As I read the next few sentences, I showed them how they could use one hand as Amos and the other as Boris; in dramatic playing they could simultaneously embody and experience *both* perspectives. I read on:

> Amos screamed and punched at Boris until he remembered he owed his life to the whale and quietly climbed on his back. From then on, whenever Boris wanted to sound, he warned Amos in advance and got his okay, and whenever he sounded, Amos took a swim.

In a brief reflection, a couple of the children inferred that both Amos and Boris must have apologized. Then when I asked if they thought they were friends one boy said they were "really good friends" because they agreed on what to do to avoid fights. There were nods of agreement as one girl said, "that was win-win."

Clearly, many children had demonstrated deep understanding of this complex passage. If I had wanted a written record I could have asked them to create a more tangible artifact by writing or drawing on their copy of the page. I could also have reflected with them on how we had comprehended and inferred meaning and then drawn connections with reading strategies they were more familiar with.

Social Curriculum Goal: How Do We Make and Keep Friends?

As a final task for the second session, I wanted the children to connect the meaning they had just been making about *Amos and Boris* with more abstract ideas they had previously shared. In doing so I shifted focus specifically to social curriculum goals in relation to friendship. Restated as inquiry questions these were: How do we make friends? What do friends do together to stay friends? How do we make friends with those who seem to be very different from us?

On the wall was a display of the children's ideas about how people make friends and what friends do together (Photograph 3.16). Toward the end of the first session, the children had reflected on their dramatic playing as whales as well as their sequencing of the events. In a brief inquiry discussion they had identified and agreed upon their ideas. I had typed up these ideas and cut up printed pages so that each statement could be used separately in addition to using their ideas collectively.

I removed them from the wall and laid out these pieces of **paper on the floor**, asked the children to work in pairs to select one of the ideas, talk together reflectively, and **stand up when they had agreed** on an example. They shared these in five-second *tableaux* after a **3-2-1 countdown**. The girls in Photograph 3.17 were showing, in a brief moment of dramatic performance, how they liked to hug to "help each other feel good." Why? Because "that makes you like each other and want to play together."

Plan to Use Teacher-in-Role

One of the most versatile tools for mediating meaning-making in dramatic pedagogy is the strategy of teacher-in-role. Unlike a drawing, a video, or children's unmediated dramatic playing, teaching in role is inherently a dialogic tool: you make meaning *with* the young people as you answer and address them in dialogue.

In previous examples I've shown how I used the strategy when my orientation was more toward building background knowledge by "limiting meaning-making" (using the words on the horizontal arrows in

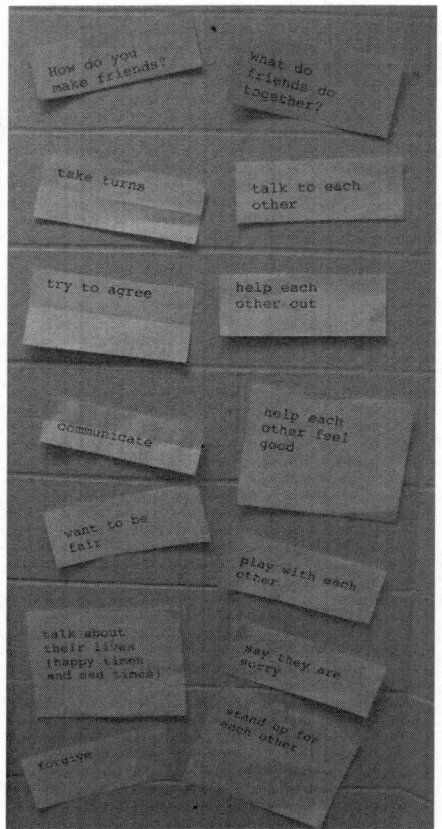

Photograph 3.16 Displaying Ideas.

Figure 3.4). In this example the orientation was more toward "opening up meaning" to develop new understanding in the exploration of inquiry questions (though at the same time, sometimes limiting meaning as people reached agreement).

Our final session focused on the 'beached whale' event and the topic of friendship. The planned order was important because the children's understanding of that event and why Amos would have worked so hard to convince elephants to help, was informed both by the background knowledge previously built and by their experience and analysis of how the friends had come through the earlier challenge to their friendship. I continued to open up meaning about friendship with the children and was able to push the boundaries beyond the uncontroversial 'feeling good' meaning that had been shared at the close of the second session.

Photograph 3.17 Friends Like to Hug.

As we gathered in the carpeted area and talked about the page we had looked at in the previous session, intending to return to our social curriculum inquiry questions on the theme of friendship I asked the children if they thought Amos should try to make friends with the elephants. The day before, in sharing their five-second tableaux the children had agreed that friends "communicate." They had also agreed that it might be harder to make new friends when people come from different cultures or are different sizes (like Amos and Boris). Though there was broad agreement that, for Amos, trying to make friends with elephants would be important to try as a first step, one child noted that elephants and mice don't speak the same language. I asked them to agree that for our purposes the animals would be able to understand each other and that we would speak in English, just like Amos and Boris. I was limiting their meaning-making by 'establishing agreed understanding' about the narrative world.

At first, I embodied an elephant that they-as-Amos could encounter (Photograph 3.18). Some of the children *sculpted* me: several showed me how to hold and move my arm like a trunk (more agreed limitations) and some delighted in illustrating elephant greeting sounds as they shared

Photograph 3.18 Teacher-as-an-Elephant.

their prior knowledge. Then all had an opportunity to slip into dialogue with me-as-the-elephant and in reflective analysis a few children made some additional suggestions and there was some agreement about how each-as-a-mouse might "communicate" and show "respect" (within the agreed limitations of our goals). Talking softly and giving a gift of food were suggested and embodied (as further limitations).

My modeling prepared the children to improvise dialogue together briefly with a partner in a space away from others: via dramatic playing, one child-as-Amos tried to communicate and persuade the other-as-an-elephant to help Boris (Photograph 3.19).

Inquiry questions are premised on opening up meaning and discovering novel diverse ideas (which at the same time limit our focus of concern). When learning objectives are restated as questions that the group is interested in, agreeing to focus on them creates a goal of sharing, creating, and thus opening up multiple possible meanings about that aspect of the topic. It also assumes the value of contextualized dissonance. In Figure 3.4 this is represented by how the right-hand arrow becomes increasingly open: some meanings may be more tentative, less clear or, if pressed, seen as less shared among the people in the group. Similarly, the increasingly faint dotted arcs represent that participants' ideas are more diverse, and that the young people are less able to expect to turn to the given curriculum for answers or to expect that shared understandings will emerge from the group.

Photograph 3.19 Children-as-Amos and -as-Elephants.

In contrast, when my orientation had been toward building back-ground knowledge in any conversation as teacher-leader I had to decide whether or not to share or agree on particular information with every-one. This was an example of how I intended to limit meaning-making by the group—not permanently, but in the context of the current focus. For example, having agreed that whales actually do communicate in singing and that in the story a whale can talk with a mouse, unless a majority of the group had been really interested at that time I would not have been open to having more than a cursory discussion about the complexity of how whales communicate with one another and with other creatures if one of the children had raised the issue. That would have been a distrac-tion from our goal.

Bringing the children together I asked only half to stand (the children-as-elephants) while the children-as-Amos sat. I gave those sitting a reason to watch and listen: "Listen carefully to what the elephants say. I'll ask you mice in a minute if you think it's going to work." Then, using *dialogue-in-role*, as-an-elephant I talked with the children-as-other-elephants (Photograph 3.20).

"We're elephants. Why should we help a whale or a mouse?" I asked. As several of the children answered me, the meaning of the

Photograph 3.20 Dialogue-as-Elephants.

elephant-mice encounter in relation to the topic of friendship was being opened up.

BRIAN: Why should I help a mouse? What's he got to do with me?
JOHN : We should help him.
BRIAN: Why? I'm not a mouse.
MARY : He's nice.
BRIAN: But he's not an elephant.
MARY : Well you should help others.
JOHN : You might need his help sometime.

Turning to the children-as-Amos who had been an audience to their peers I asked if they thought the plan was going to work. There were nods; none said it wouldn't. When I asked the children how they thought the elephants had communicated, one boy said, "He was respectful. He gave me a peanut."

With time running out, I brought the children to the carpet and read to the end of the story. Knowing that Amos and the elephants had successfully returned Boris to his ocean home, there was a satisfied pause as I closed the book.

To conclude, I asked the children to reflect verbally on what they now thought about friendship after meeting Amos and Boris and the elephants. Some of the polyphonic responses were as follows:

> Help each other out, like when Boris got hurt.
> You shouldn't care about size.
> Don't pick on anyone or they might turn on you.
> Friends help each other in hard times.
> Say you're sorry.
> Forgive people like when Boris forgave Amos for punching him.
> Get more help from other people.

I ended by asking the children to "Point to a person you can get help from in our class ... and another ... and another." The children laughed as they kept on using the tool of **pointing**. With an implicit focus on community building, I reminded them of a valuable piece of old knowledge, "We can all help each other, can't we." We concluded the session by embodying "helping each other" in an ensemble group hug (see Photograph 3.21).

A few things I remember about
DEVELOPING NEW UNDERSTANDING

- Conversations may continue when people are moving as well as sitting.
- I provide lots of multipurpose artifacts that people can use as material tools: paper, markers, blocks, cloth, musical instruments, etc.
- I invite people to make things and then use those artifacts. When I take photographs of their still images we may talk about them.
- I know whether my orientation is more toward opening up or limiting their meaning-making: interpret and infer meaning or comprehend for information?

Selecting Dramatic Strategies

Strategies are teaching tools used to mediate learning. In every task I use strategies in the sense that we engage in predictable social practices (that I've used successfully before) ranging from simple active strategies, like using the phrase, "Step forward when you have an idea," to complex dramatic strategies, like small groups creating and sharing tableaux. Strategies cannot simply be 'implemented.' The examples in this chapter

Photograph 3.21 Group Hug.

show tools being used strategically in tasks for different social and academic purposes: getting to know a group, beginning work, building background knowledge, and developing understanding while exploring inquiry questions. All can be used in creating what Sawyer (2007) calls "semi-structures" to support dialogue. In this section I step back from planning for a particular session to consider how to select one dramatic strategy over another for mediating learning in a particular task; here I don't bold and italicize dramatic strategies. I categorize by returning to the learning modes I introduced in Chapter 1.

Over thirty years ago Dorothy Heathcote (1980/1984) published her now famous list of thirty-three theatre and film "conventions" on which all subsequent books and charts of dramatic strategies are based. First in the list is "role" in the now widely used sense of a person who by convention represents someone else who is open to dialogue as if she or he is elsewhere. As Heathcote puts it, "The role actually present, naturalistic, yet significantly behaving, giving, and accepting responses" (p. 166). Teaching in role uses not only the most versatile convention but is also the most demanding dramatic strategy. Heathcote's list continues with

Table 3.2 Selecting Dramatic Strategies

Dramatic learning mode	Dramatic learning social practices	Dramatic action	High teacher structure/low student choice: whole group teacher-led strategies	Medium teacher structure/medium student choice: whole group mostly student-led with teacher support	Low teacher structure/high student choice: includes students working in 'teacher-less spaces'	Key teacher language
Dramatic Playing	Experiencing with social imagination	Stepping into imagined spaces to embody and experience as if we are in an event … and stepping out	The Sun Shines on All Those Who …/Cross the circle/ classroom as if …; Soundscape	Students-in-role interact with teacher-in-role; make model of scene	Teacher directs as pairs, threes, or small groups improvise part of event	'Shall we all imagine that we are …?' 'What might we be doing?' 'What were you doing?' 'How did it feel?'
Dramatic Performance	Showing and telling about an event as teacher-in-role or as students-in-role	Choosing to show/tell us as if we/they are in an event	Show us … and freeze	"What are you doing?": one or more students add on to teacher's/another student's action	Pairs, threes, or small groups with student-leaders show and explain tableaux of an event they've improvised; students-in-role being hotseated	'What do you want us to focus on?' 'What did you intend to show us?'

(Continued)

Table 3.2 (Continued)

Dramatic learning mode	Dramatic learning social practices	Dramatic action	High teacher structure/low student choice: whole group teacher-led strategies	Medium teacher structure/ medium student choice: whole group mostly student-led with teacher support	Low teacher structure/high student choice: includes students working in 'teacher-less spaces'	Key teacher language
Dramatic Reflection	Reflecting and interpreting an event as dramatic spectators or spect-actors	Watching and listening to others, to reflect and interpret as if they/we are in an event	Hotseating teacher-in-role; Sculpt teacher	Students interpret student-made tableau of event; add possible thoughts as thought-tracking	Hotseating students-in-role; sculpt students	'What do you want to find out?' 'What do you notice?' 'What did we find out?'
Dramatic Inquiry	Dialogic inquiry into the meaning of a topic/text including through dramatic playing, dramatic performance, and dramatic reflection	Dialoguing and inquiring into a topic/text as if we are various other people.	Continuum; Four Corners	Consciousness Threes/Alley	Tableaux with conflicting viewpoints	'What have we found out about our inquiry question?' 'What would you like to know (more) about?'

variations on still and moving images of people including as if through-out photographs or video (employed in the dramatic strategy of creating tableaux) and concludes with verbal and written conventions (e.g. dictating, reading, or writing a letter). Heathcote stresses the overarching learning purpose of conventions: "they all slow down time and enable classes to get a grip on decisions and their own thinking" (p. 166). Though conventions were employed in the teaching I describe in this book, I mostly focus my analysis on the use of dramatic strategies. Based on her work, Jonothan Neelands (1990) produced the first, and still widely used, book of dramatic strategies, using terminology that I employ, including hotseating, thought-tracking, and teacher-in-role.

I categorize dramatic strategies in Table 3.2 by their increasing social demand on the young people and in relation to the four dramatic learning modes. In the *Amos and Boris* work I used most of the strategies listed in the High and Medium teacher structure columns. The least demanding strategies for students are the most teacher structured and most limiting of participants' choices (as an amalgam of the task dimensions listed in Table 3.1). The strategies that are least demanding on students are all whole-group, teacher-led, and brief. Working with the whole group not only directly builds community it also allows me to follow these essential procedures:

- clarify tasks
- demonstrate and model what to do
- take questions
- review

I remind teachers who seem impatient with learning how to use dramatic approaches that just as it took time to learn, for example, how to read aloud to children or lead a discussion with a particular group, so it takes time to become comfortable with, and knowledgeable about, being hotseated by students. Learning how to share narratives with young people was worthwhile; so was learning how to talk with them as if I was one of the characters. Further, since using a strategy is always situated in a particular context it may be introduced gradually into existing classroom structures and social practices a few minutes at a time. This is a way to move toward becoming more comfortable using dramatic pedagogy more often.

Dramatic Playing Strategies

The younger children are, the easier it is to engage them in dramatic playing. Older students have to be supported into feeling safe enough to talk and/or move as if they are other people and/or are elsewhere. I must take the lead by modeling games and joining in to imagine with participants. Though I have classified hotseating as a dramatic performance strategy, showing a group that I can briefly move at will in and out of the world of a narrative as a character demonstrates that dramatic playing can become a 'normal' part of classroom life. It's a short step then into talking for a few seconds with people as if we are all inside the world of the narrative and inviting their questions.

Cross the Circle/Classroom

In Chapter 1 I gave an example of playing 'Cross the Circle' with the middle school students. Forming a circle of chairs with upper elementary or older students provides a sense of security. The game only requires that the students cross the circle as if they are a character in a narrative for a few seconds. Often I play this game, as I did with the middle school students, after playing an across the circle game that does not require embodiment as if they are another person, for example, The Sun Shines.

With Megan's seven- and eight-year-old children we didn't form a circle but rather gathered together in the way they were used to—on the carpet by the smart board. The equivalent of 'Cross the Circle' was 'Cross the Classroom.' They did this very early on when we all moved around the room for 10–15 seconds, as if we were whales swimming, and then came back to sit on the carpet. Several times over the sessions everyone similarly embodied the same creature/character for very short periods of time sometimes moving in the room, other times moving just our hands: as Boris, as whales meeting and greeting, and as Amos on his ship.

Soundscape

A simple but powerful way to create a shared experience of an event is to conduct the group in soundscaping. Megan's class loved to make the sounds of a hurricane just using their hands and bodies. It's more demanding to use percussion instruments. People need time to experiment with making sounds and need some direction about how to create the dynamics of sound rather than just noise.

Modelmaking

I have a box of wooden blocks that small groups of all ages have used to make models of scenes or of entire worlds. Unifix cubes can represent characters and I use construction paper for signage. Preschool children have created the wall that Humpty Dumpty fell off; college students have created a tomb for *Romeo and Juliet*. Making models can raise significant questions like, how high was the wall? Or, what was in-between Verona and Mantua?

Dialogue-in-Role

In the final session in Megan's classroom, in role as Boris I talked with the students as if they were all Amos. I-as-an-elephant also talked with students-as-elephants. Keeping it brief reduced the improvisational demands on everyone. Additionally, because of the task sequence, everyone already knew whom they were imagining, and why they were in the scene. Since some students watched others the scene had a performative dimension to it but this was only minimally demanding on the performing students because the dramatic playing was foregrounded.

Teacher Directs Small Groups' Improvisation

Like many teachers I made the mistake of beginning my use of dramatic pedagogy by asking young people to get into groups to 'act out' a story. Early on in my career as a secondary teacher I didn't realize that the arguments in groups were more often my responsibility than those of the students. Asking them to work in 'teacher-less spaces,' with little prior experience of small group work or a clear goal, was asking for trouble.

I now regard small group improvisation as among the 'most demanding' strategies of dramatic playing. Whereas most preschool children are pretending all day long and young school-aged children will often be happy to enact or make-up stories, there are two main reasons why I advise against jumping into small group improvisation without teacher direction. First, I always need to be sure that the students can already do with me any task I am asking them to do without me. Second, if children work alone in groups I must rely on either the good social health of every small group and/or on the developed leadership skills of at least one student in each group.

I did expect the young people in Megan's classroom to improvise when I asked the children in pairs to imagine that they were elephants and mice. However, I modeled the task and reduced the demands on the children to a minimum in three ways: I waited to use this strategy until the end of the third session, they only had to improvise for about two minutes with a clearly defined goal, and the children had to collaborate with only one other person chosen by Megan.

Another way to provide more structure is to direct students' actions in creating tableaux and assist them as they move into dramatic performance mode in sharing. I can guide small groups (pairs are the least demanding) using language like the following:

- You have two minutes to agree on the moment you want to show.
- How does this idea connect with our inquiry question? What do you want us to think about?

- Choose a narrator/director; if you're having difficulty deciding, the shortest person can direct this time.
- Directors, you have three minutes to sculpt everyone into an image. You take the lead here but everyone must agree with your idea.
- Relax. Any problems?
- Directors, you're also going to narrate when we share. So, now work with everyone in the group to agree on what you will say about your group image.
- Let's all practice together. I'll go 3-2-1 and you'll step into the tableau. Narrators speak the lines you are going to say.
- Relax. How did that work? Any problems? Director/narrators, we're going to do it again. This time watch closely so you can make changes.
- Let's all practice together again.
- OK, now we're going to see these one at a time. Who would like to go first?
- Everyone else can relax for now. Narrator, what do you want us to watch for? OK, so let's watch for that.
- Narrator, are you ready?
- [Assist as necessary so that the performance feels successful.]
- So, what did you notice here? What did that make you think about our inquiry question?

Dramatic Performance Strategies

If I want students to *show* ideas as well as talk about them then they must become comfortable having peers watch them perform. Brief performances are often best, not only early on.

Show Us

This strategy involves having young people move all at the same time and then freeze to 'show us' an image. It is the least demanding way to move everyone into a moment of dramatic performance. Young children are eager to be active: Megan's children were all ready to pretend to be whales swimming, sounding, and breaching. At any moment I could have moved from dramatic playing into performance by asking them to freeze to 'show us sounding,' etc. All could briefly look at a couple of frozen volunteers.

Though older students are less ready to move, they are more likely to do so if everyone does so at the same time. If high school students were studying *Moby Dick*, I could ask them (if necessary at their desks or standing beside them) to freeze to 'show us' an image that requires minimal physical movement, for example, a whaler with a harpoon. Then they could move again to show, for example, a whaler on deck of a ship, freezing to show us throwing a harpoon, seeing it hit a whale, etc. Of course, the students would have to see a reason for doing this in the world of the narrative, not just because I ask them. For example, I could use the convention of showing an illustration from a book on whaling.

What Are You Doing?

This game involves a volunteer stepping into the circle to perform an action as if s/he is a character at a moment in the story. A second person chooses to step in to ask, "What are you doing?" The first person tells them. At that point the first performer may leave the circle, moving to a new spot, leaving the second person who may walk around in the space until s/he stops to perform an action. A third person steps in to ask again, "What are you doing?" as the game continues.

After 'Show Us' this game is likely to be the easiest way to develop comfort with dramatic performance about a piece of text the students have some knowledge of. First, by standing (or sitting) in a circle we visually identify the imaginary line between 'inside the world of the story' (stepping forward to move as a character) and 'outside' (stepping out). Second, the performing and interaction demands are brief and in the control of the initial performer. As with all games, modeling how to play it is essential.

There are variations. First, the pair can have a conversation as if they are in the fictional world, to be ended when the first person leaves. Second, the person who joins in steps in as a character, e.g. as Ishmael talking to Ahab. Finally, the game can include **add-on**: the second person stays and then a third and a fourth person comes to 'add on' by joining in to create, for example, a scene with multiple crew members on deck. Unless the teacher ends the dramatic performance, the initial performer controls this by returning to the circle.

Showing Tableaux

As described above, a student who was the director during the creation of the tableaux becomes the narrator during the showing. This person directs the others in their small group to show the story they want to tell. He or she remains outside the image to mediate interpretation for the rest of the class. Rather than show tableaux as 'guessing games,' the director/narrator, with the assistance of the other performers, can tell the spectators where the scene takes place and what it is that they are about to see. Each person can identify him or herself as the character they are portraying and then step into the imagined space.

Tableau is a very popular strategy. There are multiple variations that make the strategy increasingly demanding. Showing a still image with one director/narrator and one performer is the easiest. More demanding is increasing the number of participants, bringing an image to life for 5–10 seconds without words, and then adding words that could be a caption or with each person speaking a phrase (that may be from the text). Additionally, two or more images can be presented in sequence, for example, before and after an event, or in contrast, for example, from two different perspectives. Creators of tableaux can employ conventions as if in e.g. photographs, video clips, statues, or nightmares.

Hotseating Students-in-Role

This is one of the most demanding strategies for students. However, when a student knows the perspective of a character well, seems able to move in-and-out of the fictional space at ease, and has already demonstrated that they can answer their peers seriously, then they are likely ready briefly to take on this responsibility.

There are several ways to support them. First, I may move into hotseating seamlessly when in a discussion a student begins to say something like, "Well I think she would have ..." I sometimes ask, "Could you speak as if you are that person for a moment? Do you want to come and sit on the chair?" and then, "Could we ask you-as-him/her a few questions?" Second, I can join the student. Sometimes I offer, "How about we're both the person and either of us can speak or answer?" Third, I can invite the whole group to join me in a collective role hotseating the student-in-role.

Dramatic Reflection Strategies

Dramatic reflection is the inverse of dramatic performance. As people perform they *show and tell* for spectators who *watch and listen* as they reflect to interpret and evaluate actions and events in the real-and-imagined world of the performance either from a position as themselves or as if they too are in the narrative world.

Hotseating Teacher-in-Role

Hotseating teacher-in-role is the easiest way to have students watch, listen and interpret. All of the children in Megan's class were captivated by me-as-Boris and all were interested in asking questions to find out about the beached whale.

Similarly, with high school students reading *Moby Dick* they could dialogue with the teacher-as-Ahab. Just as the children met Boris on the beach, I always have to choose, or have the students choose, where and when they might meet and talk with a character in relation to a narrative event. It is less demanding if they encounter a character as themselves. If the group wish to do so, using a collective role they could imagine meeting Ahab as if they are crew on the *Pequod* believing they may have seen the white whale. Especially if I use hotseating early on without having read much of the text it's important that I know (even if the students don't) *where and when* they are encountering the character: I need to know what information to draw on to answer their questions (and what not to refer to because the character does not yet know). For example, are they meeting Captain Ahab before or after the first sighting of Moby Dick?

Teaching young people to reflect using hotseating requires that I model for them how I move in-and-out of the fictional world. Just as I moved my body to become Boris and then returned to the classroom world, so with older students I could, for example, show and tell them: "When I sit in the chair I'll be Captain Ahab sitting on a capstan on the *Pequod* just after they sight Moby Dick. When I stand up, I'll be Mr. Brian, back in the classroom."

Sculpting Teacher/Students

Sculpting their teacher (as Megan's children did briefly with me-as-an-elephant) is very engaging for students, can be a preparation for hotseating, and is an easy way for students to dialogue about the narrative world as they create a still image of a character in an event. We can always use conventions such as creating a sculpture, a photograph, a portrait, or a memory.

As with hotseating I must be ready to model how to step in and out of the imagined scene. I can try out words and actions as if I am the character but then immediately step back into the classroom to check: "Did I get that right? What do you want me to say? What is it you are trying to show here?" etc. In our dialogue I am assisting them to interpret a character's action in an event by showing possibilities.

Sculpting one or more peers is more demanding. A 'no touching, just show' rule is especially important with adolescents. As the students being sculpted may not understand the sculptor's intentions I remain ready to ask the sorts of questions I would likely have asked if they were sculpting me.

Students Interpreting Student-created Tableau

When students interpret a still image made by peers this is likely much more demanding than meeting a teacher-in-role. First of all, they are more likely to laugh. Second, it may be more difficult because the image students make or the words they use are likely to be less carefully created than mine.

I can assist in these ways. First, I support their performance, keep any performances brief, and focus the group on reflecting. For example, using the 'Show Us' strategy I can easily move into interpreting as spectators by asking one or two of the students (or perhaps half of the group) to freeze for a few seconds, and then ask everyone else to say what they notice, what it makes them think to ask the character etc. Similarly, in sharing student-created tableaux, I can introduce a '3-2-1-freeze' countdown.

Second, agreeing on an interpretative *reason* for watching. In Megan's classroom the children-as-Amos watched the children-as-elephants talking with me-as-an-elephant. They were watching and listening for whether the elephants were going to help. After a short performance we shifted into a whole group reflection.

Third, any questions that spectators have can be answered by hotseating me or by the group as a whole. One strategy to use is ***thought-tracking***. Rather than asking the person showing the image to speak, anyone else can come up, touch them on the shoulder and speak the thoughts they imagine may be in their mind. Alternatively they could share the thoughts from where they are sitting or standing. Sharing many possible thoughts promotes a more polyphonic dialogue.

Hotseating Students-in-Role

Provided students have chosen to perform, their presentations are serious, and they do not begin to feel exposed, young people can hotseat their peers. As I noted above under the subsection on dramatic performance strategies, students need not perform alone. Additionally, everything I noted about the previous strategy applies in this case, only more so.

Additionally, when I mediate a reflective discussion (that may be brief) I can both assist performers by monitoring and seeking clarification of questions, and I can deepen reflection by using any response from the student or students-in-role as a jumping off point for whole group dialogue. I don't just leave them to it.

Dramatic Inquiry Strategies

Over time dialogue becomes dialogic inquiry when students explore a topic creating meaning across sequenced tasks. Goals may be restated as inquiry questions providing an ongoing focus across tasks, for example in *Amos and Boris*, how do we make friends? In *Moby Dick*, why is Ahab so obsessed with the white whale? In dramatic inquiry mode, young people inquire, either as themselves or as if they are other people (for example, as physicians caring for Jack, or as mice helping Amos, or as sailors on the *Pequod*) about a topic that is contextualized in a sequence of dramatized narrative events.

The following strategies are ones that are especially useful for opening up or extending inquiry.

Continuum

At the end of our first *Amos and Boris* session, as the children were getting ready to go to lunch, I asked them to line up. The children had just encountered me-as-Boris beached and had begun to wonder what to do. All were agreed that as a friend he would want to help him but they were unsure how. I asked them to stand close to where I had been lying on the carpet if they thought Amos *had* to get the help of others to be able to rescue Boris. The closer they stood to the door the more they thought he could work alone. If they weren't sure I asked them to stand in the middle. Though lunch was clearly looming in the minds of many, we did have a brief polyphonic conversation as I asked the children to tell the person beside them why they were standing there. Inviting public explanations, several children spoke. That was when it became clear that many had not realized the significance in this event of the relative size of mouse and whale. It was also when the idea of seeking out elephants arose.

I have used this strategy with all ages of students. It's a dramatic strategy when the students dialogue in role. Not only can it lead to intense sharing with everyone able to speak, once we move into public sharing the strategy makes visible one person's ideas in relation to others. Outliers have to justify their position. Further, the strategy can make *change* in understanding more visible. After exchanges, I ask people to move from where they are standing on the continuum if they have changed their mind in any way. Those who move have a chance to explain their reasoning. Finally, continuum is a strategy that can be returned to with the same question but later in the work.

Continuum is similar to the **'Four Corners'** strategy where in response to a question people go to a corner to show that they 'agree,' 'strongly agree,' 'disagree,' or 'strongly disagree,' staying in the middle for 'not sure.' Again, dialogue can lead to clarification of thinking for teacher and change in opinion or understanding by students. An advantage of Continuum is that relative positions and nuanced changes in meaning may be more visible.

Consciousness Threes/Alley

In the work on *Brave Margaret* I used Consciousness Threes as the young people in threes explored an urgent decision over what the warriors should do: fight or not fight the giant? A similar strategy is Consciousness Alley where everyone in the group stands in two lines. One side argues for going ahead with whatever idea is being considered, the other side giving a counter argument to a single volunteer who moves up and down the line in response. Again, everyone speaks at the same time, and there is a public analysis of how the person in the middle felt and how persuasive he or she found the arguments, and why.

Others call these strategies 'Conscience' Threes/Alley but I prefer to emphasize that the person in the middle may not only be considering ethical decisions of conscience, they may also be listening, and responding to, competing consciousnesses on any urgent or difficult question; they may be hearing the viewpoints of many other people in their lives not just internalized moral voices. For example, with the children in Megan's classroom we could have used the strategy to consider whether or not Amos should go to sea again at the end of the story. With high school students reading *Moby Dick* they might explore whether the person in the middle should try to convince Ahab to abandon his search for the white whale.

Tableaux with Competing Viewpoints

In writing about tableaux above, I noted how demanding this strategy can be for students, and showed how as teacher I can mediate both the creation and sharing of tableaux to support a group in finding more significance in their work. An advantage of the strategy is that students may create and present images for whole group analysis that capture more meaning than if they only used words. Further, in moments of stillness, or brief movement, these are much more significant performances of meaning than any light-hearted or superficial 'skit' focused on communicating information.

Competing tableaux can take explorations further. When small groups create and share tableaux, the images may be carefully crafted utterances that may provoke intense dialogue. Further, dialogue may lead to new understanding especially when groups share competing viewpoints on the same event. Whereas in Consciousness Threes/Alley viewpoints are reduced to words of advice, focused on one character's decision, competing tableaux can introduce more nuanced and complex perspectives and images of action. Further, when used after exploring viewpoints in other tasks, ideas presented may both summarize agreement in a small group while highlighting differences across groups when they are shared. Examples from work with other groups include the following.

Each group devises *alternative explanations* for an event. These are all possible interpretations of why something significant happened. For example, what may have happened in the past to explain why Ahab is so obsessed with finding the white whale?

Each group creates *contrasting images* showing family photographs taken before and after an event, for example the death of a character. The feelings of characters, their thoughts about events, and their relationships with one another can be discussed when analyzing the images.

Each group shows *a possible event* in a character's future that is not in the text, but that is, based on what has happened previously. These competing predictions may be analyzed for what they reveal about events, characters, or situations.

**A few things I remember about
CHOOSING DRAMATIC STRATEGIES**

- I start with the high teacher structure and least socially demanding strategies for the students and then begin to use less teacher structure.
- I consider employing a convention.
- Two good minutes is better than ten mediocre minutes.
- I plan to join in and imagine with young people.
- I learn strategies with the students and ask them how to make them better.

Conclusion: Planning is Preparing for a Journey

My advice to a reader who's like me? Start slow. Start short. Give students choice from day one. Plan to integrate from the beginning. Pretend with the kids. Read these chapters so you can see strategies in action. Take notes. Try things out. Enjoy learning!

Planning prepares for teaching that will better mediate learning on a shared journey of exploration. I often make my planning visible and to an extent negotiable. Often I write core ideas on an index card that I refer to openly. Sometimes I tell the young people when I am trying out a new game or strategy and that I'd appreciate their help and feedback. Nearly always I write up inquiry questions, that I may then revise with the group, so that we can keep these in mind as we explore a topic.

I plan as much as is necessary so that *I* feel prepared for the length of time I intend to work on tasks with the group, knowing that I can pause at any time, switch to other work, and plan in response to whatever has happened. I know I have over-planned if I am unresponsive to what is actually happening in the classroom. I have under-planned if I don't know what I am going to do first and don't have alternative possible tasks.

Nothing is more important than planning from a viewpoint that includes *all* of the young people as individuals and as a community. Then I can plan how I might participate, dialogue, and inquire with them as actual people not as an abstraction.

Finally, I try to remember that my two greatest teachers are the young people, provided I ask them, and my self, when I reflect on what went well, what went not-so-well, and what we might do tomorrow because of what we learned today.

Notes

1 An event can function as a "pre-text," as an entry point into the world of a narrative text. This core concept in the field of drama in education, or process

drama, developed by the leading scholar and master practitioner, Cecily O'Neill, explains how participants' engagement can be mediated and sustained when participants are positioned, "in a firm relationship to the potential action ... establishing location, atmosphere, roles, and situations" (1995, p. 22). Further, a carefully chosen pre-text, or event, "contains the seeds of inquiry" (Taylor & Warner, 2006, p. 10).

2   Variations are to ask students to **Go Stand By** a picture that interests them and **Sit Down** together on the floor or on chairs. The aim is to encourage dialogue and to make agreement (or the lack of it) visible.

Chapter 4

Teach for Authentic and Critical Inquiry

When my 95-year-old uncle Fred was in hospice care I returned to my hometown. Though I no longer lived in Derry~Londonderry after going to university in England, with my visits and contacts across the decades, the threads that tied me to Ireland, and to him, were still strong. I felt that connection when his eyes twinkled: "Agh, Brian, have you come all the way from America to see me?"

"Sure I was coming to England anyway," I said with a joking reference to our shared cultural expectation of reducing a sense of obligation. "How are you doing?"

"Just putting one foot in front of the other," he replied. And in his familiar laconic way he added, "Though that can be hard as I don't get out of this bed too much!"

As I savored a briefer version of one of his tales about my long-deceased parents, I touched his hand to say, "You know, I've always treasured your stories. And your wisdom. Any advice from a nonagenarian to a youngster in his fifties?"

He looked me in the eye to say with measured seriousness: "Just be yourself, Brian." Fred Logan had integrity: with me he was an honest, reliable, and loving second parent and teacher who was always prepared to question people's assumptions, even on his death bed. I've carried that standard of authenticity and critique with me into the classroom.

Authentic and Critical Pedagogy

In a bold critical statement, Parker Palmer (1997) in *The Courage to Teach* declares that, "Technique is what teachers use until the real teacher arrives" (p. 5). Until then we may be haunted with becoming the sort of teacher one of his students describes: "Their words float somewhere in front of their faces like the balloon speech in cartoons" (p. 11).

Being my self, being a real teacher, is being open to change in my understanding of people and topics while engaging in authentic dialogue to support change in others' understanding. Vygotsky (1934/1986) is emphatic: "The true direction in the development of thinking is not from the individual to the social, but from the social to the individual" (p. 36). My inner dialogue with my uncle Fred's stance on life and on me has continued beyond our last meeting as part of my ongoing critical inquiry with others into how people may learn from, and teach, one another.

As Bakhtin's interpreters, Morson and Emerson (1990) conceptualize his theory, "selfhood is not a particular voice but a particular way of combining many voices within" (p. 221). It's in dialogue over time that I, and young people, have the opportunity to combine with other voices, other worldviews, including those in texts and in memory, as we address and answer one another to develop as teachers, as learners, and as a community.

As young people use mediating tools in active and dramatic learning modes to explore topics with teachers over time, dialogue grounds dialogic inquiry that is often dramatic. To build a collaborative community of inquiry, as much as possible teachers need to work with young people as an ensemble.

In this chapter, I describe examples of authentic and critical teaching in Lorraine Gaughenbaugh's fourth-grade classroom of nine- and ten-year-old children at K-4 STEM Summit Elementary School in Reynoldsburg, Ohio. Having previously taught third grade in the district she joined this new school in 2011 to teach all classes once a week in hour-long sessions with a focus on dramatic inquiry-based study of literature, social studies, and/or environmental science.[1]

In the research documented in their book *Authentic Achievement* (1996), Fred Newmann and his associates conducted a five-year federally funded nationwide project (that from now on I refer to as 'Newmann') in twenty-four elementary and secondary schools, into the success of school restructuring designed to effect student achievement. The findings of their empirical research showed that restructuring failed, unless schools paid attention to both the intellectual quality of classroom pedagogy and the vitality of the school community.

In his recommendations, Newmann proposes three inseparable dimensions of "authentic" pedagogy as "standards": disciplined inquiry, construction of knowledge, and value beyond the school. Beginning with a pedagogical framework of social and cultural assumptions, Newmann's research confirms the significance of pedagogy focused by dialogic inquiry into a topic. Newmann shows that, with the teaching and support of adults and peers in sequenced tasks, young people will connect with prior knowledge to create substantive new understanding in outcomes that have value to them, as well as their teachers, beyond individual classroom success.

Learning is authentic when dialogue and inquiry changes understanding. As Newmann puts it, "The ultimate point of disciplined inquiry is to move beyond [prior] knowledge through criticism, testing, and development of new paradigms" (p. 25). Scholars concerned with "critical inquiry" share his transformational vision and I turn to that later in this chapter.[2]

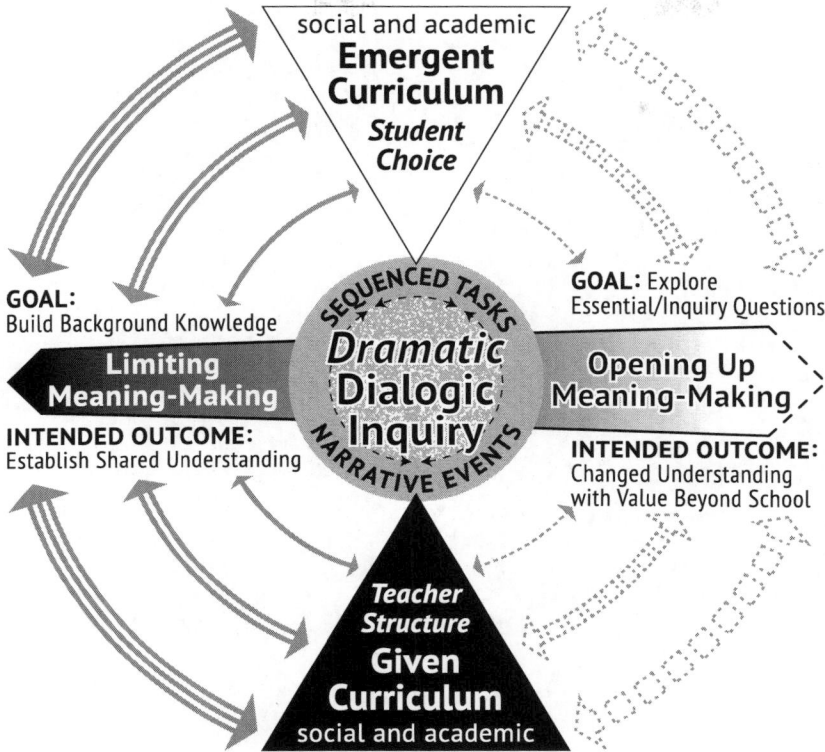

Figure 4.1 Teaching for Authentic and Critical Inquiry.

Figure 4.1 represents how classrooms may be organized to support authentic and critical learning in tasks that are both structured by the teacher and always give students choice. Using Newmann's findings, I extend the figure and ideas developed across previous chapters. In the previous chapter, as I considered planning for dialogic meaning-making, I focused mostly on dramatizing individual tasks exploring a narrative event. In this chapter I explore how tasks are *sequenced* and that a goal of exploring *essential* questions can focus dramatic dialogic inquiry across sessions. Further, in dialogue students ideally create outcomes not only of establishing shared understanding (old knowledge) but also of developing changed understanding (or new knowledge) intended to have *value beyond the school*.

Disciplined Inquiry

Lorraine is asking her nine- and ten-year-old students to consider how they might care for wounded soldiers. Immediately before I took

Photograph 4.1 Reading a Real-and-Imagined Letter.

Photograph 4.1, as *teacher-in-role* as if she was the head servant at Inverness Castle in medieval Scotland Lorraine introduced an event from the world of *Macbeth* along with an ensemble task: she tells the *students-in-role* as servants the news that the war is over in which Macbeth, their "thane" (or lord), has been fighting. One child says, spontaneously, "Hip, hip, hooray" and Lorraine encourages a group cheer. But then, with a serious tone, *reading-in-role* she reads a letter as if from the battlefield (that she had written) telling the servants that, as the injured are being brought to the castle, they must prepare to receive and care for them.

In January 2012 the students were in the midst of ten weeks of disciplined inquiry coauthoring understanding about *Macbeth*. For Newmann, inquiry is 'disciplined' both in the sense of rigor and the creation of disciplinary knowledge.

Whereas previous sessions using dramatic inquiry (described below) had been concerned with events dramatized in the play, this narrative event was implicit. Using the criteria outlined in Chapter 3, the event had 'eventness' as there was the meeting of several consciousnesses (the servants, the head-servant, the injured soldiers, as well as their thane) and 'presentness' since there was the potential that the moment could unfold in different possible directions (the soldiers may have multiple injuries, they may die or need care, the soldier's families may need to be contacted, and the celebration plans for the return of their thane may need to change). The event was a disruption in the life of the castle servants. Five minutes previously the young people-as-servants had been transforming the room in preparation for an anticipated celebration: in dramatic playing they had been focused on preparing food, practicing entertainment, and trying on fancy clothes. The sudden contrast in mood that descended as the letter was being read was a moment of dramatic surprise.

The dramatic tension inherent in the narrative event, apparent in the faces of many of the children, for the next twenty-five minutes held the students in a task of preparation for the imminent arrival of injured, and perhaps dying or dead, soldiers. As they had done since the beginning of the year they worked as an ensemble. On the board was written a shared goal, restated as an inquiry question to focus action in a sequence of tasks in the session: what will we do for the wounded (or the dead!) in order to care for them, because we feel compassion? Lorraine held five pieces of paper to provide predetermined groups a particular inquiry focus: how to care for the walking wounded, injured, unconscious, or possibly dying or dead soldiers.

Arguing that real-life situations are the appropriate holistic model for classroom inquiry, Newmann stresses that inquiry's purpose is to grapple with disciplinary problems in order to produce "intellectual accomplishments that are worthwhile, significant, and meaningful, such as those undertaken by successful adults" (p. 23). Though socially imagined, this was a real-life problem. From both the thematic viewpoint of the given literary text, broader social and physical science curricular considerations, and the personal histories of some of the families in the school whose parents were serving in the military, Lorraine believed that it was worthwhile to explore this adult topic.

The young people-as-servants were soon deeply engaged in tasks using dramatic playing mode and mediating tools that included bloodied bandages (visible in the photographs) and chairs transformed into beds. Photograph 4.2 illustrates small groups each with a clear task and a shared goal: groups collectively investigated (in preparation for sharing with the whole group) different possible ways to care for soldiers.

Students both authored understanding about the play world and explored some of the human consequences of the aftermath of the battle. For three weeks they had explored narrative events including the battle in which Macbeth had repulsed invading Norwegians, supported by a traitor, the thane of Cawdor.

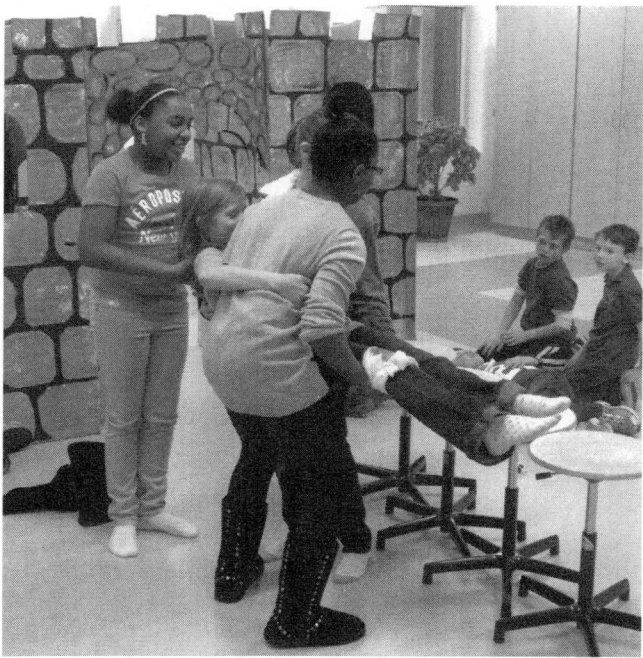

Photograph 4.2 How Will We Care for the Wounded Soldiers?

Exploring Inquiry Questions

Lorraine had chosen to inquire into 'compassion' because as one of five core values in the school (collaboration, communication, curiosity, complex thinking, and compassion) it was part of the given curriculum teachers had collaboratively developed before the school opened. She uses "the 5 C's" as cross-disciplinary themes and as a focus for informal assessment of students' ongoing social and academic achievement. Those values are displayed on posters throughout the school and contextualized in student achievement on display.

At times I ask questions intended to focus and limit meaning-making within the inquiry. As Lorraine did, I may do so either as-a-character, for example, "Servants, what do you need to prepare?" or as the teacher, for example, "Does this make sense? Do you know what to do now?" Students' responses require answers. Thus when the young people in Lorraine's classroom responded to her initial question, "Servants, what do you need to prepare?" by asking, "How many wounded soldiers are coming?" she stated, "More people than us." And when asked, "Why are we fighting the Norwegians?" she answered, "They invaded our country."

Inquiry questions can focus any dialogue. The more questioning is open-ended, the easier for students to keep conversation going. For example, are you wondering about anything? Are you curious about anything in particular? Paradoxically, many students are less likely to respond if asked directly, do you have any questions?

Questions that sustain curricular exploration over time can become "essential" (Sizer, 1984; Wiggins & McTighe, 2005). Essential inquiry questions are reworded long-term goals. Using the words of the poet Rainer Maria Rilke (1903/1993) we may "live the questions" (p. 21) as Lorraine's students did for ten weeks: Why do people kill other people? When might it be right or wrong to kill? The inquiry on this day explored an aspect of these essential questions displayed on the wall. The more questions include the following characteristics the more likely they will engage young people in extended dialogic inquiry. In the previous chapter I noted the first three 'OIA' criteria for formulating inquiry questions. I extend these below.

Questions That Are Likely to Sustain Dramatic Dialogic Inquiry

- **Open-ended** questions with no obvious answer (e.g. Why do people kill other people?) rather than 'closed' or moralizing questions with an implied right answer (e.g. Why is killing wrong?).
- **Interpretive and inferential** questions (When *might* it be right or wrong to kill?) rather than literal and factual questions (e.g. Who did Macbeth kill?).
- Questions requiring dramatic **action** in response (e.g. What will we *do* for the wounded [and the dead] to care for them because we feel compassion?) rather than abstract questions that could just be talked about (e.g. What *is* good care?).
- Questions exploring important **themes** in the narrative world (e.g. Power: Why would a person want to be a king enough to kill?) rather than less consequential ideas (e.g. What was life like for a king?).
- Questions both **contextualized** in the social world of a text and **beyond the narrative world** (e.g. Why do people, like Macbeth and Lady Macbeth, take deadly action even when they know what they do is wrong?) rather than focusing solely on particular narrative events (e.g. Why did Macbeth kill Duncan?).
- **Relational** questions (e.g. How did Macbeth's relationships with his wife, Lady Macbeth, and King Duncan, affect his decision-making?) rather than affective and individual questions (e.g. How did Macbeth feel about killing Duncan?).

Use Prior Knowledge to Build Background Knowledge

Newmann's empirical research into disciplined inquiry confirms what I showed in the previous chapter: people build background knowledge from prior knowledge about a topic while at the same time deepening understanding in elaborated dialogue. In this section I focus on a teaching orientation toward building background knowledge in inquiry through sequenced tasks; in the following section I turn to a reciprocal teaching intention of changing students' understanding.

Prior knowledge is all the potential collective knowledge that a group already knows or knows how to access about a topic—the old knowledge that could be made available in dialogic inquiry tasks. In Figure 4.1, the double-pointed arcs represent how at any time given curriculum knowledge can be shared by the teacher as well as how information, ideas, and questions, may be accessed or brought to the group by students. Additionally, authoring new understanding can make clearer the need to access additional prior knowledge.

The work on caring for soldiers occurred in Session 5. To make sense of the situation, the students drew on their own prior knowledge and on background knowledge they had built previously in a sequence of tasks. Lorraine began Session 1 as Shakespeare does, with experiencing a battle. Rather than read the opening scene, or even introduce characters, she introduced key historical and geographical information by reading a prepared **narration** that set the scene:

> This story takes place 1,000 years ago in a country far away called Scotland. It is a time of castles and knights. The story begins on a heath (a large open area where few trees or bushes grow). Another country called Norway has invaded. Two great armies meet on the heath to do battle.

Reflecting with the students, Lorraine asked the young people what they knew about battles a millennium ago and what they wanted to know: she led a very brief discussion about medieval warfare and how it was different from today. As it seemed many of the young people knew much about castles and weapons she facilitated their sharing.

Many boys provided information about swords, pikes, bows, etc., and many were eager to show how to use these as they played *Cross the Circle* contextualizing their movements as dramatic action pertinent to the narrative. For example, "Cross the circle to show us a soldier fighting in the battle between Scotland and Norway. Tell us what weapon you are using." Then, playing *What Are You Doing?*, "If someone wants to, you can come up to join in." As shown in Photograph 4.3, a person has stayed in the middle of the circle sharpening a sword and another has joined in. In their brief dramatized conversation the students shared

Photograph 4.3 What Are You Doing?

and applied prior knowledge to create an image for the whole group to see.

How much prior knowledge I present, or ask students about, may be planned and/or decided in-the-moment. The younger they are, or the less engaged by school, the more likely it is that a teacher needs to assist students to connect images of the narrative world with their concrete knowledge of the real world. For example, introducing the opening of the play to six-year-olds Lorraine did not focus on the details of weaponry but rather on the wildness of the "heath" in wind and rain. In contrast, when Megan Ballinger began with her high school students they were interested in leadership and risk-taking in battle.

Though teachers are most likely those with the most extensive background knowledge of the topic, young people always know relevant information. A prior knowledge base can be formed out of everything that I already know about the academic territory of any text plus whatever accurate (or sketchy) prior knowledge the young people are aware of. However, prior knowledge is useless unless it is selectively accessed by individuals and made available to the group by sharing it as accurate and usable information, ideas, or concepts. Telling is never enough. Nor is spending five minutes merely asking children what they know before engaging with an activity. Prior knowledge has to become visible and transformed into tangible artifacts available to the group as usable tools.

Having built mostly informational background knowledge about weapons, to engage with the event of the battle, Lorraine put students into pairs to *apply and extend* their understanding in collaborative dramatic action. In a mostly non-verbal dialogic encounter the children used appropriate imagined weapons not mentioned in the text to enact a fight. The students-as-soldiers in Photograph 4.3 are using broadswords in highly structured dramatic playing. After brief instructions, Lorraine beat a drum six times as a signal so that, without touching, pairs could move their bodies to enact improvised back-and-forth attacking and defending moves as if in a hand-to-hand fight between soldiers from each army. As they repeated the encounter several times, the young people could explore and experience in embodied imagination the use of those weapons, and the physical consequences, in the battle (see Photographs 4.4 to 4.6).

Additional strategies that other teachers have used to build background knowledge of the setting include the following:

- a **photograph** of a heath shown or projected and discussed in terms of why a battle might have been fought there;

Photograph 4.4 Students-as-Soldiers Before Battle.

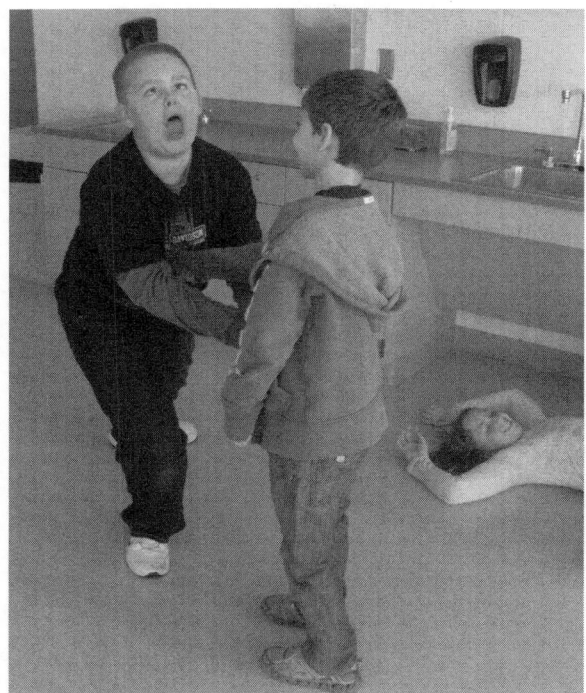

Photograph 4.5 Students-as-Soldiers During Battle.

- a *word carpet* of words on sheets of paper created by the teacher with students: what people visiting the heath after the battle might have seen, heard, smelt, or touched; students in pairs take turns leading their eyes-closed partner and telling them what they see, etc.

I find that when students are engaged by a topic invariably they are both eager to share information and are open to self-directed background knowledge building. For example, with *Macbeth* I have known students of all ages, with access to computers, do online research at home about medieval battles and castles, historical facts, and even information about cultural norms like the succession of monarchs, how kings could be chosen, moral norms at the time about beheading traitors, and assumptions about the relative power of men and women.

It takes time to organize tasks so that students can share, apply, and develop their prior knowledge and discoveries from in- and out-of-class investigations. However, I prefer to be challenged in planning a sharing than having to carry the burden of being the sole authority in the room.

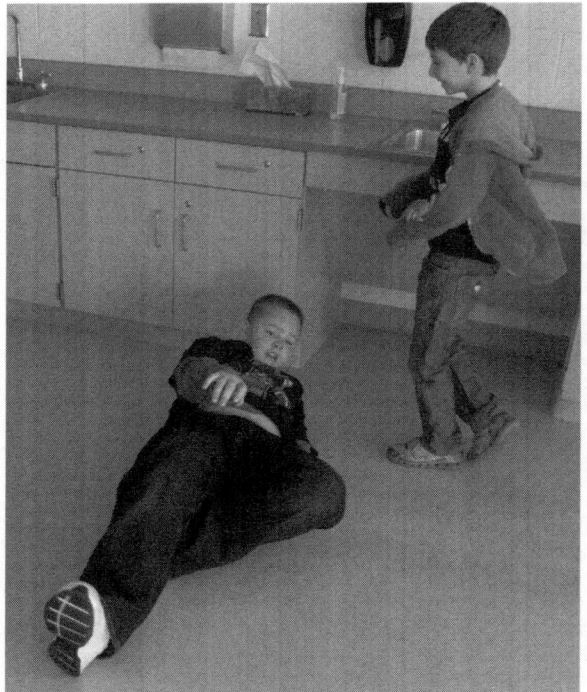

Photograph 4.6 Students-as-Soldiers After Battle.

Developing Dramatic Inquiry Skills

Embedded in Lorraine's teaching during opening tasks was continued development of students' dramatic inquiry skills. With her mediation the students revisited, experienced, and modeled for one another, skills she knew they would need to develop so that she could share more leadership in subsequent tasks as the year unfolded.

She had to remind some to "Step in as a soldier" and then "Step out into our classroom" but very quickly all were able in brief dramatic playing to move into, and then out of, the imagined world. She thanked those students who were ready to 'Show Us' and commented on their dramatic performance ability to hold still and be observed. She noted, to herself, those who were still less comfortable than others performing as if they were other people. And as they reflected, when she asked the whole group "What do you notice?" she extended generic answers by directing attention to interpret some the details of presentations: the apparent weight of a sword, the ferocity of the soldier, etc. Finally, as she posed questions like, "I wonder if it would be right or wrong to kill in a war?" she focused the group on an essential question that would guide subsequent conversations.

Deepening Understanding in Elaborated Conversation

In authentic, substantive, dialogic, polyphonic conversations that were elaborated over weekly hour-long sessions students continued to build and deepen their factual, social, and cultural background knowledge as they dialogued about battles, castles, soldiers, thanes, ladies, monarchs, and Shakespeare's language. Their dialogic inquiry was always contextualized within the events of Shakespeare's play as well as in the actions and relationships among characters.

Session 2 began with **Cross the Circle** in order collaboratively to retell what they knew about the story so far. One person who had been absent the previous week was able to learn, and ask clarifying questions, about the invasion and battle: the more eager children showed and explained their actions as they brandished weapons in combat.

To introduce the character Macbeth, Lorraine used words written on the wall that other characters use to describe Macbeth (before he murders Duncan and becomes king): brave, valiant, noble, and worthy. All had the opportunity to cross the circle to show 'brave' Macbeth, etc. Those who did not already know the words, or were unsure of their meaning, were able to experience and reflect on their meaning embodied in context as some people showed synonyms.

Then Lorraine asked students to imagine they were Norwegian soldiers watching her-as-Macbeth as some children *sculpted* her as 'brave Macbeth.' She told them that an injured soldier had told King Duncan about Macbeth's brave deeds: she would speak his words as she came to life as Macbeth in battle against the Norwegians.

Using another dramatic strategy, she *narrated her actions* to life as she moved and spoke these words from Act 1 Scene 2.

> For brave Macbeth—well he deserves that name—
> Distaining Fortune, with his brandished steel
> Which smoked with bloody execution,
> Like valor's minion carved out his passage
> Till he faced the slave.

Lifting an imagined sword on the words "brandished steel" and making an appropriate grunt with each sword swipe, Lorraine-as-Macbeth pretended to strike out at a series of opponents as she "carved out his passage till he faced the slave."

The children were transfixed and eager to discuss the meaning of the passage. They soon worked out that Macbeth had killed many enemy

Photograph 4.7 Sculpting an Image.

soldiers ("with bloody execution"), were intrigued by the word "minion," and wanted to discuss how a king could be a "slave" as they connected with their prior understanding of American slavery. As one girl said, "Just because you're called a slave doesn't mean you are one."

Lorraine then provided copies of the extract as they used **choral reading** to read the whole passage together ending with the lines she had not yet shared:

> Till he unseamed him from the nave to the chops
> And fixed his head upon our battlements.

Nearly everyone wanted to pretend they were being disemboweled! (Photograph 4.9)

One boy knew what battlements were and the children collectively inferred that Macbeth must have beheaded the Norwegian king as many delighted in embodying the action of putting his head at the top of the castle walls.

After reading the passage again in a **choral reading** now with the students making appropriate movements Lorraine asked why they

Photograph 4.8 Narrating Actions.

thought Macbeth had "fixed his head upon our battlements." One of the students inferred that, "He's sayin', 'Don't mess with us again.'." Setting them up for a later *juxtapositioning* when they discovered Macbeth murders the king, Lorraine asked, "If Duncan was to die, is Macbeth the sort of person you would want as king?" Lorraine asked them. Everyone nodded.

Newmann is adamant: as students build background knowledge they should form in-depth understanding. Rather than simply acquire information or ideas, young people must "use what they have learned to construct new knowledge ... to facilitate complex understanding of discrete problems ... around a reasonably focused topic" (pp. 25–26).

In the first two sessions students had coauthored understanding about the-Macbeth-whom-Duncan-rewards-and-trusts. When I first taught *Macbeth* to fifteen-year-old students, they never seemed to understand how Duncan would have trusted Macbeth and why the other thanes would have believed he should be king after he stabs Duncan. We had rushed forward too fast. Lorraine's students' understanding of

Photograph 4.9 Reflective Dramatic Action.

this problem for beginning readers or viewers of the play was much more complex. They were much better prepared to understand, than my class had been, how Macbeth could betray and murder his king and his friend, Banquo, as he followed his wife's advice: "false face must hide what the false heart doth know."

As Lorraine's students used the modes of dramatic learning they engaged in authentic dialogue. Newmann stresses that, as they inquire, students need to engage in dialogue that is "elaborated, complex communication both to conduct their work and to express their conclusions" (p. 26). Students should work toward elaborated communication as they use appropriate "nuanced language in extended narratives, expositions, explanations, justifications, and dialogue" (p. 26). All of these were present in these first two sessions. Consider the students' nuanced understanding of Shakespeare's language, their ability to retell a story, their comprehension and interpretation of the extract, and their brief though substantive conversations about the meaning of words new to them.

All of the learning analyzed in this section was largely oriented toward building background knowledge as students agreed on shared meaning. Though students were additionally authoring understanding new for them, in later sessions tasks were oriented more toward opening up meaning in order to author changed understanding.

Authoring More Complex Understanding

Evidence of higher-order thinking is Newmann's core standard for his second criterion of authentic pedagogy: constructing or, as I characterize it, authoring more complex understanding. In other words, unless it is clear that students have demonstrated that they have created complex conceptual understanding beyond recall of information that I have provided or merely a performance of their own existing understanding, then despite any active or dramatic task students may not have developed more than superficial meaning.

Whatever artifacts students make in tasks is evidence of the *quality* of their thinking as well as being outcomes demonstrating established or changed understandings. Superficial writing suggests lower-order thinking: recall without understanding. Sophisticated movement or a still image with an oral explanation makes visible "higher-order thinking," which "involves students in manipulating information and ideas by synthesizing, generalizing, explaining, hypothesizing, or arriving at conclusions that produce new meaning and understanding for them" (p. 33). Learners must *do* something with what they are finding out from teachers or peers, not merely listen or speak. Learners must know how to create new meaning using multiple processes, for example:

- bringing together different pieces of information (synthesizing)
- selecting ideas (comparing and contrasting)
- clarifying for a peer (explaining)
- abstracting ideas (generalizing)
- sensing a resolution to a problem (reaching toward a conclusion)
- opening up ideas (hypothesizing)

Lorraine works in a school where teachers practice the sort of "artful science" that Shirley Brice Heath (2012a) envisions. Experimental and design approaches to authoring understanding and higher-order thinking through inquiry are emphasized throughout Lorraine's school. Five aspects are widely displayed on charts: *imagine* problems and possibilities, *plan, design,* and *revise* possible solutions that you test out, and *share* results with others as everyone reflects on what they have learned. Lorraine uses the chart in her room to help children see connections between active and dramatic approaches and experimental science. Like Heath, she recognizes:

> the here-and-nowness of experience at the heart of art and science ... the making and interpreting of images and the creation of

technologies that improve image-making and cross and double-check findings given by these technologies.

(n.p.)

Her students know that creating and performing several tableaux is one example of a "design process" for sharing and comparing the results of an experiment exploring possible answers to an inquiry question. As they enact plans, students are expected to imagine and anticipate both actual material or social problems they may encounter as well as the possibilities of what they might perform. For example, in Session 5 as the children worked in small groups each had a shared goal for their task. The children in Photograph 4.10 had the objective of coming up with ideas for how they might care for a 'walking wounded' soldier.[3]

Each small group, working primarily in dramatic playing mode, was able to imagine, embody, explore, and interpret possibilities. Photograph 4.11 shows young people experimenting with how they might find out if an injured soldier was alive or dead.

Photograph 4.10 Higher-Order Thinking in Dramatic Playing.

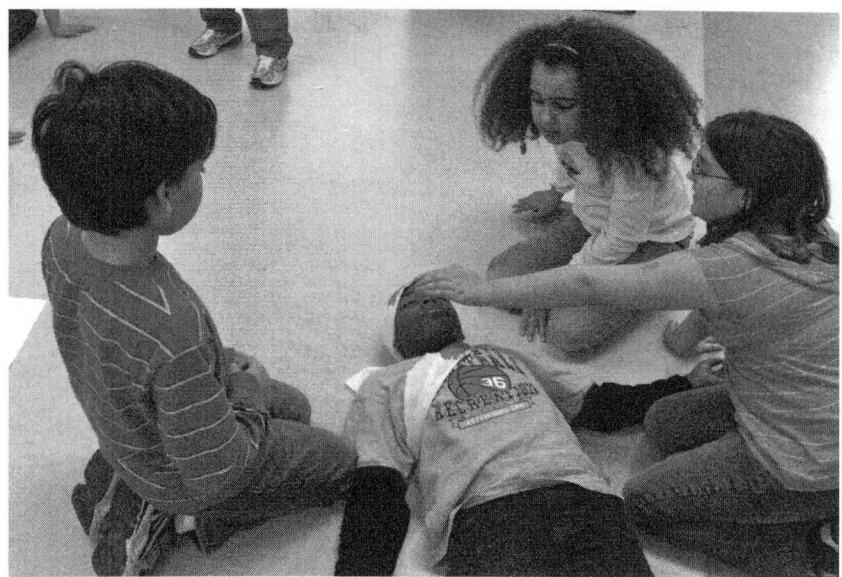

Photograph 4.11 Experimenting in Dramatic Playing.

Newmann sees higher-order thinking as evidence of students' creation of new understanding as part of ongoing disciplined dialogic inquiry in meaningful sequenced tasks. In contrast, teaching individual 'thinking skills' from Bloom's taxonomy in decontextualized tasks, or providing prior knowledge without opportunities for application, are all misguided approaches if we want students to think in order to achieve something worthwhile. Newmann laments: "Most cognitive work in schools consists of transmitting prior knowledge to students and asking them to accept it, reproduce it in fragmented statements, or recognize it on tests. Only rarely are students asked to *use* what they have learned to construct new knowledge" (p. 25, my emphasis).

The horizontal arrows on Figure 4.1 represent how, as the young people authored more complex understanding in dialogue, they were moving back-and-forth between opening up and limiting their meaning-making. They did so within and across actual and possible narrative events as they shifted orientation between hypothesizing (e.g. "What if he's not breathing?" "What if he dies?"), and resolving problems (e.g. "Give him CPR") as well as between concrete possibilities (e.g. "He needs a bandage on his head") and abstractions (e.g. "If he loses too much blood he's dead"). Of course, not all of their words or actions were 'on task'—for example, there was another girl in the group who had gone off to talk to her friend when this photograph was taken. However, based on her observations and interactions with students, Lorraine informally assessed that students were on task 99 per cent of the time. The task kept meaning in motion until they lost interest in exploring ("We're done. Can we share?").

Framing People's Perspective on Real-and-Imagined Events

Every time young people step into any event (whether in the real world or an imagined world) they "frame" their actions with a particular perspective that shapes their authoring of understanding. Heathcote (1980/1984), drawing on Erving Goffman's (1986) sociological concept of "framing", explains:

> In any social encounter there are two aspects present. One is the *action* necessary for the event to progress forward toward conclusion. The other is the *perspective* from which people are coming to enter the event. This is frame, and frame is the main agent in providing tension and *meaning* for the participants.
>
> (p. 163, my emphasis)

Significantly, for Heathcote (1980/1984) the young people in Lorraine's classroom were "framed into a position of influence":

> I find it a general rule that people have most power to become involved at a *caring and urgently involved* level if they are placed in a quite specific relationship with the action, because this brings with it inevitably the *responsibility*, and more particularly, the *viewpoint* which gets them into an effective involvement ... hooked into the *power* to think about influence ... [with] decisions to be made by the children.
>
> (p. 168, my emphasis)

Heathcote (1978b/1984) argues that dramatic pedagogy provides teachers with tools to "bring power to my students and to draw on their power" (p. 21). Framing young people in dramatic inquiry goes beyond them being able to take on a role; it can provide them with a very different viewpoint from those usually assumed in classrooms where children often have little power to make decisions, influence events, make meaning, or create outcomes that have much value beyond school requirements.

Assuming the power of head servant, with students dramatically framed as servants listening to her read a letter as if from their thane and then responding, meant that Lorraine-as-head-servant could share power and leadership with the students-as-servants in relation to sequenced collaborative tasks in the real-and-imagined world. All of the young people's movements, dialogue, imaginings, actions, and interpretations were now framed from the viewpoint of responsible servants in the castle with an urgent need to prepare together for the imminent arrival of injured soldiers; as the children played with possibilities they could develop a caring relationship with the imagined people in the event (and, at the same time, with one another in the real world). As students-as-servants engaged with this social task their thinking was "higher-order" as a matter of course.[4]

Not only were they generating and interpreting possible caring actions in response to the particular needs of wounded people in the imagined world, they were also interacting with peers and teachers in responsible collaborative ways in the real world. What it meant to be a 'student' in 'school' was being transformed. In dialogue, young people were developing understanding of self as well as of concepts.

Authoring Understanding With Students

Their inquiry question, like a 'compass' provided Lorraine, and the students, with both direction for navigating this part of the curricular territory and a focus for their thinking, dialogue, and meaning-making. As Lorraine and I moved round to assist small groups it also provided us with a standard for informally assessing their learning progress and gauging the need for tactical teaching.[5]

In addition to providing information, as we interacted with small groups we were able to affect the students' meaning-making. For example, we could assist them in:

- deciding how to go about the task
- listening to one another
- agreeing or clarifying disagreement
- showing an idea in action rather than just talking
- focusing on the intended outcome
- choosing one possible action over another
- considering another possibility
- focusing on the inquiry question

The students shown in Photograph 4.12 had been using dramatic playing to explore how they might care for a soldier who seemed to be dead. Lorraine was helping students reflect on how they might test for vital signs.

As students embodied ideas in imagined events, with adult support they had the opportunity to "hone their skills and knowledge through guided practice in producing original conversation and ... performing artistically" (Newmann, p. 24). The students' dramatic playing was

Photograph 4.12 Teaching as Facilitating Reflection.

followed by dramatic performance and reflection that deepened their ongoing dramatic inquiry.

Value Beyond Success in School

In contrast to most schooling designed "only to document the competency of the learner," in the real world adults "communicate ideas, produce a product, or have an impact on others" (Newmann, p. 26). Value beyond the school is Newmann's third criterion for authentic pedagogy: "students make connections between substantive knowledge and either public problems or personal experiences" (p. 33).

As the children in the small group considering how to care for a soldier who might be dead continued individual and collaborative experiential explorations through dramatic playing they made connections with substantive medical knowledge. Additionally, Photograph 4.13 shows one boy praying, connecting with his personal prior experience. Later, in the reflections on their performance students made both public and personal connections. Throughout, they were connecting with substantive knowledge about *Macbeth*.

In the final five minutes of the session Lorraine first directed the whole class to watch a dramatic performance by this group. The sequence of

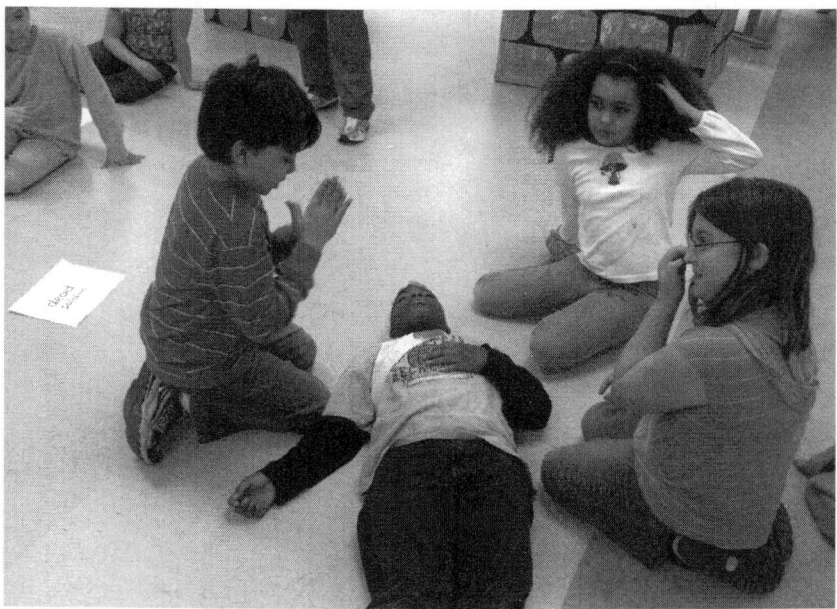

Photograph 4.13 Connecting Personal with Professional Knowledge.

dramatic playing, dramatic performance, and dramatic reflection was collectively an artifact-in-motion demonstrating both that they knew established knowledge (e.g. about testing for vital signs) and their changed understandings (e.g. about being respectful).

Soon all children participated in a polyphonic conversation focused by this contextualized response to the inquiry question: What will we do for the wounded (or the dead!) in order to care for them, because we feel compassion?

What follows is a transcript in which Lorraine and I, as co-teachers, facilitated and participated in a conversation with the students who devised and performed the tableau as if they were castle servants (these students' names are bolded) as well as with other students in the class (framing the event as if preparing for the arrival of injured soldiers).

By this session, the children were all very comfortable with modes of dramatic performance and reflection using the tableau strategy. Presenters moved seamlessly back-and-forth from showing an image to talking about it as spectators.

DAVID: This soldier is dead.
LORRAINE: You put your hand over his face, why?
DAVID: I was checking to see if he is breathing.

LORRAINE: What else?
DAVID: Checked his pulse.
DAVID: (rubbing his hands together) ... CPR
BRIAN: (addressing whole group) What are they trying to do?
MARY: Make him breathe again.

[David goes to get a blanket.]

LORRAINE: Why are you doing that?
DAVID: So people might not be as scared.
BRIAN: (addressing whole group) What do you notice is happening that you like in terms of caring and compassion?
PETER: He is putting a blanket over his head to show respect.
MARY: Doing it gentle, not hard.
LORRAINE: So they're showing compassion?
STUDENTS: Yea.
TRINA: "Hi soldier's mom."

[One of the girls in the presenting group has turned to talk as if to someone.]

BRIAN: Can you tell us what you're doing?
TRINA: His mom passed by ... I'm telling her that her son has passed away.
BRIAN: She's gonna do it respectfully.
TRINA: 'Hello, soldier's mom, your son died in battle.'
TRINA: Let's please give him a silent moment.
BRIAN: Let's do that, let's give him a silent moment.

[Without any direction, the students all stop moving to sit in a gathered silence for about ten seconds looking at the tableau. Then I move to deepen the dialogue by asking the following question.]

BRIAN: How might that make a difference for our celebration?
MICHAEL: There will be less people.
LORRAINE: Should we continue?
MICHAEL: Yeah.
MARK: For our soldiers that made it.
BRIAN: For those of you who think the celebration should go on, stand up, if you have reservations stay seated.

[About half stand.]

LORRAINE: If you are sitting down can you tell us why?
SARA: There might be a lot of food there.
STACY: If we leave the people, we couldn't just forget about them and just leave them.

BRIAN: Can you talk to the people with the dead soldier [and not to me].

STACY: They shouldn't continue the celebration, if there is a dead person that didn't get invited. We shouldn't just go on without them.

CAROL: I wouldn't go.

STACY: No.

CAROL: Because they'd be like, they'd be yelling and screaming for the person who made it and forget about the dead soldiers.

[I remind the children of the 'Hip, hip, hooray' cheer that they had all done together earlier on being told that the war was over. I begin to say the words, some of the children join in, but others begin and then stop.]

BRIAN: Would you feel comfortable doing that?

[There are murmurs of disapproval.]

BRIAN: How might you change it?

STACY: Just have a feast because you're happy and glad that they won, just say that was her son, she wouldn't want to say "Hip, hip, hooray," it would probably make her cry.

CAROL: We could say cheers for the people who didn't make it.

BRIAN: So, you'd want to take time to honor the people who didn't make it?

STUDENTS: Yea.

In an extensive authentic substantive polyphonic conversation (that included dialogue with two adults) students created deep meaning going beyond what they had previously been able to think about in small group dramatic playing and reflection. For some, understanding was transformed in relation to their feelings about the type of celebration that was now appropriate.

The work had value beyond school success (for example, in understanding a story) as they made connections with the world outside the classroom. Though they only touched on the topic, thinking, feeling, and exploring possible actions in order to care for and show compassion and respect for the wounded and the dead is a substantive topic: it bridges a public issue and what may have been, or will at sometime be, a personal experience for each person in the room, regardless of age.

Critical Inquiry

As Bob Fecho (2011) succinctly puts it, "If to inquire is to ask with sincerity, then to critique is to question with doubt" (p. 23). As he notes, despite the word's sometimes negative connotations, critique is part of constructing ideas and authoring meaning: "to call into question is not an act of treachery, but instead is an act of caring and compassion."

I raise questions with young people because I care about how they understand the world; I encourage them respectfully to question others' ideas and positions, including mine, because I want them to learn that they always have choice in how to act, respond, and frame their understanding of events.

Like Fecho, I regard critique as both an inseparable dimension of dialogic inquiry and a necessary stance in the process of becoming the sort of teacher I want to be. Calling into question the planned celebration was a tactical move designed to deepen dialogue about a budding understanding of how being compassionate of people and their families might mean that plans should change, including those in which people are invested. Immediately before the tasks outlined above, children-as-servants had begun the session trying on costumes (see Photograph 4.14) and engaging in exuberant dramatic playing to plan a banquet (complete with music, dancing, food, and entertainment) to celebrate a planned visit by King Duncan. My question *juxtaposed* their prior perspective with reflections on the wisdom of celebrations in the light of a death.

Photograph 4.14 Dramatic Playing Using Material Objects.

A critical stance, for Marilyn Cochran-Smith and Susan Lytle (2009), is a process of "building, interrogating, elaborating, and critiquing conceptual frameworks that link action and problem-posing to the immediate context as well as larger social, cultural, and political issues" (pp. 51–52). One of the frameworks focusing critical inquiry in a polyphonic conversation with one of the other fourth-grade groups that day was this: would we treat the body of a dead soldier differently if we discovered that he, or she, was from the army of the 'enemy'?

BRIAN: I just found out something ... one of these soldiers is a Norwegian ... from Norway. Does it make any difference?

ASHLEY: Why they had to die ... I can't say that.

BRIAN: Because...

TIM: They're Norwegian.

KELLY: May they rest in peace.

MICHELLE: They will always be in our heart.

TIM: I can't say it ... I wish they could come back ... but they would or probably could betray us again.

BRIAN: You wouldn't want that, would you?

LAURA: I guess, it doesn't matter what country they're from we should all be together.

MEGAN: I wish the battle never begun and we were just allies again.

BRIAN: And maybe if we get the right king we can be allies. I have a question for the people standing [those not in the tableau], are you feeling compassion for the Norwegians ... Are you feeling compassion for them? Do you show compassion for them? Should they be buried?

LORRAINE: Should we bury them?

PETER: No.

JAMES: Yes.

LORRAINE: What should we do with them?

MINA: Leave them in the graveyard and let them rest in peace.

CHRIS: Ship them to Norway.

BRIAN: Some people say we should leave them here. Some people say we should bury them. Does anybody say the body should be left for birds to eat on the battlefield because that has some-times happened.

[Some students raise their hands.]

JASON: We can give it to poor people who need food ... Cut 'em up and eat them. Give him as bait.

BRIAN: Would that be showing respect? Do we show respect for all people or just people in our army?

TIM: All people.
MINA: Every single person in the world.
CHRIS: Everyone in our army.
JASON: Everyone but our enemies.
MINDA: All people are the same they should be treated equal.
BRIAN: If you were captured by the Norwegians would you want them to show respect for you? Would you want your body to be left out and eaten by the birds?
LORRAINE: Leave them and your parents would never know what happened to you.
BRIAN: Should we show respect for them, if we want them to show respect for you? You know the Golden Rule, right?

[Some students say the rule aloud in unison.]

BRIAN: What do you think of the Golden Rule?
JASON: But I don't think that really works with enemies. Golden Rule is right but they're Norwegians, they fought for Norway and they tried to invade our land, and they weren't treating us the way we wanted to be treated. So why should we treat them the way they want to be treated?
TIM: Is it Cawdor?
BRIAN: No, Cawdor was a Scottish traitor. This is a Norwegian soldier ... Olaf maybe is his name.
LORRAINE: Martin (student lying on the floor representing the dead soldier), do you have anything to say?
MARTIN: No ... Yeah ... Curse Scotland!

A critical stance guards against didacticism from me or from students. As Fecho stresses in relation to stances with which we disagree, "The intent is not necessarily to dismiss those stances but, instead, to explore them with a critical eye to then be better able to reject, accept, revise, or adapt a stance from an informed position" (Fecho, p. 23). Critique is the mirror image of affirmation of other's ideas: both are essential, neither is sufficient.

Like Fecho, I do my best to adopt a critical stance in mutual inquiry with students that leads me to "call all stances, including our own, into question." This guides what I say in dialogue, for example when I challenged the students on the question of respect. At the same time, my own understanding of the Golden Rule was critiqued when Jason introduced his belief that only people who act on the Golden Rule themselves should be given its benefit.

The exchanges with and among the students were not moralistic and did not close down meaning-making or impose one person's views, including those of the adults. Rather, in a polyphonic conversation about an event a thousand years ago alternative views were expressed that resonated with a contemporary socio-political question about the treatment of our 'enemies' that could easily have been extended in subsequent work.

Critical Literacy

Critical inquiry, in relation to print and other texts, is critical literacy. As Hilary Janks (2010) puts it, reading critically means reading "against" as well as "with" a text. Reading with a text requires us to identify with characters and in imagination enter into events so that we can seek to understand the world of the text from viewpoints created by the author. Reading against a text draws attention to how a character frames events including their assumptions about their own and others' actions; it raises questions about the veracity or wisdom of a character's perspective.

Janks regards an examination of power and domination as central to critical inquiry: how do characters and readers use power and privilege to impose certain interpretations while minimizing or silencing others?

A character's viewpoint and assumptions about the world can be questioned and critiqued using *hotseating*. When I frame an event as a character I can deliberately present a perspective with which the students are likely to disagree. For example, as shown in Photograph 4.15, at the beginning of Session 6 the young people encountered Lorraine-as-Lady-Macbeth before she meets Macbeth on his return from the battle. First Lorraine set up the strategy. As she put on her cloak she spoke as the teacher, making it clear that, "I'm going to put on this cloak so I can talk to you as if I'm Lady Macbeth." Then, *reading-in-role* she picked up the scroll of paper (that had a script of what she was going to say on a piece of paper pasted inside) to read as a letter. At first, using the dramatic strategy of *overhearing*, the young people were able to listen in to hear Lady Macbeth talking to herself while reading a letter from Macbeth.

Lorraine combined language from the play (*italicized below*) with her own words and interpretation of Lady Macbeth:

> Yes they have been *successful* in battle and king Duncan is coming home ... *three weird creatures* have given my husband a *prophesy* ... yes he is going to be king, I will be queen. I have longed for this day, I deserve to be queen that would be great ... Duncan needs to die, Macbeth needs to be king ... why should we wait any longer? Perhaps the prophesy wants us to murder Duncan ... Macbeth is *not without ambition* but I do worry about my husband, he is *too full of the milk of human kindness* ... but if we have a plan, stick to it, and *press our*

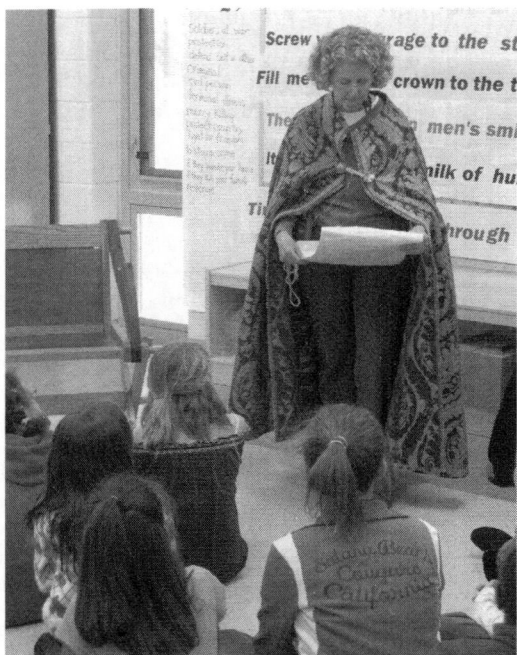

Photograph 4.15 Hotseating to Critique a Text.

courage to the sticking place we will be successful ... a plan to murder Duncan.

Stepping out of the imagined space, and introducing the active strategies of **stand if you** want to speak and **you can speak when we make eye-contact,** combined with the dramatic strategy of ***thought-tracking*** as voices of conscience, Lorraine said to the children:

> If you have something you want to say to Lady Macbeth just stand up and speak when I look at you. It's like you are voices in her conscience. Sit down when you're finished and we'll know who's not had a chance to speak to her.

She positioned the children to frame what they said to Lady Macbeth as if they were voices inside her mind. Rather than being outside in judgment, in imagination the children could step into her consciousness to make visible a possible inner dialogue.

Over half of the young people stood as she stepped back in to the world of the play as Lady Macbeth. As shown in Photograph 4.16 as

Photograph 4.16 Critical Dialogue.

she made eye-contact with different children they spoke to her and in doing so were able to interpret and critique the character's assumptions while collectively having an authentic, substantive, polyphonic conversation with the character.

JOSE:	Why do you want to be queen?
LORRAINE:	I want the power.
TREVON:	Why don't you just wait until Duncan is done being king?
LORRAINE:	I am tired of waiting.
KELLY:	How about we get the two guards to fall asleep sometime and going to his room and get 'em?
MARIA:	Should you really do this?
LORRAINE:	'Tis a tough question, but the prophesy has said it shall be …
MARIA:	How do you know it will not fail?
LORRAINE:	Screw your courage to the sticking place and we'll not fail.
JEREMY:	If you're such a good wife why would you want to kill the king?
LORRAINE:	Macbeth wants to be king in his deepest desire.
REBECCA:	I think king Duncan should stay king.
LORRAINE:	He will die somewhere.
REBECCA:	Is that why you married Macbeth?
LORRAINE:	I had plans for his greatness.

LISA:	What if the guards see you?
LORRAINE:	The guard ... it must be done in the night ... do the deed quickly.
CHRIS:	How do you think Duncan will feel when you kill him?
JOSEPH:	Why not, if you, once you make the guards sleep with something why not kill Duncan and take his blood and smear it over the guards?
LAURA:	What if you get caught?
LORRAINE:	If we stick to the plan and stick to our courage ...
ANNA:	What if I tried to stop you?
LORRAINE:	I believe the prophesy has said Macbeth will be king ... it's been foretold.
JACK:	Once people realize King Duncan is dead won't they come after you?
LORRAINE:	We must be clever ... we must be sure we wear our false face.
AUBREY:	How do you deserve to be a queen? What did you do?
LORRAINE:	Have I not been a faithful wife, have I not served my husband loyally? ... I was born to be queen, some people are you know ...
HARRY:	What if they figure out that you killed Macbeth?
AMY:	How do you know Macbeth will stick to the plan?
LORRAINE:	Who can help me to think how I can convince Macbeth?
MELISSA:	What if they that ... never mind.
TOM:	Why don't you put poison in his food, so they can find you?

Lorraine stepped out again to ask the students to shift back into the world of the classroom in order to ask the students to synthesize their ideas as they continued their polyphonic conversation.

LORRAINE:	So what do we know now about Lady Macbeth? Stand up if you have a word that can describe Lady Macbeth?

Nearly everyone immediately stood up. Lorraine asked anyone who was standing to give words to those still seated: "Stand up when you hear a word you agree with." The students then shared, and had a chance to change their words, by playing **The Trading Game**.

Lorraine facilitated so that everyone could share. (When she used language like "because" to encourage students to extend their ideas, this is shown in brackets.)

AMY:	Selfish (because) she wants everything for herself, power especially.
TOM:	A nightmare (because) she's mean and selfish and wants to kill the king.

MELISSA:	Stupid (because) she wants to kill King Duncan (because) she want to be queen (is being the queen a stupid thought?) if I want to be queen and Kim was the queen you don't just go kill her because you are jealous ... she's jealous of king Duncan (is there another word then instead of stupid?) jealous.
CHRIS:	Not loyal. She's tricking her husband.
LORRAINE:	Is she being loyal to the king?
MARIA:	Not humble.
HARRY:	Evil—she's tricking her own husband to be king.

When students seek only to comprehend a text extract they can easily assume an uncritical stance. However, when pressed to critique they may take up a detached stance with a privileged viewpoint: "That was stupid" or "I would never have done that." I remember when first teaching the play through literary analysis how much work was involved getting beyond initial generalizing abstract statements about characters, like "Lady Macbeth is evil." I never had a student use a metaphor like she's "a nightmare" and explain it clearly: "because she's mean, and selfish, and wants to kill the king." But then I hadn't discovered the power of hotseating or other strategies used to extend critique through dramatic inquiry.

In adopting a critical inquiry stance toward literacy across the curriculum, Richard Beach and Jamie Myers (2001) identify six dimensions to the process: young people must become *immersed* in social worlds in order to observe and *identify* with the perspectives of different people and situations, as they wonder, find, and ask questions that are *explored in context. Representing* data and ideas allows for analysis and *critique* that leads to a *transformation* of understanding.

The children in Lorraine's classroom had time to become immersed in the world of *Macbeth* and explore inquiry questions in context from multiple perspectives. Dramatic strategies like tableaux, sculpting, and hotseating mediated their presentation of ideas to analyze and critique. As I have shown above, they identified with soldiers in battle, castle servants, wounded soldiers, and later they would add the viewpoints of Duncan, Macbeth, Banquo, Macduff and others as they did in the example above when they first encountered Lady Macbeth.

Critiquing a viewpoint can transform understanding in a dialogic classroom if young people are able to identify with, and be affected by, that perspective. As Bakhtin (1990) puts it, I "evaluate from the standpoint of others" (p. 15). For students to identify with how another person views the world (like Lady Macbeth) doesn't mean they have to agree with that viewpoint but rather in imagination they view the world as that person does and allow the other's viewpoint to affect their understanding. As one of Lorraine's students put it, dramatic inquiry means, "I can get inside other people's thoughts."

Transforming Prior Understanding Through Critical Inquiry

Transforming prior understanding through critical inquiry is possible with students of all ages. Ann Pelo (2008) in her introduction to *Rethinking Early Childhood Education* stresses that:

> [Exemplary early childhood teachers] emphasize children's social-emotional and dispositional learning. Teachers seek to cultivate in children the disposition to pay attention to their own and others' emotions and needs. They emphasize the importance of collaboration and offer children coaching and practice about understanding multiple perspectives. Teachers create opportunities for children to think critically and engage intellectually with ideas and with each other—and to take action based on their critical thinking [and inquiry].
>
> (p. ix)

Whereas I can expect eight- and nine-year-old children to project in imagination into the consciousness of a character they hotseat, three-year-olds need more adult support to be able to critique. For Vygotsky (1978), they need to be *assisted* in creating a zone of proximal development which, for the children at the childcare center (described in Chapter 1), was in relation to how to help someone who had fallen and hurt his head.

When I used dramatic inquiry with the preschoolers some children transformed prior understanding as they critiqued a norm: 'Call the squad if someone is injured.' When the children first encountered Justin-as-Jack lying on the ground with his head in a bloody bandage, it was at the conclusion to me reciting the *Jack and Jill* nursery rhyme as I performed the story (see Photograph 1.21). Previously the children had repeatedly embodied the tale from Jack's viewpoint: all "fell down" several times, everyone had held their head, and following my lead many had pretended to cry as we recited the words "and broke his crown." I ended my dramatic performance of the story by discovering Jack on the ground: "Oh, it's Jack. He's fallen down and broken his crown!" All of the children were captivated and went quiet. On cue from me, Justin began moaning.

My intention had been that everyone would identify with the story from Jack's perspective so that now they would see Justin not only as a *man* on the ground but also as *Jack* and that they would connect with their feelings when they too had imagined falling down like Jack.

I asked the children what we should do. No one responded. I pointed out that he was moaning and that his head was bandaged. I asked, "How do you think he's feeling?" One child replied, "He's hurt." In response I asked, "What should we do if someone's hurt?" A girl said, "Call the squad" in a commanding tone that suggested a monologic repetition of what she'd heard adults say. No one disagreed. Ordinarily I would have said "yes" to this idea and moved on, but I saw an opportunity for some critical analysis bringing together two different perspectives on what to do if someone is "hurt."

In our initial dramatic playing Paul had been slightly hurt, or startled, as children and adults moved round the room exuberantly. He'd fallen over when another child accidently bumped into him; within seconds his teacher had scooped him up, held him, and his tears had subsided. I had stopped everything to check he was OK, to clarify it had been an accident, and to agree with all the children how we would move to be sure that the space was safe for everyone. After five minutes watching, Paul had felt comfortable joining in just before I introduced Justin-as-Jack.

Wanting the children to reconsider when the emergency squad *should* be called, I replied to the girl's authoritative "Call the squad" by making a reference back to what had happened five minutes previously: "But we didn't call the squad when Paul was hurt." I asked how what had happened to Jack was different from what had happened to Paul. It was only when one of the children said, "There's blood" and another said "Yes" that I sensed an implicit agreement. Taking a slight risk that I might upset Paul but wanting his perspective, I asked, "Paul, do you think we should call the squad for Jack?" He nodded, so I asked the group, "What number should we call?" Another girl replied definitively, "28542." Not wanting this incorrect information to be used (but not wanting her to feel rejected by a 'No'), I continued to adopt my accepting positioning by suggesting that this might be her doctor's office number. I went on to instruct them: "If you need to call the squad, call 9-1-1." We applied this knowledge immediately: I directed them to pick up an imaginary phone and push the buttons. When they did, I answered as if I was the operator. In seconds I was pretending to drive an ambulance and arrived ready to take Jack to the hospital.

Being critical in a dialogic classroom means that for everyone (including the teacher) meaning remains malleable and open to reinterpretation in a new context, rather than being fixed and closed to change. I intend to make my stance one of always being ready to shape understanding *with* participants. Months later I reminded Amy Rush, the teacher who had organized the visit, of this event. She said, "Oh, when we had someone cut their knee on the playground one of the children said 'There's blood. Call 9-1-1.' Of course we didn't! I felt bad for the kids but I talked with them about not always calling the squad even if there is blood. A cut knee wasn't as serious as blood on your head."

The new understanding created in thinking about Jack became prior knowledge for the children but because the teachers treated the meaning as in flux it was still open to critique and change in dialogue with the children.

Conclusion: Becoming a More Authentic and Critical Teacher

I was immersed in writing this manuscript when Dorothy Heathcote died, aged eighty-five. Read Sandra Heston's (2011) expansive obituary if you want some of the details of why she was described as "one of the 20th century's greatest teachers." Heston summarizes Heathcote's teaching philosophy:

> Her concerns were with the condition of human beings and the effects that a holistic education would engender. It was like a perpetual journey similar to the archetypal quest of the hero in that the learning is never completed and the process of becoming is always just beginning.
>
> (n.p.)

Though some gave her Olympian status or regarded her visionary work as beyond the reach of ordinary teachers, Dorothy rejected being placed on a pedestal. She was always concerned with authentic learning going on in classrooms as well as with the reality of the professional lives of educators. Her work was practical, pragmatic, and empathetic as well as critical. She was also very funny and often laughed at herself.

She wants us as teachers to be "obsessed by ourselves" in the sense that we must know "how we feel, and what we see ourselves to be" so that "we can see ourselves through children's eyes" (1980/1984, p. 23). Teaching for her was always grounded in taking up, and engaging with, the standpoints of the young people so that we may all participate in authentic critical dialogue. Teachers should challenge young people's views but do so with supportive sensitivity.

> I am engaged first of all in helping children to think, talk, relate to one another, to communicate. I am interested primarily in helping classes widen their areas of reference and modify their ability to relate to people ... I want good people to come out of [the work].
>
> (1975/1984, p. 92)

At the same time, teaching must be about who we as teachers are becoming so that we can "see what renews us ... regenerate energy and forgive ourselves" (ibid., p. 23). Dorothy once observed a fairly disastrous session of mine when I was on her course: more six-year-old children were wandering around than were engaged. It was in laughing with her about some basic errors as she told a funny story of one of her own mis-takes that I started to regroup. I could begin to critique my teaching and hear her suggestions that sparked ideas for what became a memorable, though far-from-perfect project.

When you know what you value, as I noted in Chapter 2, you know the principles that guide your teaching. In her article on "the authentic teacher and the future" Heathcote (1984) asks challenging practical and philosophical questions including: what do you stand for? Answering that authentic and critical question is a life-long pursuit but is essential because, "knowing what you stand for is the first step toward authenticity" (p. 183). She concludes this remarkable essay by quoting Alvin Toffler:

> The responsibility for change lies with us. We must begin with ourselves, teaching ourselves not to close our minds prematurely to the novel, the surprising, the seemingly radical.
>
> (p. 198)

I stand for more than the expectations I agree with students. I stand for being open to new ideas while honoring the old. For dialogue to be authentic and critical it requires that as each person listens they are ready to change and grow in understanding in response. I desire that for learners of all ages, including myself, in growing communities engaged in dialogic inquiry that is often dramatic.

Notes

1 Lorraine taught units of inquiry in relation to the sinking of *Titanic* with both a social studies and science curricular focus. In the final edit of the manuscript I reluctantly cut the section documenting that teaching. We are happy to provide the section to readers via email: edmiston.1@osu.edu or at my website: go.osu.edu/edmiston

2 The term 'critical' has many connotations in different pedagogies. I am not using it in the narrow sense of individual 'critical thinking.' Nor am I using it in its neo-Marxist sense of Critical Theory and Critical Pedagogy (a theoretical framework that has been used explicitly in the literature in drama education since at least the work of Augusto Boal). Rather, I use the term, for example as Carmen Medina (1994) uses it, to mean using dramatic pedagogy in order to engage in critical dialogue with students, so as to inquire into, and critique from multiple perspectives, social and cultural assumptions, especially in relation to narrative texts.

3 Note that they were not positioned as 'students role-playing' medical treatment of soldiers. Rather, within the event (meaningful within the world of *Macbeth* that they had explored over four sessions) young people-as-servants (who could also imagine they were soldiers) prepared for treatment of the injured. As with the preschoolers, adopting the frame made a difference to what they could do, how they dialogued with peers and Lorraine to make meaning, and how the young people identified with the task and with one another.

4 Whereas the preschool children's similar framing (dialoguing with Justin-as-Jack like physicians) had been implicit, in Lorraine's case the framing was explicit. The frame was dramatically introduced in role by Lorraine-as-head-servant when she read the letter and positioned the young people as servants with a responsible task to do. As needed, she negotiated with each small group in setting up tasks and expected outcomes: collaboratively prepare something to show us so that we will know we are ready to care for these soldiers.

5 If the session had had science learning objectives Lorraine could have provided discipline-specific background information for the students to use. All were eager to know more about wounds, treatment, and differences between modern and medieval medicine. Joining in as a co-teacher I provided information orally in response to students' questions, much of which was incorporated into their dramatic playing.

Chapter 5

Be Tactical and Strategic to Transform Teaching

> Children stumble upon an authentic experience if we teach with attention to detail and its relation to the whole.
>
> (Heathcote, 1980/1984, p. 25)

I'm in a cramped portable classroom filled with drawings and writing on display, projects in process, and twenty-four eager eight- and nine-year-old children. Along with their teacher, Amy McMunn, on an afternoon in November 2011 we're in dialogue about the meaning of an extract from the novel *Love That Dog* written by Sharon Creech as a sequence of poems (Photograph 5.1).

> At both ends of our street
> are yellow signs
> that say
> *Caution! Children at Play!*
> but sometimes
> the cars
> pay no attention
> and speed down
> the road
> as if
> they are in a BIG hurry
> with many miles to go
> before they sleep.

We dialogue about why the car drivers that they have just invented in exuberant dramatic playing and mostly humorous dramatic performances might be "in a big hurry." No one refers to the next event in the story that we had begun to explore when I had worked with the children over a week previously: a speeding driver strikes and kills Jack's dog, Sky. I notice a murmur of disapproval in the room when James, almost under his breath,

Photograph 5.1 Dialogue About the Meaning of Text.

says that the driver could have been texting. In the performance by his group of three the driver had been late, like the one I had modeled with two volunteers, however not for work but for his son's birthday party. In none of their performances had a driver been texting (Photograph 5.2).

I ask the children what they think about drivers using cell phones. There's minimal response. When I ask what could happen if a driver is texting, someone says, "He could be stopped by the police." I ask if they want to see that event and there are nods of approval.

For twenty minutes our dialogue continues as we shift seamlessly in and out of real-and-imagined spaces to explore what should happen, if anything, to drivers who are texting. I use the **Continuum** strategy several times to show them their changing views (Photograph 5.3). James-as-the-driver is stopped by me-as-the-police-officer and the children *thought-track* both of us (Photographs 5.4 to 5.5).

At one point I reintroduce voices from the previous session by re-reading the poem we had dramatized.

The *blue car, blue car*
spattered with mud
hit Sky
thud thud thud

Photograph 5.2 Dramatic Performance of "They are in a Big Hurry".

Photograph 5.3 Continuum Strategy.

Photograph 5.4 Teacher-in-Role Dialogues with Students-in-Role.

Photograph 5.5 Thought-Tracking.

and kept on going
in such a hurry
so fast
so many miles to go
it couldn't even stop
...
and
Sky
closed his eyes
and
he
never
opened
them
again
ever.

In our polyphonic conversation there are many views expressed as the children move in and out of talking in-role as if they are drivers and people who live on the street. There are moments of stillness, as when I re-read the poem, and times of confrontation, for example when James-as-the-driver, in an almost belligerent mood, denies he was texting and says he didn't see any dogs. There are definitive pronouncements, such as "you shouldn't text" and more ponderous comments: "maybe the driver was texting to say he was late."

The next day, as the children write, some demonstrate change in understanding about a topic with importance outside the walls of the classroom:

- I thought the person did not care about hitting the dog. Now I think maybe they did care but they just didn't want to face the kid's dad.
- I'm wondering how many children/animals died. I'm very shocked and I remember my mom texting. I said to stop.
- I'm wondering if the government is going to do something about speeding.

None of this authentic and critical learning could have happened if I had not (using Heathcote's words cited above) "paid attention to detail" that I could easily have missed. Having responded to James' side-comment we moved into an extended dialogue with his interpretation and "its relation to the whole" of both the narrative and our previous and evolving active and dramatic conversations. As I led dialogue as an exploration of the meaning of the poem, I was mediating the children's authoring in relation to goals that included inquiring into the poem's relevance for our lives within the classroom community and beyond the walls of the school.

Tactical and Strategic Teaching

> To name oneself a teacher is to live with one foot in the muck of the world as we find it, with its conventional patterns and received wisdom, and the other foot striding toward a world that could be but isn't yet.
>
> (Ayers, 2010, p. 11)

I experience teaching as an internal dialogue from strategic and tactical standpoints. Strategic teaching gives me a long-view on classroom life so that not only can I approach dialogue with a sense of what's possible but also with a view of what's desirable, or as Ayers puts it, "what could be but isn't yet." Strategically I pay attention to my plans as I look back to where we've come from and forward to where we could go. At the same time, when I am tactical I am close-up responding to the actual realities that I encounter in dialogue having walked into my own or other people's classrooms—"the muck", or the marvels, "of the world as we find it."

> When I teach **strategically** I am paying more attention to the broad goals that guide my classroom practice. Teaching **tactically** I am paying more attention to the specific tools I am using in pursuit of these goals. Teaching tools (including those traditionally and in this book referred to as 'strategies') are used strategically and tactically. In choosing tools I exercise tactical vision (a short-term selection and assessment of the use of tools in-the-moment) as well as strategic vision (a long-term determination of which tools in a sequence of tasks will best accomplish my goals). The two are not separate but are rather reciprocal practices. The more artistic my teaching the more I experience 'bifocal vision' with tactical and strategic viewpoints in a dialogic unity.

If planning provides a map of a learning terrain, teaching is exploring with a group as we learn in the time and space of actual territory. Teaching is a craft with predictable routines, frequently used strategies, modes, and other mediating tools that I carry into every classroom with my planning map and compass of inquiry questions. But teaching is also an art when I selectively use and adapt tools, choosing how to answer people in-the-moment in order to shape whatever meaning is actually being made between us, as opposed to the learning I wish was happening or assume occurs.

In the classroom, a strategy is any predictable practice used to regulate, control, and limit classroom behavior or action, including dialogue, in order to achieve a social or academic goal or intended outcome. The tools I may use strategically range from the sophisticated and dramatic, like teacher-in-role, to simple active decision-making practices, like using the phrase, "Step forward when you know what you're going to do." In contrast, a tactic is any tool used as a "calculated action" that takes advantage of the "cracks that particular conjunctions open" here-and-now (de Certeau, 1984, p. 37). Students, and teachers, can use tactics to 'bend the rules' or to 'get things done' in-the-moment since rules, procedures, and plans cannot predict the changing social reality on the ground.

Colin Lankshear and Michele Knobel (2002) have proposed "steps toward a pedagogy of tactics" that begin when we "*recognise* learner tactics where they occur and [to] build creatively and constructively upon them." They suggest that as teachers, "it is possible to consciously refine one's own tactics in solidarity with those of others [in the classroom]" (n.p.).

I teach tactically when I attend to, build on, and often seek out, the unpredictable "cracks" in *meaning* that inevitably open up in social interactions in both the real and real-and-imagined worlds. James' tactical side-comment about texting was a crevice in the apparently stable shared understanding about drivers' actions. My response was tactically in solidarity with him. With 'bifocal vision' in my subsequent teaching I was also strategically paying attention to the goal of understanding the narrative while tactically building creatively and constructively *with* his idea as I coauthored more understanding with the entire group.

Teaching and Learning as Improvisation

Teaching can be transformational for students' learning when, as Sonia Nieto (2005) stresses in *Why We Teach*, we improvise with people to "make the extraordinary out of the ordinary." As she summarizes, improvisation is "creativity within structure" (p. 211). Considering we are 'only pretending,' improvising dialogue as if we are characters in a fictional event is an extraordinary feat.

Keith Sawyer's (2004) research illustrates how "in collaborative classrooms, new knowledge and insights emerge from exploratory discussion" when teaching is curriculum-based "disciplined improvisation" (p. 19). Sawyer (2007) shows how people improvise within a subtly balanced "semi-structure" that is planned yet open to participants' ability to choose responsive action (p. 29). Planning possible structures for dialogue both contains and allows meaning to change.

Tina Fey (2011) clarifies the significance of being open to others' ideas when she stresses the life-long consequence of improvising in meaning-making: "studying improvisation literally changed my life ... it changed the way I look at the world" (p. 82). She describes the core 'rules' of improvisation: "Agree with your partner and add something of your own" (summarized in the phrase 'Say Yes, and ...').

> The Rule of Agreement reminds you to 'respect what your partner has created' and to at least start from an open-minded place. Start with a YES and see where that takes you. As an improviser I always find it jarring when I meet someone in real life whose first answer is no. "No, we can't do that." "No, that's not in the budget." "No, I will not hold your hand for a dollar." What kind of way is that to live? ... To me, YES, AND means don't be afraid to contribute. It's your responsibility to contribute. Always make sure you're adding something to the discussion. Your initiations are worthwhile.
>
> (pp. 84–85)

Planning to 'Say Yes, and ...' as much as possible to students' ideas is an essential *tactical* teaching stance anyone can adopt that significantly promotes dialogue.

In my experience, as Amy's children did, nearly every group of young people will readily agree to a 'Say Yes, and ...' expectation. With older students, or groups that have tolerated negative patterns of put-downs, I may have to work harder for agreement so that they accept the importance of the rule and are prepared to try applying it in both imagined and everyday interactions. When I've illustrated alternatives, 'Say No!' or 'Yes, BUT ...,' (sometimes with moments of melodramatic performance!), I've always had people nodding when I ask if, like me, they don't like feeling put down. Whole-group collaborative tasks, especially playing popular games, give people the feeling of why the social practice makes sense and how it can build community: everyone shares a sense of supported achievement.

An adult who improvises with students is a more responsive and effective teacher. As Sawyer (2007) stresses, when a leader is an active participant she or he functions "more like a peer than a boss" (p. 34) who is also a "catalyst and facilitator" (p. 173). At the same time, as a collaborative group member a leader engages in "deep listening for new ideas," "builds on ideas," supports the equal participation of others, focuses on the task, and is open to making mistakes (pp. 14–15). Though I did not highlight the process in previous chapters, every example illustrates dialogic interactions contained within planned semi-structures.

As Mary Catherine Bateson (1989) puts it, in *Composing a Life*, the art of improvisation involves "combining and recombining familiar and unfamiliar materials in new ways ... in response to new situations" (pp. 2–3). The more familiar I became with strategies, modes, and other mediating tools the more I could combine these with the unfamiliar and unexpected ideas and suggestions of students. Using dialogic inquiry over time, as Bob Fecho (2011) stresses, I had to learn how to extend dialogue as an active meaning-maker and "summon my authority to garner a range of response, to posit questions, to propose alternatives ... providing tools through which current and future dialogue [may] be achieved" (p. 25).

Cecily O'Neill (1995; Taylor & Warner, 2006) has shown how improvisation lies at the heart of dramatic pedagogy. I came to understand much more about the practical implications of her artistic approach to teaching when I was fortunate enough to work closely with Cecily over several years. During this time, I was privileged to participate in her graduate classes, observing and analyzing her teaching, and when she co-advised my dissertation, to begin to understand more about the art of teaching through what she had begun to call process drama.

Improvisation, Positioning, and Authorship

In the previous chapter I stressed the significance of 'framing' students with a viewpoint of responsibility. Framing extends beyond people taking on a role. When we desire to change how young people view their selves as 'students,' framing is strategic teaching. Using bifocal vision, *how* I frame people strategically is grounded in tactical decisions. When I regard students respectfully, with equality, and with a right to be in a safe space then I treat them as such, use language and actions that show my belief in equality, and I do not, for example, have to wait for students to be respectful for me to respect them.

Heathcote (1980/1984) stresses that if I want students to frame their selves differently, then in addition to changing how I *view* students I must *position* young people in such a way that they are likely to change how *they* frame events.

> One cannot endow people with a commitment to a point of view, but often by placing them in the response position they begin to hold a point of view, because they can see it has power.
>
> (p. 164)

In every interaction with people I not only provide information I also communicate my assumptions about their power to act: this is social positioning. As Bakhtin stresses, "The expression of an utterance always ... expresses the speaker's *attitude* toward others' utterances and not just his attitude toward the object of his utterance" (cited in Norris,

1994, p. 86). Peter Johnston (2004) puts it like this [with a word added by me], in his book on the significance of how the language we choose affects students' learning and their view of their selves as 'learners,' as well as shaping our learning community.

> Teachers can position children as competitors or collaborators and themselves as referees, resources, or judges, or in many other arrangements. A teacher's choice of words, [movements], phrases, metaphors, and interaction sequences invokes and assumes these and other ways of being a self and of being together in the classroom.
>
> (p. 9)

Social positioning (Harré & Langenhove, 1998) is unavoidable in dialogue and teaching. Every task is an answer to this question: who is positioned as competent to speak, act, and make meaning? How I position each student, and students as a group, carries messages about what actions I assume are *socially* possible and expected in any task, as opposed to what is *logically* possible to say or do. Further, my positioning carries meaning about what I assume is possible *dramatic* action in relation to a *narrative event* in contrast to what is possible in relation to an everyday event (Edmiston, 2003). As Harré and Moghaddam (2003) put it, positioning both limits and opens up "the repertoire of acts one has access to ... [because of] what they mean socially" (p. 5). What acts are possible are determined by a cluster of explicit or implicit rights, duties and prohibitions that may be understood within a "positioning triangle" of a position, acts, and event (p. 6). For example, it was clear in how I positioned James that it was entirely appropriate for him to act in a belligerent way in talking to me-as-a-police-officer who had stopped his car but not in dialogue with me-as-teacher in the classroom. Further, everyone in the class knew that moving in the room, raising questions, and dialoguing with anyone was welcomed.

Dorothy Holland and her colleagues (1998) have shown the interrelationship between extended improvisation, social positioning, and how people may change how they view their self in relation to how they act in a community: "using the resources available in response to the subject positions afforded one in the present, improvisation can become the basis for a reformed subjectivity" (p. 18). In other words, as adults and young people improvise and act differently in the classroom (in both real and imagined spaces), over time each may change how they understand their self as a 'teacher' or as a 'student' along with awareness of their agency, how their actions can make a difference in authoring meaning, including about their selves. Holland is emphatic that, "Human agency comes through this art of improvisation" (p. 272).

In more strategic teaching this long-term view informs all the social practices that are established across sequenced tasks. I intend as much as possible to position students across time with agency as collaborators, improvisers, and as on a shared journey of dialogic inquiry as co-explorers and co-authors of meaning and understanding. That's how I desire that they understand their authorship when working with me and with their peers. What authoring meaning actually looks like and means for participants in particular tasks is created as people choose words and deeds and responses in ongoing dialogue that shapes and creates understanding.

In more tactical teaching I am as deliberate as I can be with how I position groups and particular people in-the-moment as competent, resourceful, and socially aware authors in dialogue. Because James had come up with the idea of texting, I assumed he was ready to take on a leadership position, which he was. At different times I position myself, for example, as a resource (I took on the role of the police-officer), a supporter (I encouraged the children to take on whatever roles interested them), or a challenger of ideas (as the police-officer I asked tough questions) but always (when I employ my bifocal vision) nested within a strategic social positioning of equality, equity, collaboration, and impro-vised exploration (we repeatedly paused to consider the meaning of what we had done and to agree on what to do next).

Dramatic Positioning

Dramatic pedagogy exponentially extends my positioning choices, pos-sibilities for improvised dialogue with students, and their opportunities to take action. In an imagined world, I may position my self in relation to the group as if we/they are characters or people with perspectives on the world very different from those of everyday life.

Dorothy Heathcote's (Heathcote & Bolton, 1995) "mantle of the expert" approach to education extends the collaborative positioning of a group through an 'expert' framing (as we did in Lorraine's classroom in relation to the injured soldiers) but strategically over weeks or even months so that people may develop not only deep expertise in relation to whatever curricular areas shape goals and intended outcomes but also a changing view of their selves and their agency. Cecily O'Neill summa-rizes the educational goal in her illuminating introduction:

> The students are empowered not by giving them a spurious "free-dom", but by encouraging them to accept constraints within which they will work to encounter challenges and take decisions from a position of increasing authority and knowledge. From the firm foundation provided by the teacher the students gradually begin to

take control of the imagined context, a control they have earned in a context they have helped to create. They become experts—experts at learning.

(Heathcote & Bolton, 1995, p. ix)

Whenever I position young people as we dialogue in any classroom I do so with a similar long-term strategic assumption of promoting their authorship by shifting as much choice, responsibility, and authority to young people as possible. That framing enfolds my tactical positioning of students in any exchange. Occasionally I have the opportunity to develop a mantle-of-the-expert approach to dramatic inquiry over time (Beach et al., 2010; Edmiston & McKibben, 2011).

When teaching tactically I am deliberate about making very visible my 'real' collaborative positioning when I 'step out' and before I 'step in' to any real-and-imagined space (as I did as the police-officer). Making very clear the 'double-voiced' nature of dramatizing is crucial so that I don't unintentionally confuse participants about how I am 'really' positioning them. Similarly, participants of any age must learn to be clear with peers when they are 'only pretending.' An image I carry with me is of using a puppet. Though people treat a puppet as if it were real, everyone knows the difference between the puppet and the person who is the puppeteer.

It all may seem very complicated but the perception, experience, and negotiation with students is as simple as young children agreeing to be Jack and Jill and having fun pretending to go up a hill together. Or, on the playground when children ask their teacher (who they know values their interest in stories enough to play with them) to be the giant up the beanstalk so that they can shriek with delight on being chased and enjoy laughing about the event with their friends.

When people know that dramatic positioning is 'just pretending' they experience it nested within whatever everyday social positionings have been established. Thus, students know that I'm not 'really' positioning them as a gruff police-officer, a giant, an elephant, or a murderous monarch. Rather, in dramatic dialogue young people and I may "play with positionings" (Edmiston, 2008) in order to explore how they (and I) *might* answer in dialogue with the viewpoints of imagined others. In dramatic dialogic inquiry, that is always improvised, each may author more complex understanding about narrative worlds and about our selves, our agency, and our relationships than is possible only in the real world.

Teaching Modes for Active and Dramatic Learning

How I socially position young people for learning can be conceptualized as shifting among different teaching modes that are often intersecting and

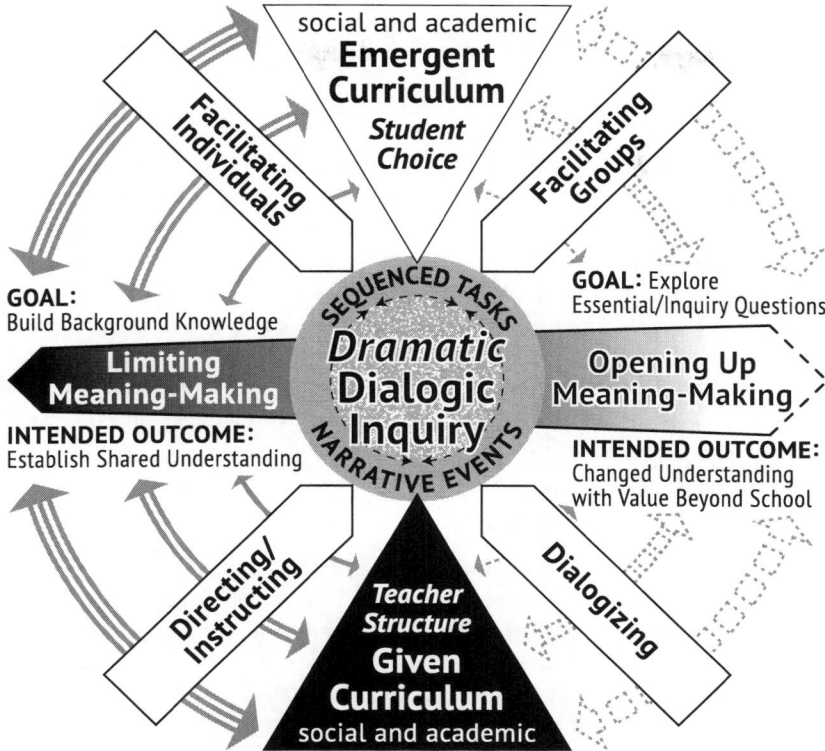

Figure 5.1 Four Teaching Modes for Active and Dramatic Learning.

overlapping. The four teaching modes that I regard as core are drawn in Figure 5.1 (my model of teaching for active and dramatic learning) as arrows touching the circle representing the classroom learning space.

Dialogue, which may be dramatized, is at the center of teaching and learning when learners author understanding in dramatic inquiry into the meaning of narrative events.

Learning is mediated by whatever tools are used in the different active and dramatic learning modes, alluded to in the circling dotted arrows. My teaching, always in relation to modes of learning, affects the classroom space and thus the lived, perceptual, and conceptual experiences of the participants (including me). My teaching creates the conditions for students' experiential, performative, reflective, and inquiry learning.

In planning I decide in advance the tools to use strategically in tasks. I plan for learning in response to my perception of the given and emergent social and academic curricular needs and always in relation to the goals and intended outcomes of sequenced tasks focused on exploring narrative events. I plan tasks that are carried out in the dynamic tension between how much structure I create and the choices students have.

Teaching tactically, I don't lose my strategic vision but rather fore-ground what's happening here-and-now over my attention to plans, goals, or intended outcomes. Tactically, I may seamlessly shift among the four teaching modes as I select tools and strategies in response both to young people's actions and to my perception of the emerging needs of the group. At other times, one teaching mode clearly predominates for students, for example when I facilitate individuals or small groups writing for an extended time or when I am giving clear instructions before a task. As an analogy, when people talk or write as their communicative purposes change they foreground different rhetorical approaches that may or may not be recognized by others, for example, focusing more on exposition, persuasion, description, or narrative.

Teaching as Facilitating Dialogue

The two teaching modes shown at the top of the diagram are teaching as **facilitation**. I negotiate with students, and intervene as needed, in order to facilitate tasks so that information, skills, and ideas can emerge from the students to be applied with any given knowledge in context as they reach toward achieving a goal or creating an artifact as an outcome. The main purpose of facilitation is so that young people can access, share, and use their prior knowledge while authoring meaning in particular tasks using various learning modes and tools as they dialogue. This process is represented in Figure 5.1 by the double-pointed arcs.

Teaching more tactically, I only facilitate as much as is necessary. Learning to watch groups or individuals at work and only intervene as needed was an important stance for me to develop as a teacher. I developed a practice that helped me learn to intervene only in response to what I actually saw or heard. I intentionally stood and touched the wall with my hands not letting go until I saw something important enough to warrant an intervention. I discovered that people could often get along quite nicely without my input. At the same time I could then be more tactical in deciding who might actually need assistance.

Because learning is primarily social, **facilitating groups** is my dominant teaching mode (though often in combination or closely sequenced with other modes). At different times during a session I tend to structure tasks for collaborative work in whole group, pairs, and small groups.

At the same time, because no one enters or exits the classroom with the same knowledge or perspective, everyone has to make individual sense as they experience, share, reflect, and inquire in dialogue. The intent of **facilitating individuals** is to create opportunities for each person to access, apply, and be able to share their prior (and developing) knowledge and unique viewpoints. The children in the classroom of Megan Rogers Frazier could share their individual ideas in every task and had repeated moments of personal reflection after sharing. As examples, apart from reflective conversations, they each wrote down and talked about what they thought it meant to be a friend, and wrote their own illustrated stories as concluding artifacts.

Students are likely to form more complex understanding when I sequence tasks so that in dialogue over time they move back-and-forth between collaborative and individual meaning-making. Doing so means they may build new meaning in response to different perspectives, not just those they walked in the door with or that they encountered in a single event or in one other person's interpretation.

Making a tactical teaching move, at any moment I may shift from a whole- to an individual to a small-group configuration, in response to the meaning students are actually making (or not). For example, when the graduate students in the class I wrote about in Chapter 1 were inquiring into how to justify active and dramatic teaching to administrators, we agreed on some basic principles in whole group (e.g. use language that administrators understand) and then moved into pairs to apply the principles in particular imagined situations relevant for each individual (that they later wrote down). As a roving spectator to their conversations I listened in for an example that could illustrate the idea and checked in with the pair before refocusing the whole group to reflect on one brief performance that I helped direct. I also listened critically for what was *not* being said so that I could ask questions designed to facilitate reflective meaning-making about, for example, the wisdom of locating explanations of dramatic approaches within teaching toward meeting highly valued academic curriculum goals.

Four Teaching Modes

- **Facilitating groups.** When I facilitate group collaborative tasks young people draw on what they already know as individuals and as a group as well as on what they may discover as they create and collaboratively experience meaningful shared outcomes and author meaning. I step back to watch and listen, intervening only as needed to keep a task going productively. To the extent that they build on one another's understanding in dialogue young people open up meaning for one another as they collaborate on achieving shared meaningful goals.
- **Instructing/directing.** Instructing and directing young people is essential to set up tasks, model expectations, and, as necessary, to

maintain engagement. My teaching is focused on students' under-standing of some important information or idea or knowing an aspect of a necessary skill so that they may begin or proceed with a task to achieve an agreed outcome. I introduce information, ideas, or practices, especially in response to questions or comments from any students expressing an interest or a need. When I instruct or direct I only require minimal meaning-making by the students as individuals and as a group: I provide knowledge largely in the form of 'answers' not open to much debate in terms of meaning.

- **Facilitating individuals.** Facilitating individual meaning-making, skill learning, or information gathering has a quite different (though related) purpose from facilitating group coauthoring. Whereas collaborating groups necessarily build some new ideas and open up meaning, in individualized tasks students mostly share what they already know. The focus of this teaching mode is on individual responses so that each may access and apply their prior knowledge in an individual task, that later may be shared. Though they may have questions, young people's prior knowledge will tend to have fairly fixed meaning for them. Subsequent collaborative tasks can build on the meaning young people individually author.

- **Dialogizing.** When I dialogize[1] I intend to open up meaning for indi-viduals and the group through dialogue that would be unlikely to happen without my intervention. Whereas facilitation sets up the *students* to make meaning, dialogizing is active teaching as I participate in dialogue with the young people to coauthor meaning *with* them. I use this teaching mode for shorter periods of time but potentially it has the most effect on group dynamics and meaning-making. When I shift into a dialogizing mode I intend to open up and destabilize meaning by, for example, raising questions, juxtaposing two or more view-points, affirming dissensus, and promoting dialogue in order to cri-tique, rethink, or reframe some prior, given, or apparently fixed or finalized understanding about a view, topic, process, or text.

Teaching as Active Participation in Dialogue

When I use the two teaching modes shown at the bottom of the diagram I am an active direct participant in dialogue with young people rather than only facilitating their dialogue with one another. I strategically pay attention to the social and academic given curriculum and make tactical decisions about minor or major interventions intended to assist people to explore or extend an understanding as part of their reaching toward a goal or achieving an outcome that I believe is important.

When I **direct** or **instruct** I shape process and introduce content. As needed, I model, set up, or modify learning tasks in response to goals and intended outcomes, as well as students' emergent individual or social needs. When I direct and instruct tactically I especially do the following: help young people focus on a task, an agreed objective, or on the process of dialogue; provide information or suggestions in response to students' direct or implicit questions.

Hotseating a character is a very effective way to instruct by providing contextualized information from a particular viewpoint on events. Tactically, it's relatively easy to ask whom they would like to talk to and respond accordingly. Then, having students work out their questions in advance both gives me time to prepare answers and allows for a whole group dialogue prioritizing questions and clarifying what they need or want to know. Though I am a participant I have to be careful not to make meaning *for* the young people that I want *them* to dialogue about, for example, when I am asked for a interpretation. I must keep meaning in motion. For example, if the children I wrote about in Chapter 4 had asked Lorraine-as-Lady-Macbeth one of their essential questions, for example "Is killing right or wrong," a definitive yes or no answer would close down meaning. Turning an answer into a question usually keeps the dialogue going (for example, "My husband is a general who has killed in battle. Is that right or wrong?"). So does an ambiguous answer true to the character's viewpoint (for example, "I don't choose to think about questions like that"). Both provide statements for subsequent analysis in reflection.

Though some groups need a great deal of direction and may expect a lot of instruction, others require relatively little. The less a group needs my input the less I use this mode though I didn't realize that possibility as a young teacher because I was over-directing, doing too much instruction, and not enough listening and watching. Getting groups and individuals to take more responsibility for their own learning is a long-term project built from task to task though supported by my stance that students are competent to take on more responsibility and then assisting them as necessary to act responsibly. Now, when I am able to work with a group over time I expect that once they learn a new strategy they will be able to use it with less input from me the next time. For example, though some of Megan's children had to learn to transition from the real to the imagined world, by the second session with the exception of one or two individuals they all moved seamlessly in and out of the world of *Amos and Boris*. I could then focus on assisting those young people, not by singling them out, but tactically by paying attention to them during any transition, often standing close-by and looking at them when giving a direction, and thus facilitating them to be among the first, and not last, to respond to my instruction, "If you can hear me, clap once. If you can hear me, clap twice …".

In the **dialogizing** mode I intend to extend dialogue by introducing a new perspective the young people are not currently considering that I believe is important for them to answer. When I dialogize I may set up, or adapt, a task. Or I may just ask a pointed question. The overall purpose, as Holquist, in his commentary on Bakhtin (1981), describes it is this: "dialogization" is when language or ideas "become relativized, de-privileged," so that we are aware of "competing" interpretations of the same thing (p. 427). Dialogizing introduces an additional point of view, another way of interpreting an event or making sense of an idea, and thus deepening understanding by making it more complex. A dialogizing stance, using Cecily O'Neill's words, includes me "searching for strategies which unsettle, create ambiguity, and force students to struggle with contradictions" (cited in Taylor & Warner, 2006, p. 21).

At its simplest, I tactically make a dialogizing teaching move by asking a carefully worded question that successfully provokes dialogue (not a monologic response). In Lorraine's classroom, as the young people were spectators to the group showing how they would care for an injured soldier, I evoked a transformational dialogue by asking, "How might that make a difference for our celebration? Should we continue?" As we dialogued, in responding to an alternative perspective on the party they had just planned, as they stood up over half of the students demonstrated they were rethinking their assumptions about celebration in the context of a death.

I may also make a dialogizing move through switching tasks. For example, with the middle school students (described in Chapter 1) tactically I used the *Consciousness Threes* strategy so that individuals in the middle of the conflicting voices telling them what to do could experience, and in dramatic action had to answer, the juxtaposed positions about whether or not to attack the giant.

A more complex, though highly versatile and effective, way to introduce a competing viewpoint is tactically using the strategy of *teacher-in-role*. Now a perspective is located in the consciousness of a character, contextualized within an event, with whom the young people can not only talk but also critique. In Lorraine's classroom if we had had more time, tactically I had wanted to take on the role of a parent of the soldier so that the young people would have to answer someone in mourning rather than talk in the abstract about the consequences of a death.

I find it important to recognize which teaching mode I am foregrounding, though tactically I frequently shift briefly among modes or add a mode. For example, facilitating any group work I may momentarily facilitate individual thinking by asking people to stop, think for a moment, and jot down a question or an idea. Or, as I facilitate a group discussion when I give any information or help with process I am instructing/directing and just by responding in any conversation I may begin to dialogize.

Because the purpose of teaching is to effect learning, my attention must always be on what the students are really doing and the actual meaning they are making as well as the understanding we have made and could make.

If people are so open to new ideas that there is no traction between their views or if they are not considering knowledge that I believe is important (moving to the right on the horizontal line in Figure 5.1) then I may introduce some new limits in their meaning-making by establishing some 'old' knowledge. That was what happened in Megan's classroom when I shifted tasks to establish some important shared understanding having realized that the children did not know how whales swim and again when they didn't understand the problem of being beached.

Conversely, if I realize that people have limited their meaning-making (moving to the left on the horizontal) or seem to have assumed or established an understanding that I assess is problematic, I can move to open up the process especially by introducing a new perspective that may dialogize meaning as participants create some new understanding. In Megan's classroom, when the children-as-mice seemed to have thought talking to an elephant would be easy for mice and had not considered how to build trust, I moved into taking up the perspective of an elephant with them to challenge their thinking as I facilitated dialogue in a whole-group exchange.

Teaching Modes and Strategies

In Table 5.1, I categorize selected active and dramatic strategies by teaching mode. Teachers have found Table 5.1 a useful checklist extension to Table 3.2 (where I categorized strategies by learning mode and by increasing social demand). In planning and teaching (whether strategic or tactical) it's useful to have an array of strategies to consider. Rather than add commentary or examples I direct readers to the descriptions of contexts in which the strategies were used (listed in the index).

Dimensions of Tactical and Strategic Teaching

Since teaching is always for learning, each teaching mode can be conceptualized in relation to the active and dramatic learning modes. I use strategies within tasks to promote, support, and extend dialogue in relation to the topic, narrative events, goals, and outcomes. When I view my actions and utterances tactically, my teaching potential is shaped by the

Table 5.1 Active and *Dramatic* Teaching Strategies Categorized by Teaching Mode

Facilitating individuals	Facilitating groups
Vote From Your Seat	Choral Reading
Stand/Step Forward When/If You …	Sun Shines on All Who …
Go Stand by …	Zip Zap Zop
Amplify	Red Ball, Yellow Ball
You Can Speak When We Make Eye	Social Atom
Contact	Talk to/*Show* Your Neighbor
Cross the Circle/Classroom	Group Storytelling
Show Us …	Continuum (stand and explain)
Sculpting Teacher/Students	*What Are you Doing?*
Thought-tracking Teacher-in-role	*Collective Role*
Thought-tracking Student-in-role	*Ritualized Action*
Interview a Partner	*Teacher-in-role Dialogues with*
Hands/objects-as-Puppets	*Students-in-role*
Walking-as-a-character	*Teacher Directs Small Groups' Improvisations*
Writing-in-role	*Hotseat Students-in-role*
Narrating Actions	*Pairs-dialogue-in-role*
	Modelmaking
	Soundscaping
	Create Tableaux/Still Image + with words
	and/or movement
	Show Tableaux

Instructing/Directing	Dialogizing
If You Can Hear Me, Clap Once	Trading Game
3-2-1 Countdown	Continuum (move and explain change)
P2P Reading	*Consciousness Threes/Alley*
L2L Reading	*Hotseat Teacher-in-role (to critique)*
Echoing Back	*Tableaux with Competing Viewpoints*
Counting-off	*Juxtapositioning*
Paper/Photos on Floor	
Photograph/Video Projected	
Modeling	
Narrating	
Word Carpet	
Reading-in-role	
Puppet Show	
Overhearing	
Hotseat Teacher-in-role (for information)	

affordances of whatever learning modes the young people are using or that I might introduce.

Table 5.2 is a grid with summary information about possible tactical teaching in what I think of as different 'dimensions' of each teaching mode. Though Table 5.2 shows a grid of teaching dimensions, the reality in the classroom cannot be reduced to boxes. In this section I provide examples of a few of the dimensions though I hope that, combined with the notes in the table, this is sufficient to illuminate more specific aspects of tactical teaching in relation to active learning modes and *dramatic learning modes* (that I reference via italics in the table).

The unpredictability of being tactical and needing to improvise is what makes teaching exhilarating for me, though sometimes scary. A significant advantage of having learned from my wide experience across many classrooms teaching people of all ages is that I am a much better improviser now than I was thirty years ago: the fear factor has been diminished and contained through the confidence I have in thinking and acting with bifocal vision in teaching that is both tactical and strategic. That's hardly surprising since we get better at what we spend our time doing, especially when we reflect. So, for instance, I'm hopeless at video games but I've become quite proficient at playing the fiddle ten years after picking up my father's instrument.

To illustrate tactical teaching in which I made very deliberate interventions, I use examples from the two sessions I led in Amy McMunn's classroom before the one I referenced at the opening of this chapter. I analyze my thinking at moments of tactical decision related to the overall meaning being made in the whole session. I use brackets to reference the dimensions of whatever teaching mode/learning mode was foregrounded, for example (instructing/dramatic playing). Additionally, I may reference a particular teaching strategy, for example (instructing as teacher-in-role/dramatic reflection).

Negotiating to Introduce a New Perspective

Over three sessions working with Amy McMunn's class I explored part of the world of *Love That Dog* via extracts from poems in which Jack tells how he chooses Sky at an animal shelter but later sees him killed in a car accident. In the first session sixteen of the university students in my Autumn 2011 graduate class were able to join us after school one day in October with eighteen of Amy's students. We met in the music room so that we would have more space than in Amy's classroom. My teaching was largely strategic for the first forty-five minutes because I was able to follow my planning map closely.

After brief introductions I had begun with the children sharing answers to an inquiry question: What do we love to do (or would love to do) with

Table 5.2 Dimensions of Teaching

Teaching Learning modes	Experiencing *as dramatic players*	Showing/telling *as dramatic performers*	Reflecting and interpreting *as dramatic spectators/ spect-actors*	Inquiring *as dramatic inquirers*
Directing/ Instructing	I can provide direction or information: "Let's do this ..."	I can direct others; I can perform information: "Here's what I know"	I can give information and support the reflecting/ interpreting process: 'Look here. What do you notice about ...?'	I can consider with the group what they may need to know or do
Facilitating groups	I can bring energy, ideas, tools, structure, etc., as needed as the group collaborates: "Let's all ..."	I can shape, deepen, or extend a performance: "3-2-1-freeze"; "I have an idea ..."	I can give feedback to the group on process: "What I've noticed is ..." and content: "What do you think so far?"	I can shift task, return focus to goal or inquiry question, make a suggestion to the group, etc.
Facilitating individuals	I can move around to support and collaborate with whomever seems to need assistance: "Can I join in?"	I can publicly collaborate with individuals: "I can work with you, if you like ..."	I can amplify an unheard view or support a minority viewpoint: "Did you hear this idea? What do you all think?"	I can personalize or equalize tasks so all may participate in inquiry
Dialogizing	I can support an emerging new perspective in the flow of exploration: "Yes!"	I can address a group from a new perspective "Yes, and ..."	I can answer one perspective with a conflicting perspective, "Yes, but ..."	I can design a task to consider more than one of the perspectives in or on event(s)

our pets? And why? Everyone had either currently or previously had a pet: they liked to stroke cats, chase dogs, and laugh with animals. Why? Answers included: to play together, be entertained, something to do, and teach them tricks.

I had introduced the fictional world through the following tasks: games ('Cross the Circle' and 'What Are You Doing?'); reading a poem; sculpting to model, and then creating and sharing humorous moving

Photograph 5.6 Improvising Dialogue using Puppets.

tableaux of 'what we [would] like to do with our pets'; and writing from a template based on one of the poems. All of this was in preparation for the event I had selected to enter in imagination when Jack went to the shelter with his father and chose Sky.

In Photograph 5.6 the young people are improvising dialogue in pairs using beanie baby dogs as *puppets*. One is moving the puppet while the other is speaking as if she is the dog. We had just read the part of the poem in which Jack (as the narrator) describes his visit when he had imagined all of the dogs jumping up and saying, "Choose me. I'm the best one."

We drove and drove
until we stopped at a
red brick building
with a sign
in blue letters
ANIMAL PROTECTION SHELTER
And inside we walked
down a long cement path
past cages
with all kinds of
dogs

big and small
fat and skinny
some of them
hiding in the corner
but most of them
bark-bark-barking and
jumping up
against the wire cage
as we walked past
as if they were saying
Me! Me! Choose me!
I'm the best one!

I had stopped reading before Jack chose Sky. Their joyful exuberance is clear in the photograph. Using dramatic performance they are trying to convince visiting teachers-in-role as prospective pet owners, like Jack, to "choose me."

As I watched the children I was tactically mapping out a plan for what I might do next. I had planned no further than the young people imagining choosing a dog; they would experience two of the consciousnesses in the event (Jack and chosen dogs). I was trying to decide whether, and if so how, to introduce a new perspective (the dogs that were not chosen). The work to this point had been joyful but emotionally sentimental. I wanted to dialogize their experience through introducing the perspective of the dogs that are not chosen. Should I read the end of the poem where Jack in stark realism says that the unchosen dogs will be killed (instructing/reflecting)? Should I work in role as the shelter director (instructing as teacher-in-role/reflecting)? Though I was tempted to spring a dramatic surprise on them I thought better of that given that I was working with eight- to nine-year-olds I did not know and whose parents would be arriving in ten minutes.

Tactically I decided I had to negotiate with the children (directing/inquiring) so that they would not suddenly have to face the topic of death but could choose to do so (or not).

I had planned that the university students would reflect and analyze how convincing the children had been and to ask the children to add on their comments about what they liked about their dog (instructing/reflecting). Children gave sentimental attributes like "cute," "funny" or "loveable." I asked the children to put down the dogs they had picked up previously (instructing), I read the section of the poem when Jack chooses Sky, and I asked the children-as-Jack to pick up a dog—all chose the same one again (instructing as teacher-in-role).

I told the children that the story had a sad and a happy ending and asked if they wanted to hear the sad ending (instructing/reflecting).

All seemed to agree that they did. But in case, I offered that they could cover their ears as I read the rest of the poem; one of the university students did so. Now that they all had chosen and knew what would happen, I read the rest of the poem:

> And that's when we saw
> the yellow dog
> standing against the cage …
> as if he were saying
> Me me me! Choose me!
> And we did
> we chose him …
> And the other dogs
> in the cages
> get killed dead
> if nobody chooses them.

Photograph 5.7 shows *me-in-role* as the shelter director carrying on a tray the beanie baby dogs that the children had previously passed over as I again spoke the final four lines of the poem (dialogizing as teacher-in-role/dramatic reflection) and watched closely to see how the children responded.

Photograph 5.7 Dialogizing as Teacher-in-Role.

I asked the children individually to invent why the dogs might not have been chosen as they looked at the tray (directing/reflecting). I modeled that one had a missing leg. Some repeated my idea while others imagined dogs that were blind, deaf, and sickly. Their language contrasted with their previous 'cute' words. Then, as I walked by, repeating the words from the poem, everyone took a dog (dialogizing as teacher-in-role/dramatic reflection). Tactically, I had to stop and start again because of some giggling. I acknowledged that it might feel a bit silly with me holding beanie baby dogs on a piece of plastic but I asked them if they could imagine real dogs when they looked. I paused to let the moment settle and I continued when I felt their seriousness.

Our dramatization of the second half of the poem was an embodied experience by the children in *juxtaposition* with their dramatization of the first half: 'choosing the previously unchosen' was contrasted with 'choosing the best.' In both cases they picked up dogs in their hands but the meaning made was quite different. This introduced some experience of dissonance between viewpoints so that the children could have begun to critique and reframe their ideas about loving abandoned animals.

There were still dogs left on the tray. If I had had more time I would have turned to the question of shelter animals that get "killed dead" (facilitating whole group/inquiry). There was stillness as I alluded to that fact when I again repeated the final lines of the poem.

Some parents had already arrived to collect their children. Wanting the children to reflect individually to author meaning about the session, I asked the young people in a final task to say and/or show what they might do to care for the dog (facilitating individuals/dramatic reflection). Many shared both medical procedures, like "put its leg in a cast," and caring actions, like "hold it and love it." Then, wanting them to connect with and build on the understandings we had agreed at the beginning, I returned to the white board as we read together, and the children dictated additions to, their previous ideas (directing/inquiring). I could assess that their understanding was now more nuanced. What do we love to do (or would love to do) with our pets? "Give them baths so they don't get fleas." "Comfort them so they'll not feel lonely." Why? "They show love, for example by licking your hand." "They become part of the family and accept you as you are." "And as one boy said about caring for his dog: "I feel like I'm needed."

Taking Charge as Director/Dramatic Performer

In the second session, a week later, I largely followed my planning map until near to the end. After introductions, we improvised in **Group Storytelling** as those who had previously been present created the story of Jack and Sky, one phrase or sentence at a time (facilitate whole group/

performing for reflection). Those who had not been present could ask questions. We played **What Are You Doing?** to share moments from the story so far. The children loved showing playing with their pets (facilitate whole group/dramatic performance for reflection). After reading (facilitate whole group/reflection) one of the poems several times **L2L** (reading in a circle line-to-line, each person reads only one line) and having whoever wanted to add an accompanying *soundscape,* I brought in blocks, legos, and construction paper for *modelmaking* (facilitate pairs/dramatic playing and reflection).

> My street
> is on the edge of a city
> and it has
> quiet music
> most of the time
> whish
> meow
> swish.
> My street is a THIN one
> with houses on both sides
> and my house
> is the white one
> with the red door
> ...
> At both ends of our street
> are yellow signs
> that say
> *Caution! Children at Play!*

The children, working in pairs each with a few lines to focus on, worked collectively to build a model of a scene, the street where Jack lived (Photograph 5.8). When I realized I had not thought ahead so that we could have more than one house for Jack I negotiated with the children. Two pairs had already begun on Jack's house so I asked them if they could work together. They seemed happy to do so. For those not working on the signs, I suggested that they create houses where Jack's neighbors lived.

I had planned to activate the scene and bring it to life with a whole group performance, but not *how* I would do so. Up until that point my facilitation had turned the tasks and meaning-making almost entirely over to the young people. Individuals recalled what they knew of the narrative as they told, showed, and answered the questions of their peers. I had directed our shared L2L reading of the poem but they had been able to say "stop" in order to ask any questions. Putting them in pairs they

Photograph 5.8 Modelmaking.

had transformed their interpretations into a model using dramatic playing and reflection and the blocks, etc., as tools.

I asked them to walk around to look at the model they had made of the scene (directing/reflection). Everyone made positive comments and could ask questions about other people's work (Photograph 5.9). I could tell they felt proud of the model that covered a large area.

As they were appreciating their work I was planning. I read to myself the remainder of the poem that would introduce an additional perspective—the consciousness of Jack watching the accident.

The *blue car, blue car*
spattered with mud
hit Sky
thud thud thud
and kept on going
in such a hurry
so fast
so many miles to go
it couldn't even stop
…
and

Photograph 5.9 Whole Group Reflection.

Sky
closed his eyes
and
he
never
opened
them
again
ever.

Strategically, I knew that having a serious shared experience of the accident would be essential for them. I made several tactical decisions. First, I had a small blue car in my pocket and though I had briefly considered asking one of the children to use it I decided not to because I hadn't identified someone who could take on such a central emotionally charged role without preparation and practice. I thought about taking one of the children aside but they were all so engrossed in making the model that I didn't want to do that. Second, though I had planned to have them read the poem, I realized that they needed to *hear* the words of the poem and not read them; paper in their hands would be a distraction from experiencing a performance of the narrative event. Third, though I had asked people to create an image of Jack's house I decided not to ask any of the children to view the event as Jack because of the emotional closeness of the perspective of watching your pet be killed; I decided to distance the experience by asking them to view the event as a neighbor. Then they could feel the dramatic tension by *viewing* the event from a perspective parallel to Jack's, as spect-actors living on the street who could only watch but couldn't act to save Sky.

These tactical decisions were foregrounded in my teaching as I took charge to direct and perform (directing and dialogizing using narrating, reading, and a toy car tool/dramatic reflection). I asked everyone to move to wherever they imagined they would live or liked to be on the street, if they lived on Maple Street. I said if they were by Jack's house to imagine they were someone who wasn't Jack. Using their *hand-as-a-puppet* I asked them to move their hand to where they were when they heard the accident. I asked them to invent what they-as-a-person-on-the-street could see out of their window that night, which they did. Then I produced the blue car, placed it at the end of the street, practiced speeding it down the road without running into any of the houses, as I **narrated** how one day Jack, his family, and some of his neighbors saw "a blue car, spattered in mud, in such a hurry."

As the car sped by for the third time, I read the poem. There was stillness.

Without disturbing the somber mood *I-as-television-reporter* held up an imaginary microphone and spoke as if I was on television (facilitating individuals/dramatic reflection): "There was an accident today on a side street at the edge of the city. A car struck and killed a dog. I'm here to talk to some of the people who live here about what they saw."

Then, I-as-the-reporter asked the children-as-people-who-lived-on-the-street what they had seen and how they felt.

> There was a blue car. It was speeding.
> I heard the dog yell. It was horrible.
> There were flashing yellow lights. Didn't he see them!
> I'm really angry.

Strategically, I knew to end with the whole group in a circle. Tactically, as it was time to go home I could not have them leave upset or angry inside Jack's world. I also felt they needed to experience some 'light' to illuminate the moment of 'darkness' we had just visited. Intending to dialogize their meaning-making, I wondered how I could refract one view through the other and then realized I could do so by adapting the opening game '*What Are You Doing?*'. I gathered the children but now I asked them to show, "the memories Jack had of Sky that he'd never forget" in a variation: What *were* you doing? I fed them the line "I'll never forget ..." as they responded. Speaking in the past tense introduced a sense of looking back from an accident that changed Jack's life. At the same time we could all laugh as a few children performed joyful embodied images of lively, happy dogs and owners.

> I'll never forget:
> ... feeding him treats
> ... scratching his head
> ... saying his name.

The session and the children had come full circle.

Some Core Strategic Questions About Tasks to Promote Bifocal Vision

Strategic:

How do these tasks promote our goals and intended outcomes?
How are we building community?

Tactical:

How am I positioning students?
Should I shift teaching modes?
Can I give more choice to promote more agency?
Is there another learning mode, strategy tool I could introduce?
Should I introduce another perspective?

Strategic Planning, Tactical Responses, Building Community

Not long after I began working with Cecily O'Neill at Ohio State I was eager to find a possible site for some practical work. I visited the middle school classroom of Jean, a teacher I had recently met, knowing that her twelve- and thirteen-year-old students had been studying a topic that I knew a great deal about, European medieval life. On the day I turned up they were talking about a version of the story of Robin Hood they had been reading. Five minutes into the lesson, to my surprise Jean suggested I take over. Unfortunately, I ignored my intuition that was telling me to return after some planning time as I mentally grabbed at a couple of ideas to implement.

The students were in chairs-with-wings laid out in a horseshoe. After a brief introduction, I asked them if they would like to imagine they were the 'merry men and women' in Sherwood Forest. With only a minimal sense of agreement, no attempt to embody a fictional role, and no negotiation about what I did next, I said I would go out and return as if I was someone else. I left my chair, walked away and then turned around. I now had the attention of the whole group as I changed my posture and spoke, "I've run away from the Sheriff of Nottingham's castle. I want to join Robin Hood's band. Do you know where I can find him?" One of the boys who had been talking with his neighbor said, "How do we know you're not a spy?" I denied this and tried to tell him that I was an outlaw. "You're a spy," said the boy again. As he pretended to fix an arrow and pull back a bow several other boys did the same. And when he made the sound of a whistling arrow and said, "You're dead" the others laughed and also pretended to shoot arrows.

Two minutes after beginning, I was dead in the world of Robin Hood and felt humiliated in the world of the classroom. Jean took over and I started wondering where I had gone wrong. I've been mulling that over ever since in reflections that help ground me in humility.

I had made several tactical mis-takes that began to come into view as I compared my disaster with Cecily's artful practice. Unlike with Amy's class, I had not negotiated with the group what was about to happen. Though the boys were actually going along with my scenario they were taking it in a direction I had not anticipated. Tactically, I didn't know what to do next. Whereas in the final session with Amy's class I had affirmed the idea of the boy who introduced the divergent view of a driver texting on a cell-phone, with these middle level students I opposed the boy's spy idea. Rather than answering with a "Yes, and ..." stance by either stepping out of the world of Robin Hood to ask if they would like to try and find out if the man was a spy, or by staying in the fictional world and promoting dialogue by saying something like, "What makes you think that?" I found myself unintentionally in an oppositional positioning.

In her 1989 *Language Arts* article, Cecily outlines some of the ways in which a teacher, intent on promoting dialogue and transformation in learning, has to become more of an artist in using dramatic pedagogy. I'm still working on developing these abilities.

> To carry out the kind of teaching which is transformative and dialogic ... the teacher/artist requires flexibility, ingenuity, personal creativity and an ability to exploit opportunities as they occur ... curiosity, the ability to focus on critical reflection, the strength to cope with uneasiness, uncertainty, and unpredictability, and considerable tolerance of ambiguity.
>
> (Taylor & Warner, 2006, p. 108)

In addition to my tactical mis-takes I had also made a huge strategic error. Without realizing it at the time, I had not followed the basic principle I stressed in Chapter 2: always begin working collaboratively with the whole group to make core values visible. Rather than negotiate a shared entry into a real-and-imagined space I had assumed that by telling the young people where we were that they would go along with my positioning of them in a fictional space. I had used an instructional mode rather than the mode of facilitating the whole group.

If I had already adopted that principle in my stance I could probably have recovered from the mis-take by tactically shifting roles, my physical location, and my positioning of myself in relation to them. In reflecting and analyzing what had happened with Cecily she had said, you could always ask, "So what will *we do* with the body?" Positioning myself in alignment with them could have opened space for a collaborative dialogue either about dramatic action in the barely imagined fictional space and/or as ourselves focused by a possible inquiry question.

Teaching Affects Agency in Real and Imagined Worlds

How a teacher positions him or her self in relation to young people and creates opportunities for everyone to improvise in imagined spaces affects how people position and understand their selves, their authorship, and how they may act in the real world as well as in real-and-imagined spaces. In other words, the social imagination of active and dramatic pedagogies can be highly significant mediating tools for developing all participants' agency, teachers as well as students.

Whereas young children tend to be impulsive and young people in general may selfishly react tactically, as teachers we can assist students to act more strategically as well as tactically and thus develop their authorship and sense of agency in relation to others. Such awareness can only begin to develop when people *choose* to act and respond in dialogue, and the younger the better. Significantly, all dramatic action is chosen words and/or deeds. In summarizing significant research, Johnston is clear that as a teacher, "Drawing students' attention to their successes and showing them how their decisions and strategic actions were responsible for them, increased children's perceptions of their ability and the effectiveness of their focused efforts" (2004, p. 39). This is what Jill, Lorraine, and Megan Ballinger all did in reflective dialogue with their classes and with individuals.

Developing students' authorship requires the bifocal vision of both tactical and strategic teaching. We must dialogue with young people in the actual world of the classroom, or as Maxine Greene (1995) describes it, we must be "wide-awake" with "our awareness of what it is to be in the world" (p. 35). At the same time, in imagination we are not stuck with the way things are. "Imagining things being otherwise may be a first step toward acting on the belief that they can be changed" (ibid., p. 22).

Strategically, Jill Sampson, Megan Ballinger, Lorraine Gaughenbaugh, Megan Rogers Frazier, and Amy McMunn, all acted to create the future they imagined for their classes: more collaborative, generous, caring, and inclusive. Their vision developed as they reflected on prior experiences. All planned accordingly and taught strategically with those social goals in mind alongside any academic goals. In strategic teaching I pay most attention to the whole—I look back and forward to see the unfolding nature of the work in the present. But strategic teaching alone is inadequate. In tactical teaching I pay attention in-the-moment to the responses and needs of the people with whom I improvise in dialogue, but whose vision of the work is unlikely to be as holistic as mine.

As I noted in Chapter 2, Jill tactically dialogued with her group as a whole in an extended 'real' conversation and Megan Ballinger repeatedly changed the actual classroom conditions in response to what students said and did so that none were excluded and all could include themselves in the ensemble tasks of their ongoing dramatic inquiries. Lorraine's tactical and strategic teaching also focused on individuals as part of the community, including developing the authorship of six-year-old George.

> Six months ago I found George quite a challenging kindergartner. He seemed to have little self-control, frequently interrupted, and constantly required my immediate attention. Other activities seemed not to have captivated him but I could imagine him enjoying the battle scene with which we would begin our exploration of *Macbeth* and medieval life. I was right.

Lorraine anticipated that George would be captivated by events in the narrative. Like the older children in the first session (described in Chapter 4) George relished wielding imagined weapons with a partner: using the tools of a drum beat and repeated action he had been more controlled in his movement than she had seen previously. However, Lorraine did not anticipate the focused attention he would command in relation to the rest of the classroom community that first occurred in the following session.

> Because so many events in the narrative pivot on the power of a medieval king, one of my goals was to begin to understand the power a noble had over his (or her) subjects if they became the monarch, like Macbeth when he is chosen to be king by the other thanes

following the death of King Duncan. I imagined the power to command servants at a banquet to be one of the events in the story with which children in kindergarten could easily relate. In the second session I planned to play 'Show us ...' as an entry into the event. The children like moving and then freezing. In this case I planned that they would all show 'eating,' 'eating at a banquet,' 'servants,' 'servants bringing in food,' 'nobles,' 'nobles eating,' and then 'kings and queens.' With some explanation, for example of the word 'banquet,' five minutes into the lesson the children were hooked, having already embodied in dramatic action the different perspectives of servants, nobles, and royalty.

Lorraine had a throne and crown ready for the monarch. Tactically, she decided to ask George to sit first as if he was the king. Noticing that waiting was difficult for him, but building on what she had seen the previous week, she wanted to see how he would handle the responsibility. Her decision was momentous.

He wanted to be called King George. As soon as he sat down, his whole demeanor changed. He was calm, pensive, and patient, not at all the George that frequently disrupted. I asked the class what the nobles would *do* after a king was chosen. One boy said they would kneel. I interpreted that that would be showing their respect. One girl said they'd bring gifts.

Over five minutes, as George personified dignity in a *ritualized action* that created a mood of regal authority, the others came forward to kneel in turn. Lorraine interpreted their actions as "swearing loyalty to the new king" as the children invented gifts and used appropriate language such as "I give you my sword" and "I give you a ring, your majesty."

After about half of the children had come up, King George said with solemnity, "I'm hungry. I want some food." Speaking as myself, because some students had not yet had a chance to kneel I asked him if he could wait a bit. George looked at me with a steady gaze as he said, "A king should not have to wait." He was right! Some of his peers responded immediately producing an imaginary tray with food that he pretended to eat. The banquet continued with King George in command of the situation and then with others taking on the role of the king.

Positioned with the authority of a monarch, George had to be the center of attention. He took up the role with seriousness, framed the situation by taking on responsibility, and adopted a commanding air that positioned his peers, his commanding self, and Lorraine, appropriately. Lorraine accepted how he-as-a-king positioned her and supported him. Because of his dramatic action, everyone could better collaborate to imagine and improvise a narrative event that was significant both for developing community and in authoring understanding about the topic. The most memorable images that his peers had previously had of George were in a tantrum on the floor or apparently aimlessly running around the room. After this occasion, everyone had powerful images of George positioned in control of himself in relation to the whole group and in a role that was central in framing a unifying experience. O'Neill (1995) illuminates this transformative power of dramatic action:

> Every dramatic act is an act of discovery and our acknowledgement of our humanity and community, first in the drama world and then in the real world.
>
> (p. 152)

In subsequent sessions George was always ready to take on roles with authority in the real-and-imagined spaces of any "drama world." Building a relationship with him, Lorraine could assist him to change his relationship with the group, and thus the George he is now becoming in the real world.

> On that day he finally became a valued member of the community, not a distraction. Since then his demeanor has changed and now I expect him to want to join in tasks. Being disruptive has become the exception rather than the rule as it was before. In the following weeks he would beam when I would tell him how helpful for our ensemble he had been as the king. He would love becoming the king for a few seconds when I would address him as "your majesty." Some of his peers would do the same. Though he 'has his moments,' as many of his peers do, I now see him as part of the group. The other day when they were working on computers I noticed people being patient and helping him calm down when he was starting to really act out. When we sat on the rug he made us all laugh when he said, "I like your hair, Mrs. G. Grey is my favorite color!"

Dramatic pedagogy can open up windows of imagination for all participants that present alternative viewpoints. For young people they may 'see' their selves, their peers, and their choices differently. As teachers we may 'view' students differently and affirm them when we value their actions. We may better recognize that no one is a fixed entity and that authorship means every person can grow. New viewpoints open up new possibilities and ways to position one another, frame events, improvise, dialogue, and embrace our agency to change our selves, our relationships, and our world.

> Only when the given or taken-for-granted is subject to questioning, only when we take various, sometimes unfamiliar perspectives on it, does it show itself as what it is—contingent on many interpretations, many vantage points, unified (if at all) by conformity or by unexamined common sense. Once we can see our givens as contingencies, then we may have an opportunity to posit alternative ways of living and valuing and to make choices.
>
> (Greene, 1995, p. 23)

Conclusion: Teaching with a Sense of the Whole in Relation to the Parts

Megan Ballinger reminds me that learning to teach is as much of a journey as teaching to learn:

> It's hard to teach in this way, but it's worth it. I would never have wanted to stay as the teacher I was going into my own classroom. Teaching is a journey and I'm looking forward to where I end up next.

Dramatic pedagogy is an art. When I teach as an improvising artist with bifocal vision I pay attention to details and their relation to the whole. As a combination of all previous figures, Figure 5.2 presents an image of the ideal interrelationship between the whole, a classroom community, and the parts: active and dramatic teaching for learning through dialogue about events in tasks that explore our humanity.

I experience three primary aspects of the whole in relation to the parts: the energy of a group in one task relative to others; the changing quality of the polyphonic dialogue in the group; and how different groupings create a sense of the movement of individuals being part of the whole.

Tasks feel effortless when a group has focused energy. Energy ebbs and flows dynamically so I try to sense a group's energy not only as we improvise but also for how it may change. I can affect, and to an extent shape, group energy by moving back-and-forth from more motion toward more stillness and/or from more sound toward more silence. At the same time I can affect the mood by shifting attention toward the lighter or darker side of life. That sense of energy flow is what I most held on to in Amy McMunn's classroom to shape our movement among moments of exuberance like pretending to play with pets or speeding in a car to being still to be interviewed or to think about the loss of a pet.

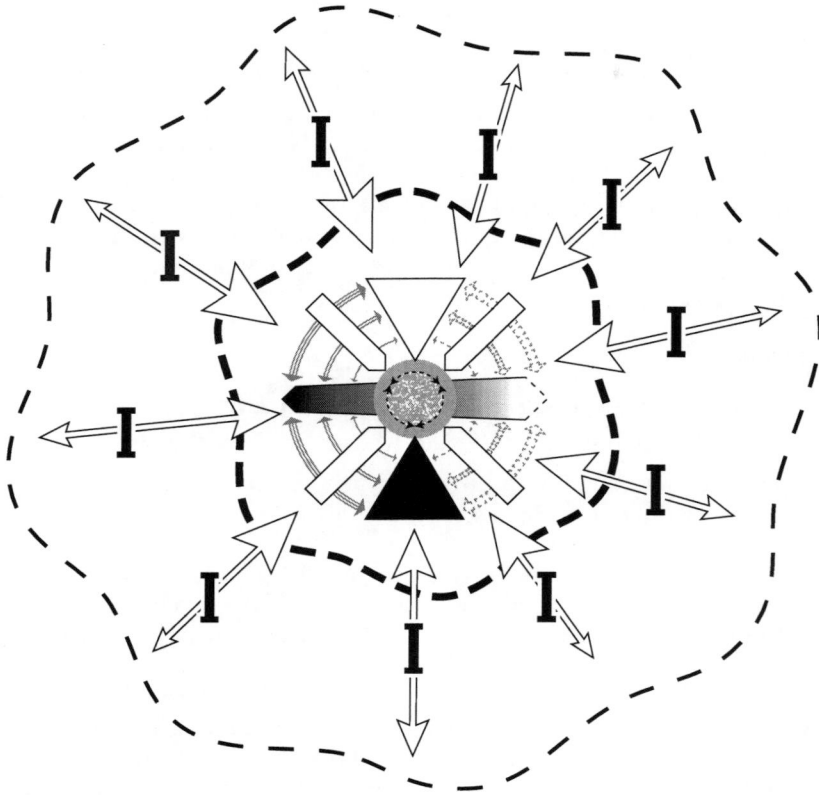

Figure 5.2 Teaching and Learning while Building Community.

Dialogue feels like the 'pulse' of teaching and learning. As people dialogue with me and with one another they make layers of meaning about
an event, more widely about the topic, and about themselves as a group
and as individuals. Imagining the center circle of learning modes and the
horizontal double-headed arrow of ongoing dialogue in Figure 5.2 in
perpetual motion within a developing ensemble, in any group there is
always an authoring tension between an opening up and a limitation of
meaning-making as understanding is being developed and affected by my
teaching. When I teach artistically I am being responsive at the same time
to my sense of evolving conceptual understandings as well as to the lived
and perceptual process of meaning-making by the students (represented
by the circular arrows and arcs). The teaching modes provide me with
dynamic tools to be tactical in the questions I pose, the statements I make,
or the tasks I introduce. I ask myself how anything I say may affect the
meaning being made. Will it open it up or narrow it? Does the group

need information? Do they need to talk or should I ask a question? When I am tactical as I facilitate or participate in ongoing dialogue I intend to keep meaning vital and in motion.

Moving back-and-forth from working as a whole group to individual and small-group work feels like the 'breath' of teaching and learning. Facilitating a 'breathing' movement between social and individual groupings is essential not only for meaning-making but for changing people's shared sense of being part-of-the-whole. Teaching tactically I mix up groupings, give everyone a chance to work with everyone else, while all the time nesting individual, pair, and small group work within a sense of *us* as a living breathing community with coherence, not necessarily in agreement on meaning but in agreement on valuing a shared experience of togetherness. At the beginning and end of a session, a sequence, or the year we are always together. In both Amy's and Megan's classrooms we began sitting together on the carpet and ended with a group hug. The overall sense of being a whole, when a group works as an ensemble, feels like a collective in-breath as we gather and a joyful out-breath as we depart.

> Our classroom is comparable to a work of art. It is a nexus of living meanings ... an individual thing detailed from the vague infinity of the background that heightens the sense of humanity ... its details, particularities, individualities—all are contained within a piece of the whole ... they are the backbone of the whole. They are necessary of its understanding. The whole contains meaning in and of itself and confers meaning to its parts.
>
> (Traugh, 1986, p. 109)

Note

1 Dialogize is pronounced 'di-a' as in dialogue, has an emphasis on the 'a,' with a 'soft g' as in logic, and 'ize' sounding like 'eyes': di-å-log-ize.

Chapter 6

Assess What You Value in Achievement

When I was a beginning assistant professor at the University of Wisconsin-Madison Elizabeth Ellsworth agreed to partner with me in a teaching fellowship program funded by the Lily Foundation: she came to watch me teach and I attended a couple of her seminars. We met several times over coffee, first to agree on what we wanted to achieve, and then to compare notes after visits. We each reported on what we'd seen students doing, talked about what we had liked, asked pointed or naïve questions, listened to the other explain intentions, enjoyed our different ideas, and gave each other suggestions to try out. This was assessment that I really valued. Dialoguing with Liz helped me in moving closer to achieving an authoring goal I was committed to: I wanted to become a better teacher.

When I ask teachers what they think of assessment the mood invariably darkens. These are some of the comments I've heard:

- We have two weeks of assessment next week so no time for teaching.
- The kids are so good but they can't sit still for that long.
- I hate not being able to help the students.
- If they could do what we did in class they'd do much better.
- No teacher would make up tests that set out to trick kids.
- A mother called me and said her daughter was having nightmares.
- They make me feel like they don't trust me as a teacher or the kids as learners.
- If the scores don't go up my job may be on the line.
- I can't get the students to care about the assessment.
- The best thing I've done is to treat it as a problem-solving game; I tell them that the testers aren't interested in your thinking: find evidence from the text.
- I don't learn anything useful from the test results.

The teachers' responses are mostly referring to standardized, state and district, high-stakes testing. As a beginning teacher in England assessment was largely only my responsibility: I continually assessed informally and, except when students had national examinations at sixteen and eighteen, in collaboration with colleagues I created formal assessments at the end of the year. Now, in the US, assessment is big business with teachers positioned increasingly as test implementers to achieve outcomes largely disconnected from the needs of the people in particular classroom communities. Of course, testing is only one form of assessment. However, the well-documented problem is that in too many places testing has become the only form of assessment that is valued; or worse, testing has become the only achievement valued. Testing has become the demonic tail wagging a curriculum dog in danger of becoming a hellhound.

This chapter is not about testing. So I won't outline the follies of cultivating the culture of testing and its practices of measuring, sorting, and ranking children, teachers, and schools as if they were factory widgets. I'll let the conclusions of the National Research Council, a blue-ribbon committee of the National Academies of Science, speak for me (Hout & Elliott, 2011):

> Nearly a decade of America's test-based accountability systems, from 'adequate yearly progress' to high school exit exams, has shown little to no positive effect overall on learning and insufficient safeguards against gaming the system.

In this chapter I consider some of the uses and challenges of authentic informal and formal assessment practices. I use the term evaluation as a broad synonym for assessment. Though people differentiate between assessment (the gathering of information about learners' achievements) and evaluation (the use of that information to make value judgments about learning or learners) the distinction is not universally applied. First, many assessments are used to evaluate. Second, like Astin (1991), I argue that an "institution's assessment practices are a reflection of its values" (p. 3). In other words, assessments are always evaluations in the sense that I assess what I, and/or others, value in students' achievements and people assess whatever has been achieved based on particular values. What is important is not the term you use, but the values you hold that inform the practices you follow to assess achievement.

In the classroom I want to assess students' meaning-making as much as possible as part of ongoing dialogue with students and colleagues. In contrast, standardized tests value independent, decontextualized, and disembodied mostly test-specific type of thinking, in order to create a product graded impersonally that has no value to the young people and minimal value to me in terms of improving my teaching. Standardized tests are inauthentic because they are separated out from authentic learning tasks and practices.

I use examples from Megan Ballinger's ninth-grade English language arts and literature classroom of sixteen fourteen- and fifteen-year-old students in a Columbus, Ohio, central city high school where 98 percent of the students come from high-poverty homes and a similar number are African American to explore this (Edmiston, 2012). In April–May 2012 I was a visitor when Megan studied with her class *The Other Wes Moore: One Name Two Fates*, by Wes Moore (2011).

The assessments that Megan uses are authentic primarily because they are integral to tasks that resemble the complexity of social activities in real-world contexts in which adults demonstrate their abilities and assess their effectiveness in achieving their objectives (Janesick, 2006). For example, her students began to read critically in the way lawyers read descriptions of a crime scene in order to write a report that might affect the verdict or sentencing of the accused.

Like Megan, I value learning in community as people dialogue and I want to know what and how people *are learning* so that I can adapt my teaching, and if necessary goals and intended outcomes, in order to extend their achievements (this is formative assessment). To assess progress she also wants to know what young people *have learned* at the end of a session, a week, or a year (this is summative assessment). And because she values learning in both the social and the academic curriculum she needs to assess what young people achieve in terms of both process and content. Additionally, she wants to share with the students much of her ongoing assessment and invite students to self-assess their learning. And finally, she wants to assess the effectiveness of her teaching so that she can improve. Though formal assessments are important, ongoing informal assessments are the most useful in changing teaching in response to what and how students are achieving (see Table 6.1).

Bob Fecho (2011) names a danger for teachers, like Megan, who must use standardized assessments but who are committed to building honest relationships with young people: "unless learners are engaged in the process, assessment is largely monological ... it is mostly something done to the disempowered" (p. 32). Megan offsets the disempowering effects of standardized testing with her attempts to dialogize the testing culture: she lets the students know that though she has to administer tests she does not use the results to judge them and she's prepared to have some honest dialogue about her frustrations. Additionally, she uses authentic assessment as a way to support their learning and improve her teaching and she asks students to self-assess. Like Jayne White (2011), Megan values "authentic authorship" because each young person is valued as "a co-author in her learning rather than an object for manipulation" (p. 64). Further, and again like White, to better appreciate the personalities of the young people as learners, Megan embraces "polyphonic means" of assessment. In an ongoing polyphonic dialogue she wants to hear the views of many: peers, parents, other teachers, visitors like me, and those of the students themselves. She wants assessment to work for her and the

Table 6.1 Informal Authentic Assessments

Assessments	Examples of achievement
Thumbs up/across/down to show …	you've understood directions; how you/we are doing right now
Vote From Your Seat to show in response to any question …	disagreement (sitting), agreement (standing), high agreement (hands raised)
Stand up when you have … /Take a step forward when you have …	an example to share; agreed with a partner on a question to ask
Stand by a photograph/word/phrase on the floor/desk to …	show what interests you; write a question you'd like answered
Stand on a continuum to show …	relevant information, e.g. number of people in your extended family; your current response to an inquiry question
Sit down when you have …	asked a question; found another person who agrees with you
Complete the self-assessment rubric to show …	your perspective on your level of achievement: exceeds/meets/fails to meet agreed objectives
Hand in an index card as you leave	three things you've learned; a question you'd like answered

young people, not the other way round. Assessment can be a tool for building a more inclusive collaborative supportive classroom community.

Ways to Categorize Assessments

Quick feedback on achievement (**informal assessment**)

Systematic assessment (**formal assessment**)

An assessment in which two or more people collaboratively author understanding (**dialogic assessment**)

What and/or how people are achieving (**formative assessment**)

What and/or how people have achieved at the end of a session/unit/year (**summative assessment**)

Assessments that use particular criteria (**criterion referenced**) and assessments placed on a 'normal distribution curve' (**norm referenced**)

The assessment of an outcome in which people demonstrate, or perform, their understanding (**performance-based assessment**)

How you assess what and/or how you've achieved or are achieving (**self-assessment**)

Dialogic Assessment

I have used Bakhtin's metaphor of authorship throughout this book to emphasize that meaning is always composed, improvised, constructed in social relationships, is in process, and may be contested. As people author understanding in dialogue, they shift back-and-forth from limiting meaning to opening it up, or using Bakhtin's (1986) terms, toward 'finalizing' or 'unfinalizing' understanding. Any understanding derived from an assessment is no different. An assessment task may be closing down or opening up my understanding of young people and/or their understanding of themselves as learners.

When I recognize that authoring views about students is a messy process without certainty, this allows me to see my understanding of young people as always in process. I may identify patterns of their meaning-making while also remaining open to new possibilities, always affected by my interpretation of what has, or has not happened, each day.

I had wanted Liz Ellsworth to attempt some assessment of achievements in my teaching and I respected not only her feedback but also her educational values: her ability to assess was affected by our relationship and vice versa. As she and I dialogued about teaching, one trusted person provided another with feedback not possible to gain alone. Each of us had different viewpoints and interpretations of 'good' pedagogy that when shared in dialogue allowed us both to develop more complex understanding of our teaching and pedagogy in general. Our informal assessment was formalized, to an extent, in our note taking. This was not one person in a hierarchical "finalizing" judgment of another but rather a meeting of equals, despite any power and status differential: this was dialogic assessment. It is possible to assess in this way in schools as well as in university classrooms.

Using Bakhtin's (1986) notions of "dialogue," "surplus of vision," and "outsidedness" to understand our authoring process, Liz could 'see' things that I could not see, and vice versa, because we each were 'outside' the social world of the other's classroom yet had been welcomed in to dialogue about our experiences and reflections over time. What each 'saw' in the other's classroom, and how we 'heard' each other's comments, depended on how we conceptualized teaching and learning and what we each valued in becoming a 'better' teacher. In this sense, our assessments were also evaluations because our stances on good teaching depended on our criteria of 'good.' I left each meeting looking forward to our next exchange, changed by our dialogue: I had more clarity about the session she had observed yet overall I left with more questions than answers about pedagogy.

Achievement, Values, and Dialogue

As teachers we assess achievement. What students actually achieve is different from any goals or intended outcomes, noted in my model of active and dramatic teaching and learning (see Figure 5.1). Goals, for example learning objectives, provide students and teachers with direction in tasks. Intended outcomes, for example artifacts like writing, are our expectations of tangible records of achievement having completed tasks. But, actual outcomes are always different. What has to be assessed is what young people actually achieve, and that will always go beyond any piece of paper. I can look for achievement in a student's social as well as individual verbal participation in a process, and in drafts of work, as well as in any completed product. Artifacts that can be assessed include records of performances of established and changing understanding as well as any written documentation. I also know that my assessment is always incomplete and that I must always make sense of any achievement while paying attention to the social and cultural context in and out of school.

The more closely we can connect tasks with student achievement the more useful the task is likely to be as a formal assessment. Examples of tasks used as formal assessments from Megan's classroom include the following: highlight words in a text extract to show comprehension and comment to show an inference; create and perform your understanding of an event; write a letter. All fulfilled academic curriculum requirements and Megan's given social curriculum expectations. The young people had choice, though it was limited. For example, they could *write-in-role* from the perspective of any character in the book, *The Other Wes Moore: One Name, Two Fates*, as if to the parole board at the prison where Wes Moore is incarcerated or as themselves to Wes or the author of the book.

The more transparent our criteria, for example in a rubric, the clearer to the students what we value in terms of how and what we want them to learn. And when we use the same criteria over time the more predictable and consistent are our expectations of their achievement. Table 6.2 is the general rubric Megan used for both students' self-assessment and her assessment in relation to approximately fifteen sessions focused on *The Other Wes Moore*. What she values is clear: social participation, asking questions, embodying the viewpoints of the characters, collaborative understanding, inferences, making connections to life beyond the classroom, and providing evidence to justify an evaluation.

With ongoing informal assessments the achievements and criteria we value become more explicit for us, as well as for students, as we dialogue with young people and, if we are able, with colleagues. Criteria from a rubric are values that can guide informal assessments of process or product. So are classroom expectations. Having agreed on the following expectations, including the wording, following a discussion with the

Table 6.2 Assessment Rubric

Exceeds expectations	Meets expectations	Below expectations	Evidence
I volunteer to participate	I actively participate	I don't show that I'm engaged	
I ask my peers questions	I ask my teacher questions	I do not ask questions	
I move and speak as more than one person	I move and speak as someone else	I only speak as myself	
I help others understand	I show I understand words in the text	I do not show understanding of the text	
I connect two inferences and/or ideas	I make an inference with reference to the text	I do not go beyond the text	
I connect the text to others' lives as well as my own	I connect the text to my life	I don't connect the text to my life	

group when they first met at the beginning of the semester in January 2012, Megan posted them in the room: respect yourself and others; listen to one another; talk out problems; no play fighting, gang banging, or yelling; come to class prepared.

How I position young people in dialogue *always* has an evaluative dimension that may affect students' attitude to any of their achievements and their evolving self. Ellsworth argues that, "the terms of an address are aimed precisely at shaping, anticipating, meeting, or changing who a student thinks she is" (Ellsworth, 1997, p. 7). The more whatever I say is heard as an evaluative assessment by students, the more I may clarify or imply the weight and value that I (and perhaps others, like principals or potential employers), place on what a student has made, said, or done. How I position, address, and answer, students can make a difference both in how they value themselves, and me, in relation to past achievements and how they are likely to approach subsequent tasks, view goals, achieve intended outcomes, and develop agency in the classroom community.

Some Informal Evaluative Comments from Megan's Classroom

Some people missed that. Quiet please, let's all listen to him? (Values social participation; references classroom expectation of listening.)

That idea makes sense. Can you put your finger on a phrase in the text that supports what you're saying? (Evaluates as meaningful but needing to demonstrate that have found evidence; references rubric.)

Hey, no yelling please. That's not helping. (Negatively evaluates; references classroom expectation.)

You are so helpful. Thanks. (Positively evaluates participation that helps others; references ongoing positive evaluation of helpfulness.)

One thing we've not thought of yet is how to write to people who don't know what we know. Any ideas? (Evaluates whole class response as needing to go further; references academic idea of audience.)

Informal assessments affect relationships and are affected by them. Any utterance or any artifact I make is emotionally and socially interconnected with my sense of self and my relationship with another person, if I care about their evaluation.

On the first day that I returned to the classroom after an absence of ten days, I joined Megan as she moved round the room assisting individuals as they wrote letters on laptop computers she had checked out for the week. After greeting Aaron with a smile and a general affirmation about the quality of his work ("You're doing great, Aaron") she sat and began to read aloud a draft of a letter, that Aaron had printed out, written by Aaron-as-Woody, Wes's friend, to the parole board. She shifted her chair and her body posture slightly saying, "Now let's read as if we're parole board members reading your letter. OK?" After reading a couple of sentences she-as-a-parole-board-member asked a clarifying question of Aaron-as-a-parole-board-member; as they talked, Aaron orally provided additional important details about his argument that as Wes' life-long friend he would support him if he were to be released. Megan then shifted her body and language back into talking-as-teacher, pointed to a line in the letter and said, "Can you add on here in your own words." Aaron had a sudden, strong emotional and physical reaction. He sat back, turned away, and said, "I ain't doin' nothin'." Megan reached out her hand toward him, leaned forward, lowered her voice and said warmly, "I'm sorry, Aaron. I didn't mean to upset you. Aaron, can you look at me?" He did. She continued, "What you've written is great. I shouldn't have said 'in your own words' because you have—this is totally your own work. I'm sorry. I meant, can you add on what you just *said* when we were talking as the parole board members. That was a great argument that you made. I want you to remember what you just said and add that to your writing. Can you do that? Do you need any more help?" As she moved on to the next student, Aaron returned to the computer and revised the letter. When Megan and I reflected later, she explained:

> Aaron holds on to things. He was so mad at me six weeks ago when I showed him he'd plagiarized in a report. I'd told him he couldn't just cut and paste off the internet; he had to rewrite in his own words. I'd asked him to change it but he wouldn't. It's hard for him to admit that's he's wrong. Today when I said 'add in your own words' I think he thought I meant that he'd copied the letter from somewhere. That's why I apologized. Otherwise he could easily have done nothing.

Dialogizing Assessment

When our assessment is dialogic we remain open not only to ongoing assessment through dialogue but also to reexamining, or dialogizing, our assumptions about students' abilities and the reliability of any assessment of their achievement.

Though Megan had accurately evaluated that Aaron had plagiarized six weeks earlier she did not assume that he would necessarily do so again. Rather, in the intervening time the high quality of Aaron's work had dialogized her prior understanding of him. Yet, for Aaron the previous event clearly affected his assessment of his teacher's assumptions about him. She had to reassure him not only about their relationship but also about how she evaluated (and thus valued) him as an author.

Every time I assess another person's work I develop my relationship with them and my understanding of them and their achievements but my knowledge is always partial: I evaluate from a viewpoint that, to a lesser or greater extent, changes in subsequent dialogue. Ellsworth quotes Shoshana Felman on the transformational possibilities of pedagogy: "Learning happens when the answer is bound in effect to displace the question and when what returns to itself radically displaces the very point of observation" (1997, p. 18). Megan's initial teaching position was how to help Aaron with his writing but his answer displaced her question: she shifted to see Aaron in the light of a six-week old event and to assess his work in relation to the past as well as the present.

When as teachers we "adopt a dialogic stance" toward assessment, White argues we are "released to see in ways that celebrate uncertainty" (2011, p. 63). This requires a "re-vision" of assessment practice as "authentic authorship that takes place in a messy pedagogy of not knowing" (ibid., p. 64). Ellsworth (1997) agrees: "We teach with no knowledge or certainty about what consequences our actions as teachers will have" (p. 17). Not knowing where Aaron was coming from as she assessed his writing allowed Megan to remain open to make an emotional connection to him through a shared past event, in relation to a pattern she had observed in his general approach to learning ("It's hard for him to admit that he's wrong"), in order to understand a present outburst ("I ain't doin' nothin'") and tactically to assist him to move forward ("Can you do that? Do you need any more help?").

The following example illustrates how Megan allows young people's answers to revise her assumptions about students' abilities, her assessment of their achievements, and how she addresses them in response. Photograph 6.1, taken about fifteen minutes into the second session, shows Megan in dialogue with Dayvon. After some introductory games, everyone is reading a single page extract from *The Other Wes Moore*. The extract is the author's retelling of the events of the murder for which the 'other Wes' was convicted. The students' task is to underline in red anything they think suggests Wes was guilty and in yellow anything that suggests he could be innocent as well as to write what they can infer.

Megan has just sat down to check in with Dayvon who has underlined several lines but written only a few words on the paper. She's listening to him talk about what he has underlined. Though this is his first day in the classroom in a month and only his fifth day this semester, Megan has a relationship with Dayvon as a member of the classroom community. Like the other students in the class after nearly four months he trusts her to be

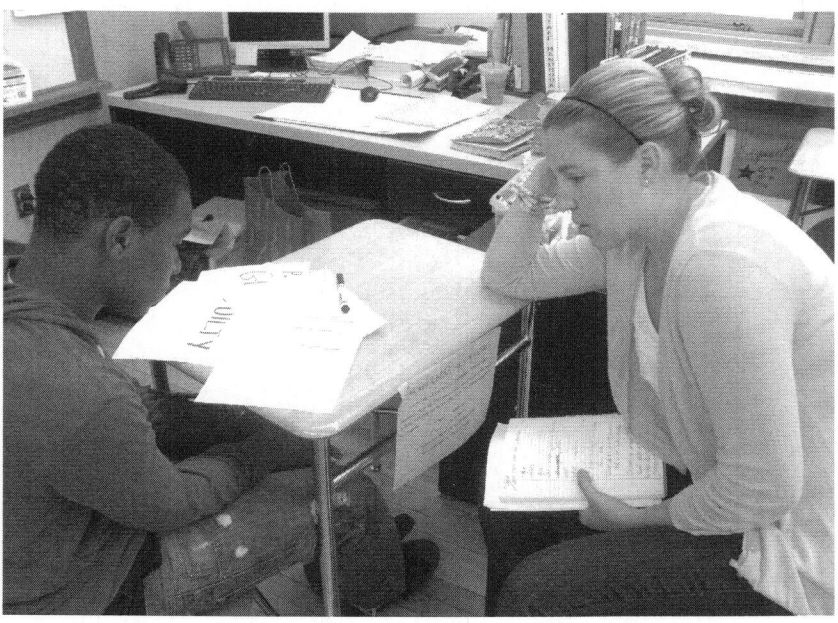

Photograph 6.1 Assessing in Dialogue.

supportive, non-judgmental, helpful, and caring. She treats him with respect and addresses him as an equal, not in terms of disciplinary knowledge but in terms of dignity.

As she listens she realizes that both her current and her prior assessment of his reading ability were unreliable. He knew much more than the incomplete sentence he had written. And though Megan had assumed from his test scores and his disengaged demeanor that he was a reluctant 'low' reader she's just learned from him that he's actually read the copy of *The Other Wes Moore* that she gave him on the day he had been suspended. This was a book that she thought he would relate to but she had no expectation that he would actually read it cover-to-cover since he had never given her any indication in previous class sessions that he could do so. The narrative tells two parallel tales of young African American men who, like Dayvon, grew up in a 'housing project' and as teenagers were caught up in the criminal justice system. Both from Baltimore, Maryland, and now aged twenty-seven, one is in prison serving a life sentence for murder without the possibility of parole, while the other is a decorated marine, a former Rhodes Scholar, and the author of the book.

When I took this photo, Megan and Dayvon were talking about the passage that along with the other fifteen students in the class he'd just read. As she listens, asks a question, helps him clarify his understanding of what might have happened in the event, and listens again to his response, she realizes that Dayvon not only comprehends the passage but also that he remembers, connects with, and has opinions about other events in the narrative.

This is the sort of dialogic assessment I value most: it occurs *between* people who trust one another in this context and who are ready to engage in honest dialogue about a particular focus, hear another's views, share and shape understanding, and in Megan's case, change a previous assessment even when it requires questioning a prior assumption.

Here is assessment grounded by the principle that assessments are unavoidably inadequate and incomplete. More important for Megan than any assessment of students' work is her relationship with them. Rather than believe that we can ever fully know a person's abilities from any assessment, White (2011) argues that teachers should "immerse themselves fully in dialogues of uncertainty with their students and to generate truths that are less concerned with outcomes than an appreciation of other." The aim is to "develop a fuller appreciation of the learner as a personality in their own right" (p. 49).

Though Megan keeps anecdotal narrative records on her students, she knows that these are not necessarily much better at assessing ability than testing data. Though they might not realize it, anyone else looking at Megan's records would always have incomplete assessments. White (2011) writes about contemporary early childhood assessment practices in

New Zealand where "learning stories" are required by a government committed to high quality 'holistic' assessments. She reports on a key research finding that even where complex qualitative narratives with accompanying visual documentation are required that include the voices of children and observing adults, "only those aspects of teaching and learning that would meet the approval of external agencies were exposed in written form" (p. 56). This was true for Megan. For example, knowing that the school and district was only interested in test score improvement she did not officially record her anecdotal notes or document students' comments that illustrate their understanding about how their learning is affected by the policies and culture of the school.

Authentic Assessment Tasks

For over twenty-five years many professionals, researchers, and educators have sought to develop more 'authentic' assessment tasks designed to provide a richer and more complex approach to understanding, and support the development of, students' learning and progress.

Newmann (Newmann & Associates, 1996) defines authentic achievements as "intellectual accomplishments that are worthwhile, significant, and meaningful such as those undertaken by successful adults" (p. 23). Grant Wiggins (1993; 1998), an early proponent of authentic assessment, or what he also calls "educative assessment," puts it succinctly when he identifies two key ideas in authenticity: context and judgment. "What we should be assessing is the student's ability to prepare for and master the various roles and situations that competent professionals encounter in their work ... the real, 'messy' uses of knowledge in context—the 'doing' of a subject" (1993, p. 202).

Dissatisfied with the usefulness of typical standardized tests, the results of which have increasingly been used in high-stakes evaluations, the objective of the authentic assessment movement has been to champion authentic tasks that include achievement as part of young people's ongoing classroom activities (Janesick, 2006). An assessment task is only 'authentic' when it is integrated into ongoing intellectually demanding and socially supportive teaching and learning classroom community activities and achievements that relate to the world outside the classroom.

Newmann's five-year research study evaluated the success of school restructuring designed to effect student achievement and confirmed, in relation to social studies and science teaching, the obvious but too often overlooked truism that teaching, achievement, and assessment are all interrelated. You can't think about assessment without connecting it to desired outcomes. Nor can you separate out assessment from the tasks students engage with, and the quality of the classroom community that includes the relationships between and among students and teacher.

Collaborative Tasks as Authentic Assessments

In the world outside schooling people mostly live and learn collaboratively. If we want to prepare students to be able to work with other people, plan in teams, and assess their work with peers then our classrooms must be similarly organized as communities of social learning.

The theory of learning underlying this book is social. Vygotsky's social constructivist theory has huge implications for assessment. Vygotsky (1978) argued that it is more important to assess the 'buds' or 'flowers' of learning rather than the 'fruits' (p. 86): teachers need to assess what people can do *with* others in a 'zone of proximal development' (or ZPD) that they cannot do alone. A teacher needs to know the leading edge of students' learning because that's where teaching is most needed. In a ZPD, that is always context specific and always changing with interactions, people's abilities that are in the process of developing become more apparent: functions that may develop more fully tomorrow may be visible today though currently in an embryonic state.

One of the courses I took when I was a student teacher included dramatic pedagogy. In the final session, when we participated in a whole group improvisation as if we were on a boat, I engaged the teacher-as-the-captain as if I were the first mate. My sighting of an island led to her, with my assistance, launching a rowing boat that we directed as everyone set off to search for buried treasure. At the end of the session, Tina gave me an oral assessment: "you were good at leading the group. I think you should learn more about using drama." She could see the 'buds' of potential in what I was able to do *with* her that I was not yet able to do alone, and that I myself could not see. She was right. As I learned from the ideas and practices of others those buds flowered and eventually developed into the fruits that today are my current knowledge of active and dramatic pedagogies.

Megan sees the buds of potential in her students. For example, an early piece of writing was "a letter to yourself in ten years time." Sheree had written (with spelling as in the original):

> I see you as a good hard working young lady you should be still in college. You should have a good paying job, getting your PhD so you can become a nurse. I see you haveing your own house playing your bills with NO kids. I see you taking care of your parents and you little brothers. You gotta take care of your grandparents cuss you no they gonna need you.

In the classroom, Sheree worked diligently to craft and revise her *Wes Moore* writing that was among the strongest in the class: well argued and developed, with supporting examples, and showing insightful critical analysis of their work on the text.

Though Sheree, like the other students, lives in a neighborhood with violence, drug dealing, and homeless people (that many students wrote about in "Where I'm from" poems) as well as many caring and resourceful adults, unlike many of the other students she has an articulated positive vision for her future. With support, Megan believes Sheree can achieve academically. Though she had been suspended mid-semester for escalating a fight in the class, Sheree's academic performance can be high. Megan put Sheree in contact with one of the counselors who helped her plan ahead for a possible internship at a local hospital.

The connections between young people's academic performance, their relationship with adults and peers, and the academic social practices of the classroom community are very apparent with Megan's students. Sheree provides a compelling example. In a summative self-assessment at the end of the semester, she wrote in answer to the question, "How were you feeling about the academic content?": "OK" at the beginning and middle of the semester but "good" at the end. In response to the question, "How were you feeling about yourself at the beginning of the semester?": "I was feeling dumb." In the middle: "a little on the down side." At the end: "smart, bright." And in response to "How were you feeling in relationship to others in the classroom?" she went from "OK" to "kinda good," ending with "good." Megan agreed with Sheree's self-assessment.

> At the beginning of the year she was so antagonistic and mouthy. She had great ideas but she just did the bare minimum to get by. I could tell she wasn't going to trust me right away, it was going to be a gradual process. Asking her to do a self-assessment then would have been pointless. I tried to talk with her and joke around, encourage her, and show that I cared about her success. The work on Wes was so significant because she was able to be a leader, especially when she could be an attorney asking questions—she had never asked questions before in class. It was amazing how she kept encouraging others, and bringing people into the dramatic performances, including Aaron, who always sat out. When she asked how long we were going to work in this way and I told her we were continuing for a month, every morning she wanted us to get started.

Mary James (2009) argues that embracing Vygotsky's learning theory means that teachers must assess how learners "build knowledge as part of doing things with others" (n.p.). Consider the unfairness and incompleteness of attempting to assess Sheree's ability, and those of her peers whom she cajoled into participation, while ignoring her social relationships and her potential for development.

James' analysis of paradigmatic differences in approaches to assessment suggests a sort of 'generation gap.' Vygotskian assessment is what

James calls "third generation assessment." In contrast, testing is "first generation" assessment that attempts to assess 'what has been taught' and assumes Behaviorist stimulus/response and information processing theories of learning: if it was taught properly then it should have been learned. But direct instruction is most often the only teaching valued. A Piagetian Constructivist theory of learning underlies "second generation" assessment that seeks to document individual sense making. Individual facilitation by an adult is the teaching mode privileged; assessment is concerned with understanding constructed by young people working *alone*: the child is learning, so document what he or she is demonstrating that he/she knows.

In Megan's classroom the young people were learning the literacy practices of reading and writing as they collaborated with peers and their teacher. Many of the collaborative tasks documented throughout this book could be used to assess what young people can do when working with peers and/or adults. Other tasks could assess what they are able to do on their own. When individualized tasks are created in relation to prior or subsequent collaborative contextualized tasks they are authentic assessment tasks. For example, the task in which Dayvon, Sheree, and their peers read a text extract alone, built on a previous dramatization of the text as a whole class and other active and dramatic explorations of its meaning in relation to the world of the book.

Additionally, collaborative whole group tasks make it possible for young people to create shared ensemble experiences that are impossible to have alone: the playing of group games, the experience of building and shaping meaning in dialogue, and the creation of imagined social settings and interactions. These might be thought of as 'fourth generation' assessments: the success of group tasks assesses how well the group functions as a community. What norms seem accepted by everyone? Who takes a leadership role? Who opts out? Is anyone ignored or excluded? How do people deal with dissonance?

Standards for Authentic Assessment Tasks

Newmann conceptualizes high-quality intellectual authentic achievement across the curriculum as a primary goal of education for all students. Three main criteria apply both to teaching and assessment tasks: authoring understanding, disciplined inquiry, and learning that has value beyond schooling.

Value Beyond the Classroom

Students' achievements should have value beyond the classroom and school as an institution, in terms of the topic, issue, or problem being studied, and the audience for whatever outcome the young people create (ibid., p. 24). The more valued an achievement by students and others, the more useful and reliable any assessment of that achievement.

Engagement with Topic and Audience

Topics should have perceived value for the learners as well as for others outside the classroom. Young people will only see value in anything they achieve if they are *engaged* by the topic and the inquiry tasks. Megan knew that because individuals are frequently absent in the school, where there is a widespread jaded view of schooling among the students, both the choice of topic and her planning of initial 'hooks' for the students were crucial. Students had to choose to step into the imagined world of a text or the work would be over before it had started.

Megan had selected the story of *The Other Wes Moore* carefully. As with Dayvon, she expected all of the students to identify with the world of the book, and with at least some of the characters, relationships, situations, and events. She was right. At the end of first session everyone in the class, with perhaps one exception, had demonstrated their interest in continuing. She assessed their interest using the active strategy **Vote From Your Seat** as a performative assessment tool. Photograph 6.2 shows

Photograph 6.2 Vote From Your Seat.

students responding to the question Megan posed at the end of class: do you want to continue? Sitting meant 'no,' standing meant 'yes,' and raising one or more hands meant 'definitely yes.'

Everyone had stood except Aaron, the only person who identified as White in the room. Megan later explained. "He doesn't like to show he agrees. If you say up he'll say down." I had noted his apparent oppositional stance during the first session: he had sat in the corner, had said "I ain't readin'" when I had helped give out the page of text to everyone, and he didn't respond when I said "You can look at the pictures if you like." Yet he had watched, made relevant comments, read, and on several occasions moved and participated in whole group tasks. However, in contrast with most of the students who joked with those they had developed friendships with in the class, Aaron largely engaged with tasks in parallel with his peers rather than collaboratively. He was not the only person to sit out. As Megan explained, "With some people, just being there at 7:30 in the morning, and not getting into an argument is an achievement. Sometimes I insist that they get up but usually as long as they're not stopping other people learning they can choose to sit out."

When the young people had first entered the room ninety minutes earlier, they had encountered a cut-out image of a body on the floor. It was intended to suggest a crime scene they might have seen on a television detective show. As Megan greeted them, a few, including Marquis shown in Photograph 6.3, chose not to sit at one of the desks spread round the perimeter of the room. He asked about the cut-out. Megan explained that the new topic was a story about a robbery and a murder. Some were intrigued enough to ask a few questions. After morning announcements via the intercom, Megan laid out on the floor photographs from the book, showing scenes from the life of the Wes Moore who is now in prison. She asked the young people to look at the photographs and pick one up that interested them. As is apparent in Photograph 6.4 their level of interest was only moderate and the energy level was low.

Giving out a text extract on a single sheet of paper (shown in Photograph 6.1) did provide an individual focus but it was not until the young people were up on their feet and talking that the group interest and energy levels rose significantly. Megan allowed the students to self-select five groups to read collaboratively one of the five paragraphs. Their task was to dramatize part of the event described. This was a challenging performance task that assessed both their abilities to comprehend and infer as well as their ability to work together.

Photograph 6.5 contrasts significantly with the previous two photographs taken twenty minutes earlier. The young people are dramatizing part of the fourth paragraph:

A black-gloved hand reached out the window [of the stolen car] holding a handgun and let off three shots, striking Sergeant Prothero

Photograph 6.3 Choosing to Stand.

[an off-duty police-officer employed as a security guard at the jewelry store] at point-blank range.

All groups to some extent first used the mode of dramatic playing as they read words and moved around as if they were the characters. All moved into dramatic performance mode to show a dramatization to the rest of the class who all watched intently; most verbally participated in whole group reflections as Megan introduced an inquiry question: should the case against Wes Moore be reopened?

Before, during, and after their collective dramatization of the robbery, Megan answered their many questions to provide them with key factual information including the following: four men were found guilty; all were sentenced to life in prison without the possibility of parole; Tony Moore, the half-brother of Wes and four years older than him, fired the shots and pleaded guilty; Wes claimed mistaken identity. Toward the end of class the students asked inferential questions that included these: What happened next? How could an eye-witness identify Wes if the robbers

Photograph 6.4 Low Group Energy.

wore masks? Why was Wes charged with murder if only Tony shot the gun that killed Sergeant Prothero?

By the close of the first session the students were hooked. Their connection to social worlds beyond the classroom was clear. Some talked about local crimes and one girl the next day told me privately that her father, who was in prison, like Wes had been arrested with his brother but claimed his innocence.

Assessing Engagement

After my third visit to the classroom I introduced the following dynamic tool that I have used with other teachers to assess student engagement both in a single session and across sessions. Megan immediately embraced it. We used this tool in conjunction with a slide show of photographs I took in class.

Photograph 6.6 shows Megan's representation of the relative engagement of the sixteen students on her roster in a classroom sociogram using

Photograph 6.5 High Energy Dramatic Performance.

Photograph 6.6 Sociogram Assessment.

headshots of the young people cut from printed-out photographs and a manila folder representing the classroom as a social space. The closer toward the center Megan placed a photograph the more she assessed the students were engaged. At the center were Marquis and his friend, Troy. Photographs touching represent some relationship between students. As we dialogued she moved photographs: she recounted stories from earlier in the year as we discussed some of what we had noticed in class. As we talked we viewed a slideshow of classroom photographs on my computer. The two elevated photos illustrate Megan's changing understanding of two students in particular who she realized were more engaged than she had assumed: shown 'looking down' on the classroom are Dayvon and Aaron.

Photograph 6.7 shows Megan's assessment of group engagement just over two weeks later. She felt the group was more cohesive. Marquis is still at the center. Dayvon has not been present. Aaron and Sheree are closer to the center.

Megan holistically assessed individual and group engagement with the topic in general as we talked about possible audiences for their work. She connected her observations and memory of the sessions with her analysis

Photograph 6.7 Sociogram Assessment Two Weeks Later.

of the photographs and related specific assessments to her unfolding assessments over the semester.

The third session had been interrupted several times including by tornado and fire drills that removed us from the classroom. During the ten minutes of undisturbed time, Megan played one of the students' favorite games that both maintained a connection with the story and confirmed her assumption that the young people identified with some of the themes. She adapted **The Big Wind Blows** to connect with characters and events in the story. In playing the game, their moves across the circle were related to the world of the text. Nearly everyone crossed the circle for the following: ... has a sibling who got you in trouble; ... has got a sibling into trouble; ... knows someone in prison.

Students were more interested when they realized that some of their life experiences intersected with the lives of real people in the story. Where Wes Moore was incarcerated and it might be possible to write to him? Megan and I talked informally with several students about how to locate the prison and write to an author. This conversation helped establish an authentic audience for the writing that followed the opening sessions.

Assessing Disciplined Inquiry

All 'successful' adults read, write, and communicate about texts. However, a cultural barrier Megan had to combat in her classroom was the students' literacy expectations. For much of the previous decade their encounters with texts were via inauthentic tasks: the purpose for reading, writing, or talking had been imposed by a curriculum guide, the intellectual demands were low requiring mostly literal comprehension via worksheets, the students often did not feel connected with the world of a narrative, what they did with their understanding of a text was minimal, and the only audience for sharing understanding was themselves or the teacher, often in an evaluative context. She was struggling to shift their whole attitude to text and approach to meaning-making.

Since the beginning of the semester in January, disciplined inquiry had been a norm to which Megan aspired. The most engaged the students had been was for two weeks in March when she had used active and dramatic approaches in studying short extracts from *Macbeth*; I had visited for the introductory session. Students' achievements included character analysis in 'flyers' for the play that Megan displayed at an open house. She had not had time to repeat summative assessments that she had done the previous year in a longer study: create plot summaries in the form of short video trailers for movie versions that we had shared in a professional presentation.

When I planned with Megan, she was eager to return to a dramatic inquiry-based approach as the group had not been very engaged with a recent integrated STEM project that was not promoting inquiry-based learning. As she holistically evaluated the group, she talked about what she hoped they would achieve. She identified particular academic and related social goals, with the former as outcomes in alignment with the new Common Core State Standards:

> They tend to jump to conclusions without really looking for evidence in the text. It's important that they read more closely than they usually do. And they tend to follow the majority: if one person gives an opinion, a lot of people just go along with that and won't change their minds. A lot of students get overwhelmed trying to read a whole novel and have lost interest by page 10. Their most developed writing is personal narratives in their journals but they need to write something beyond those. They need to achieve:
>
> • more accurate comprehension of text (including comparison across text extracts)
> • more justifiable interpretations of text (especially using inference)
> • writing beyond personal narrative from different points of view
> • writing in different genres such as note-taking, a report, a letter, or a description of a scene
> • talk in support of these goals

An authentic assessment task involving reading, writing, or talking requires students to use language in situations resembling those of the real world where authoring meaning results in some meaningful visible achievement. Students need to be able to show they can use inquiry methods appropriate to the discipline being learned, which in English language arts includes communication in multiple ways.

Megan saw potential in the factual story of the 'other' Wes Moore for disciplined inquiry with her students. Following his conviction in 2001, Wes Moore is in prison without the possibility of parole. However, if legislation were to be passed, like that pending in Louisiana at the time of writing, his case could be reconsidered. Megan made it clear that it was entirely possible that in the future this could happen. The question she wanted them to consider was whether or not they believed he deserved a review. Over a period of nearly three weeks the students' work was guided by the following essential inquiry question written on the board: should Wes's case be reopened and taken before the parole board?

Supporting Students' Reading

Many of Megan's students, though in high school, still struggled with decoding text; 'scaffolding' through group support assisted them in reading more accurately. Before being required to read a text extract individually they invariably read the text socially. At different times, Megan had previously led whole group brief reflections following **P2P reading** (read a brief extract round the circle from punctuation mark to punctuation mark several times; students can say 'Stop' at any point to pose a literal or interpretative question for the group), **choral reading** (everyone reads a brief passage together), and **echoing back** words as she read (students echo back 'scary words' or 'strong words,' etc., as appropriate to the meaning) (RSC, 2010).

The students were supported in their reading of *Wes Moore*. They began with a single stand-alone page focused on a core narrative event (the author's description of the robbery) that could be understood with minimal background knowledge or information about what comes before or after in the narrative. In small groups they read one paragraph and presented dramatic performances in sequence; everyone encountered the extract as a whole. All heard the whole passage read, could follow along, saw still and moving images related to the text, could ask and respond to comprehension and interpretation questions.

Dialogue About Text

Active pedagogy assumes that to assess comprehension and interpretation readers need to *do* something meaningful with the understanding they are making as they read any text. Echoing back is a simple tool for instant collaborative active interpretation. Making artifacts, such as models, drawings, writings, can show understanding and explanatory talk can be part of any assessment. Traditional discussion tends to privilege, and only make visible, the more verbal and confident students who already have mental images.

Dialogue as part of dramatic pedagogy occurs in social spaces where young people may collaboratively create and view embodied images as they experience, show, and reflect on the meaning of a text. That was the aim of the dramatizations (then and subsequently) that on that day were presented using a loose frame, as if by lawyers to a jury at the trial. The first text extract was verbally introduced, and then referenced by Megan, as if it was a transcript from an eyewitness presented in court as evidence interpreted by lawyers for the prosecution, for the defense, and by the jury.

Photograph 6.8 shows the text extract along with an authentic-looking court document Megan created recording the sentence from the trial of Wes Moore intended to help frame the dramatic performances. She shared the latter document with some of the young people who had shown interest in the charges against him, reintroduced it the following week, and used the header to create a template for writing a recommendation to the parole board that also served as a summative assessment.

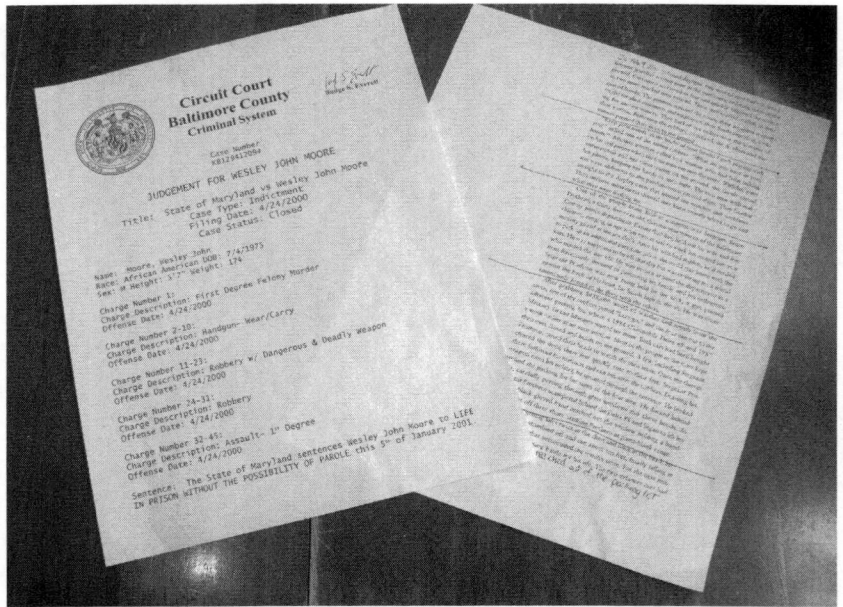

Photograph 6.8 Text Extracts

Megan had verbally told the students the standard that a jury has to apply in considering evidence (that in a later session was discussed in more detail, written up on the wall, and used to evaluate dramatized responses to another text extract): the prosecution must prove guilt 'beyond reasonable doubt.'

Using the ***teacher-in-role*** strategy with which the students were already familiar, Megan signaled a shift into the imagined space in which the narrative would be read and interpreted as she stepped in and out of the imagined world of a courtroom.

> Anytime I sit in that chair, I will be the judge and when I stand I'm Ms. Ballinger. The jury may ask questions to the lawyers to further understand what happened in the scene. So, I'm going to read the paragraph then they will show their image. We need to decide whether or not Wes Moore is guilty of the crime of murder.

The students showing the first scene had begun and ended while their peers were still moving seats to sit like a jury. Rather than move on, as the students seemed to expect, Megan addressed the class and with some cajoling the students showed the scene again as she read the paragraph, *narrating their action.*

MEGAN: (reading as students enact the scene) On February 2, 2000 in broad daylight, two masked men had run into J. Brown's Jewelers waving guns at the customers, ordering them to the ground. Customers screamed in fear and quickly followed the orders as two more masked men entered. These men carried mallets in their gloved hands. The gunmen scanned the room, their weapons trained on the terrified customers and employees, their heads swiveling, looking for any movement. Mr. Lee will you explain your evidence?

RAMONE: They robbed the store with a mallet. A big ass hammer.

TRAVIS: To break the glass obviously. Can't beat nobody with it.

MEGAN: Let's go back to those questions and ask the lawyers. Ladies and gentlemen of the jury do you have any questions? What did you think, lawyers?

JUSTIN: I want to get this over with.

MEGAN (beginning to read again from the passage):   What words do you see here?

JAMES: Terrified customers.

Some students, like James shown in Photograph 6.9, were reading along closely but most had lost focus.

Megan moved on to the dramatic performance of the next scene, shown in Photograph 6.10. As you can see, the young people had moved their chairs to sit like a jury watching small groups present. The presenting group had previously set up a desk, gathered jewelry from friends, and moved their bodies as they had collaboratively used dramatic playing to embody their unserstanding of the paragraph.

After the last performance with only a few minutes left, Megan-as-judge addressed the now highly animated group before finally playing **Vote From Your Seat** to assess their commitment to continue.

MEGAN: Any questions for Mr. Haley?

JUSTIN: Guilty.

MEGAN: If you think he's guilty what makes you think that?

JUSTIN: He is obviously guilty—he held a gun to his head [reading] "a gun pressed against the back of his head!"

MEGAN: Anyone else?

JOHN: I think they're guilty because they planned. They knew what they was doin'?

SHEREE: They purchased cars a week before they did the robbery.

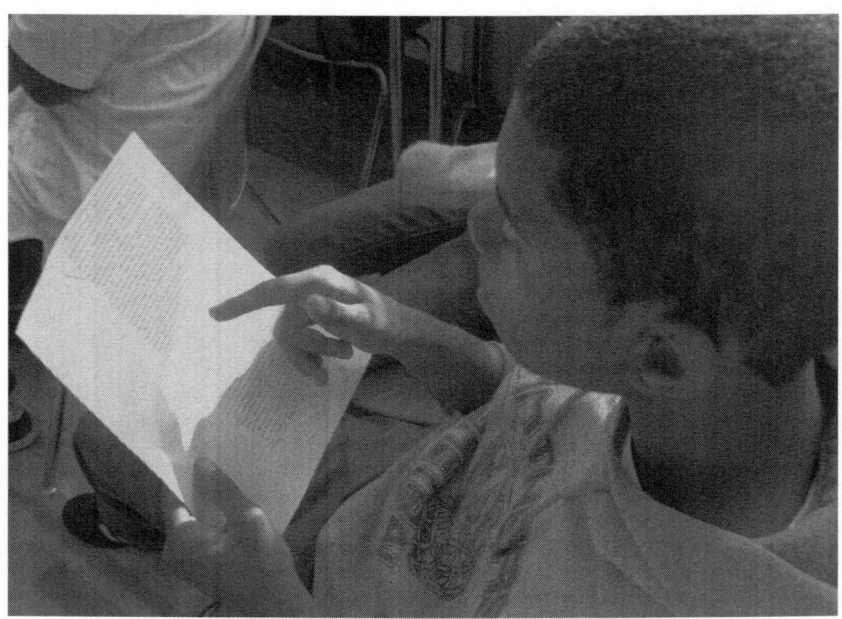

Photograph 6.9 Reading Text Extract.

Photograph 6.10 Dramatic Performance and Reflection.

MEGAN: But does that make them guilty of murder? Should Wes spend the rest of his life in jail? Should the case be reopened?

MARQUIS: They ain't got no evidence.

JAMES: Tony got life.

JUSTIN: They obviously had enough evidence, so it shouldn't be reopened.

The students' dialogue in response to her questions was an informal assessment of individual's literal comprehension ("he held a gun to his head"), reasonable inferences (purchasing the cars meant it was planned), and unreasonable inferences ("They ain't got no evidence"). However, the dialogue focused by this text extract was intended to accomplish more. As the students worked collaboratively with Megan, they were positioned in the narrative world as needing to read text more closely than for the literal comprehension they were used to in school. She questioned their interpretations and encouraged productive dialogue and disagreement.

At the same time Megan made clear the close reading stance she was promoting: within a real-and-imagined context, where the need to do so was implied, they had to find evidence for an interpretation rather than jump to conclusions.

None of this would be sustained, of course, unless the students developed a desire to read and dialogue about the story of Wes Moore. As can be seen in Photograph 6.11, taken the following day when everyone without exception had copies in their hands, students were eager to read extracts from the book. For the first time that year, many of Megan's students checked out copies of a book to take home.

Critical Inquiry, Reading, and Writing

The following day, as the students arrived, I asked several students for advice. Megan had brought in two jackets and some costume jewelry to represent some key evidence at the trial: jewelry traced from the crime scene, with Wes's DNA on it, was found in the pocket of his jacket. In Photograph 6.12 Marquis, in a variation of *sculpting*, has just tried on both jackets but on consulting some of the photographs of Wes decided that a leather one was more likely to be his. I explained Wes' story that his brother Tony, who had confessed to shooting the off-duty police-officer, had borrowed his jacket; he had touched the jewelry but claimed he had not been at the crime scene. As I talked with him, Marquis used these tools to embody two interpretative possibilities: Wes or Tony placing the jewelry in the pocket. Several of his peers had joined us and tried on the jackets.

Photograph 6.11 Engaged by the Story.

After morning announcements, Megan asked the students to complete the Class Participation Rubric in Table 6.1 as a self-assessment of the previous day. Sitting in a circle, with a moderate degree of investment she asked them to respond to the first question on participation using **Vote From Your Seat**. With some cajoling everyone stood up and several raised their hands showing they had volunteered. Megan explained that she wanted everyone to meet or exceed expectations on each criterion.

Taking the second criterion she praised them for asking questions the previous day and noted the importance of everyone asking questions of one another as well as of her so that they could help one another. Asking everyone to stand she said they could sit when they had asked, or answered, a question about the previous day's work. Students said the following:

- How do we know that Wes pulled the trigger?
- Man, we about to open this up because nobody knows.
- How do we know it was Wes and his brother?
- The killers had masks on.

Photograph 6.12 Dramatic Playing with Different Interpretations.

- It never said about who saw the cars pulled off or if anyone noticed the car pull off.
- It also say that they had just bought a car from a auction and it was the same getaway car.
- What if Tony lied?
- Why the case was closed without that much evidence and proof?

As Dayvon had not been present the previous day, Megan moved into an informal assessment of their collective memory of what they knew about the story. Using the active strategy of **group storytelling** she asked everyone to tell one detail and anyone, especially Dayvon, could say 'Stop' and ask a question. As their voices became heated as they disagreed about an interpretation (whether or not Wes was the fourth person present), Megan asked who in the story might have an opinion on that. They agreed that they wanted to talk to the arresting police officer so Megan agreed to be **hotseated** as him as if at the time of the arrest and before the trial.

Photograph 6.13 shows Megan-as-the-police-officer being questioned by the students. She is looking at Marquis who was leading the questioning. Not surprisingly, given the dramatic playing he did at the beginning of class, he focused in on the jewelry adding on another possibility beyond those he had considered previously. What follows is an extract from the transcript.

MARQUIS:	How do you know someone ain't put that jewelry in his pocket?
MEGAN-AS-POLICE-OFFICER:	Very unlikely.
MARQUIS:	I said, how do you know if one of his friends knew the police was over his friends and snuck the jewelry in Wes pocket?
MEGAN-AS-POLICE-OFFICER:	We got two black kids that already got a record.
MARQUIS:	So you think they are guilty because they are black and have assault records?
MEGAN (standing up):	I want to make it clear that I'm being the police-officer and *I* don't have these racist ideas. OK? (sitting down)
MARQUIS:	Yes, why would you say he's guilty?

Photograph 6.13 Hotseating Teacher-as-Police Officer

MEGAN-AS-POLICE-OFFICER:	Like I said, previous actions. All I know of being a cop for twelve years. All I know is their history. One guy attempted murder at fifteen so he's not capable of committing murder?
MARQUIS:	What would you think of two white kids?
MEGAN-AS-POLICE-OFFICER:	If they had the record like these two, probably.
MARQUIS:	Oh, you said, probably! So why do you say that? You said probably to the white kids. You said definitely for the black kids.

Megan had used this exchange to introduce more factual information (Wes had a criminal record of attempted murder following a fight with a knife). She also showed her willingness to address the issue of race as they considered the evidence against Wes. Marquis had critically evaluated the language Megan used and over the following two weeks he remained very interested in the reliability of the evidence against Wes.

As some students were expressing interest in the book from which the extract came, we gave out copies to whoever wanted them. Photograph 6.11 is emblematic of the intense interest of the students for five to ten minutes before Megan brought the students together for a very focused discussion with books and text extracts in hand, in which students expressed more competing interpretations. She explained how the book had come to be written as a memoir with a parallel story of the 'other' Wes Moore that the author wrote following several years of contact with Wes in prison.

To continue the dialogue, but make their positions more visible to one another, and to her, Megan used the **continuum** strategy that the group had used on previous occasions. Everyone was asked to stand on an imagined line between guilty and not guilty. They were spread out with most toward guilty. Megan asked the young people to talk with those around them to explain why they were standing where they were. Competing interpretations were shared that individuals had authored in informal discussions with the adults in the room, looking at photographs, and their previous reading including information about Wes' brother Tony, his relationship with Wes, and the necklace in the coat. When a question arose about what he had been charged with, Megan gave out copies of the judgment (shown in Photograph 6.8).

Megan then returned to the text extract used the previous day (shown in Photograph 6.8) and asked the students to sit, read, and highlight in red (for suggests guilty) and yellow (for suggests not guilty) adding some writing alongside. As Chris Ray, who was observing, noted, there was "an incredible amount of intense concentration" as Megan moved round to work with some students one-on-one.

As part of their disciplined inquiry over two sessions the students had engaged in the sort of authentic assessment tasks envisioned by

Newmann: in the way professionals do, they were reading and marking text, writing notes, and making their ideas visible as part of critical dialogue about issues of concern to them that are important beyond the classroom.

A verbal altercation between two students suddenly erupted that Megan dealt with by talking with Janice who then left to recover in the bathroom. For the final five minutes Megan led an inconclusive but very honest discussion with the class. Some of the students expressed their frustration about what they perceived as Janice's superior attitude. Megan made it clear that she expected them to resolve disagreements without being mean to one another. Everyone agreed to try to walk away if they felt angry. Though the mood had darkened, the following week the students were again deeply engaged; Janice chose to work alone.

Toward the end of the session four days later, having read, dramatized, and dialogued about several other text extracts in the interim, Megan again used the **continuum** strategy. Marquis was closest to the middle. The most vocal reason given by those clumped up on the guilty end was that Wes had been found guilty at a trial so he must be guilty. Megan used a dialogizing tactic.

She ended class by showing a short segment from YouTube on the aftermath of the verdict in the Rodney King trial. That day was the twentieth anniversary of the L.A. riots and some of the students had seen the coverage on television. She asked them if they thought the police officers were guilty or not guilty of an unreasonable use of force: no one said, not guilty. When Megan said the officers were found not guilty there was a visible double-take in the faces of some the young people. The block had already ended as Megan said, "Do you think race could have made a difference to the outcome?" Marquis, and a few others, were nodding as they all left the room.

Assessing Achievement as Part of Authoring Understanding

Tasks that assess achievement must be meaningful to students, part of ongoing authoring of understanding, and not an add-on disconnected activity.

For Newmann, there are two aspects of authoring to consider in assessment tasks. First, how will the students organize information they acquire and new ideas they construct? In other words, making meaning requires more than just finding out factual information, or having a realization; people need to use mediating tools to create artifacts. For example, teachers can provide physical materials, conceptual frameworks, photographs, and text extracts that students can use to mediate making connections between prior knowledge or established understanding and new ideas as they write, draw, create tableau, talk, etc. Second, what alternative viewpoints or approaches do students consider? One perspective is inadequate; authoring requires you to dialogue with and from additional perspectives.

Organizing Meaning-making

Some of the organizational tools available to the students included physical ones: individual folders where they could store copies of text extracts that they had either highlighted or to which they had attached post-it notes, along with drafts of their writing.

Additionally, to make shared connections more visible and accessible, Megan created a display on the back wall recording key information, conceptual ideas like the relationships between characters, inquiry questions, as well as students' post-it notes with their questions, ideas, and developing understandings (Photograph 6.14). Also visible on the right of the photograph are references to social tools: their ideas on the qualities of the community they had wanted to develop during the semester and the class expectations that everyone had signed.

Every active or dramatic strategy and learning mode was a potential tool for creating understanding in relation to the story of Wes Moore, provided students were actively and respectfully involved in dialogue as they imagined they were elsewhere. Just as with other strategies, not all students were initially engaged by dramatic pedagogy but eventually all were though not necessarily all at the same time. The closer dramatizations connected with actually reading and writing text extracts the more

Photograph 6.14 Organizing Meaning-Making.

the young people could use active and dramatic strategies as tools to achieve the literacy outcomes Megan desired for the students.

Oral and Written Authoring

Marquis entered the classroom in January with minimal literacy skills.

> Marquis' strengths lay in talking and doing rather than reading and writing. So I wanted to build on those. He was a leader in the group but initially in a negative way: he often shouted out distracting comments that produced laughter in the group. It wasn't until we began the active and dramatic work on *Macbeth* that he completely changed and was ready to be a positive leader. Like many others in the class, when he did read he decoded and assumed that literal comprehension was equivalent to understanding. His writing was very minimal, filled with mechanical errors, and he resisted editing or revising.

Marquis wrote the following personal narrative in an open-ended assignment in the first week of the semester after extended discussions on community in which he was vocal. This was in response to the following prompt: describe one problem you see in your community and what you could do to begin to work toward a solution.

> A problem in my community is there is two many fighting Ande people is getting iritled [irritated] over it Ad two many people failing and homeless people we should all work togather to solve it.

Megan clarified the literacy goals she developed for the class, and Marquis, after the first week:

> I decided on class goals of close reading and writing as meaning-making. In relation to Marquis, he had a hard time organizing his thoughts especially on paper. I wanted him to work on extending writing from a single paragraph with one idea to more than one idea in several paragraphs. Though I did address with him some of the mechanics of writing, especially run-on and fragmented sentences, I paid only minimal attention to those. Mechanical problems are relatively easy to fix in one-on-one conferences but they take a lot of time and it's ineffective unless students are working with writing that means something to them.

Marquis' final piece of **writing-in-role** in May was a six-paragraph revised recommendation to the parole board—a new genre for him (persuasive writing) and not a personal narrative. Megan had required that the students write from a viewpoint supporting and one opposing reopening the case.

Just engaging in writing with minimal teacher support was a huge achievement for Marquis. As Megan noted, "At the beginning of the semester he'd have put his head down if I had asked them to write something this long." Megan also noted that, "Marquis often has a tough time recalling details after reading" yet this writing happened weeks afterwards. This is his first paragraph:

> I think he should be in jail for life because he killed a cop and robed a jewery store and he also held people at gun point and had the people scared out of there mind and then the two cars they bought at a auction earlier that day where found burned on the side of the road.

This writing shows memory recall, accurate comprehension, identification of the main ideas, and synthesis of the first extract read in class. In addition, he restated a phrase in his own words ("scared out of there mind" echoing these words from the book, "terrified customers"), and he connected to an idea not in the passage (Megan had told him about the burned out cars).

In his second paragraph, Megan was impressed that, "He's applying what he knows to create a strong persuasive argument that he doesn't personally agree with." Marquis formed and wrote from a perspective he resisted. He had continued to champion the idea (that he wrote about in the rest of his piece) that the DNA testing results did not mean that Wes had been in the jewelry store when coupled with the fact that the robbers wore masks and that the Moore brothers shared clothes.

> I think he should stay in jail because his DNA was found on a neckless that was stolen from a jewry store and he had a leather jacket that the hostages saw when he was in the store and because of the record that he had back in the day.

Finally, impressive as the six-paragraph piece of writing is for Marquis, his writing does not show the inferring and critical analysis that he demonstrated when authoring orally and socially. For Vygotsky, his social and verbal achievements reveal the leading edge of his literacy development. Marquis could continue to grow in a literacy classroom with a patient teacher who can see his potential in social interactions and provide him, working with his peers, access to active and dramatic tools to use in conjunction with reading and writing text extracts.

Taking Up Alternative Viewpoints in Dialogue

The text extracts that Megan selected described events with multiple viewpoints. For example, the first extract (the description of the robbery and killing) included the viewpoints of the four accused, the victim of the shooting, his wife and five children, and the cashier in the jewelry store.

Other extracts included the viewpoints of Wes' mother, his brother, his friend, Woody, the mother of his children, Alicia, as well as the police officer and the victim when Wes had been arrested years earlier with a knife in his hand.

However, having alternative viewpoints in a text is quite different from young people taking up different points of view as they engage in dialogue. The examples above reveal some possibilities, as well as challenges in promoting the taking of different perspectives in dialogue using dramatic pedagogy with a group with volatile commitment.

In face-to-face interactions it's often clear when people are not in dialogue. Yelling, shoving, and verbal put-downs, classroom behaviors that were prevalent in January, negate dialogue. Megan had worked hard to counter the prevailing culture at the beginning of the semester: by the end of April the shared expectation was that people always tried to hear what another person had said and respond. Dialogue goes further.

Dialogue is not people talking while stating their opinions even if they are pretending to be someone else. Nor is it a teacher presenting a viewpoint or talking while telling students that they need to listen—that's monologue. For Bakhtin, dialogue requires that you enter into the viewpoint, or consciousness, of another person and allow their perspective to intermingle with yours. That's what active listening promotes. It's also why dramatic strategies can be so effective as tools for taking up another point of view, not to become a character, but for a while to talk, think, and frame the world from within another's consciousness. It's often easier to imagine from the viewpoint of a character in a story than from the perspective of a peer.

Genuine dialogue is transformational because your consciousness is changed, 'doubled,' or 'dialogized,' so now you see the topic differently.

Dialogue is not restricted to verbal interactions. Dialogue can be understood as happening in reading when we imagine from the viewpoint of characters and have conversations with them. It happens in writing when, as the author, I stand outside the voice of my narrator and I imagine a dialogue with the audience reading my words. Active and dramatic pedagogies are dialogic when they make literacy dialogues more visible and young people engage with them as they make meaning.

Shifting Viewpoints in Dramatic Pedagogy

In Chapter 3 I applied Ellsworth's idea of "events" as "ruptures of continuity in the status quo" to fictional encounters, but for Ellsworth pedagogy itself can critically challenge the status quo in the classroom, not just in fictional situations. As I argued in the previous chapter, every interaction is a social positioning in a triangle of position, act, and event that makes clear what acts are possible in any situation referenced. Negotiating the introduction of new pedagogies is no different.

How the young people in Megan's classroom authored meaning about each text extract was affected by how they felt positioned pedagogically. For Megan's students, dramatic pedagogy was a "rupture" in their expectations of teaching and learning. It took time for them to become comfortable with being more physically active, dramatic, and dialoguing with peers as part of collaboratively building a community of learners in which their achievements could go beyond their prior expectations.

Justin was one student who resisted authoring using active and dramatic approaches. He was an A student who had worked out how to 'do school' and get by. He was making meaning but initially with very little dialogizing. Megan notes:

> He came in as one of the highest achieving students. He wanted to work by himself, get his assignments done, and then talk with, and distract, Mano and Lenka. He was very antagonistic: if I asked him to please stop talking he'd snap, "I wasn't talkin'". I thought he didn't like me though every day he'd come in first and sit down. I'd always say "Good morning" and at the beginning of the year he wouldn't acknowledge me. I'd ask him how he was doing and try to make him laugh. Eventually he started talking about what he'd been doing instead of me always initiating. Now I have a pretty good relationship with him and he's more likely to help than distract others.

In contrast to Marquis who immediately took a leadership role with *Macbeth*, Justin had sat in the corner and talked with Mano and Lenka. When they began the *Wes Moore* work none would get up though they watched. He was adamant from the beginning that Wes had been found guilty by a jury and said several times "Why are we doing this? He's guilty." He didn't share any questions about the text extracts: he didn't seem to be able to find any ambiguity in the narrative.

Megan reported that Justin's demeanor completely changed over the semester: "Now he's part of the group and he takes more time with his assignments." In his summative self-evaluation he reported that he had found the academic content originally "easy" but that it had become "more fun" and "less work" by which Megan assumed he meant less boring. Originally he was feeling "bored" but now "better." And in relation to the rest of the group he began "never" working in small groups but now it was "more fun work" to do so.

A turning point for Justin was during a session in the second week of the Wes Moore work. The reliability of the DNA evidence on the necklace found in the jacket was still intriguing Marquis, and now others. Megan asked those who were interested to devise and then show a short scene to answer this question: If the necklace hadn't been put there by Wes how could it have got in his coat pocket with his DNA on it?

Justin, Mano, and Lenka didn't take part. As the others moved into dramatic playing mode for three minutes, Megan gave them the text extract to read that she was about to share with the group. In the book, there is little discussion about the necklace. However, Megan found a relevant newspaper story from the June 9, 2001 *Baltimore Sun*, about the trial, with information not in the book. She created a short extract to read.

Parcha McFadden, Wesley Moore's girlfriend had testified before a grand jury that a necklace found at the scene belonged to Wesley Moore. But she recanted at Moore's trial, testifying that she had been pressured by police to say the necklace belonged to Moore. Moments after the hearing, she was arrested and charged with perjury. A police technician testified he found Moore's skin cells on the necklace.

Megan then helped the small groups prepare and present scenarios for their peers to interpret. Moving into dramatic inquiry mode, and using the **Vote From Your Seat** active strategy, the audience-as-the-jury were asked to respond to this question: is this a possible scenario? Justin joined in several times to vote, standing when Marquis and Martin presented their idea, as shown in Photograph 6.15. Marquis-as-Tony had borrowed the jacket to go to Philadelphia. He came in, hung it up and left. Martin-as-Wes put on the jacket, put his hand in his pockets looking for his wallet, pulled out the necklace and said, "What's this?"

Megan introduced the newspaper report that they read together. It was Justin who said that Parcha could have been pressured by the police to say the necklace was Wes' when it wasn't. Another student said that she could have been mad at him and not realized how damning her testimony would be. Justin thought that it could have made a difference to the jury. Photograph 6.16 shows the polyphonic quality of the group dialogue.

Megan asked everyone to write inferences on their sheet. Justin wrote: "She could have said the necklace wasn't Moore's but she could have been pressured by the police to say it did belong to him."

The following day, Megan introduced an extract from an event in the book that told of a crisis moment for Wes. He had been selling drugs (though he maintained not taking them), but under pressure from his friend Woody, and Alicia, the mother of two of his children, he had decided to go straight. His performance had been exemplary on a six-month Job Corps training scheme after which he did get several jobs. Unfortunately, "the only thing consistent with these jobs was that none of them paid more than $9.00 an hour." Megan notes:

We had a lot of conversation about that. Justin said you could barely live off that on your own never mind if you had four kids and a girlfriend.

Photograph 6.15 Dramatic Performance for Reflection.

Megan introduced the *Consciousness Threes* strategy to promote more dialogue about this event. The question was: should Wes stay with his job or go back to dealing drugs. Everyone experienced all viewpoints: as Wes in the middle, as the good angel, and as the bad angel. Justin worked with Megan and Sheree (see Photograph 6.17).

Justin's final paper for the class was a well-crafted Recommendation to the Parole Board showing his depth of comprehension, analysis, and synthesis across multiple text extracts. The first half laid out a well-reasoned argument for why his case should not be reopened; it amplified points Justin had initially made in expletives from the side-lines. The second half is the more interesting, not just because it shows his ability to infer across texts but especially because of the significance of his references to both dramatized scenarios in which he had participated.

Wes attended every one of his classes at Job Corps. He graduated near the top of his class. The program led to him having legitimate

Photograph 6.16 Polyphonic Dialogue.

Photograph 6.17 Consciousness Threes.

jobs in landscaping, construction, and food service. Although these jobs didn't really pay him enough to provide for his family, <u>I don't believe</u> he wanted to go back to selling drugs because he had to do what he had to do for his family and he'd gone to Job Corps. He wanted to be there for his kids. He wasn't the best father but he tried. Finally, he should be given a chance for parole because of the evidence. The DNA evidence that was found wasn't even found at the crime scene. His DNA evidence could have got on the necklace another way, for example not strong but possible: he could have picked it up and thought it was his piece of jewelry. Also the evidence that he fled to Philadelphia. He had family there, so he most likely went there to visit his family. So this evidence is not very reliable. And the evidence provided could go either way. No body described he was there. It's not 100%. The case could be reopened.

Whereas Justin began the work on *Wes Moore* locked into one viewpoint and resistant to any dialogue, he ended in a position of doubt. He moved from "He was found guilty. Why are we doing this?" to "the evidence provided could go either way." Justin had clearly taken up alternative viewpoints to the point that his understanding had been transformed.

Conclusion: Assessment as Authoring Understanding About What We Value

I value using active and dramatic pedagogies in assessment because they provide teachers not only with tools that extend how they may assess, but also because at the same time young people across the ability range may achieve more than is possible using other approaches. In addition to the usual classroom tools of paper, pens, and computers, students have vastly more tools available to them so that they may connect meanings they create in the classroom to the world beyond school, inquire in a disciplined way, and take up other perspectives in dialogue.

Active and dramatic pedagogies extend the possibilities for teacher dialogue with students in tasks that can have authentic assessments embedded in them. We can move in, out of, and among, the experiences and analytical viewpoints of fictional characters in imagined spaces. Dramatic pedagogy allows us more easily to shift how we address and position students in relation to events, including troubling events that connect with experiences they may or may not have encountered in everyday life. Reading *The Other Wes Moore*, Megan addressed many topics: caring mothers, absentee fathers, siblings, friends, romantic partners, drug dealers, robbers, murderers, crime victims, police officers, prison officers, and members of a parole board. Collectively, the young people had personal or family experiences in all of these domains. Though talking openly in class was too exposing, in personal exchanges and in writing individually students did allude to echoes in their lives.

Megan used all of the types of assessments listed at the beginning of this chapter within her framing of students as competent and capable of learning and achievement. Throughout the semester she used formative assessments, especially informal assessments that were part of every task, to allow her to track how students were achieving. These were criterion referenced because she knew the social as well as academic criteria she was using to assess. Additionally, she repeatedly expected students to self-assess in reflections on achievement and progress. Assessments were invariably dialogic performative assessments as students worked together and/or with her to *show* what they knew in tasks that were active and often dramatic. At the end of the semester their writing was both a summative assessment and, to the extent that she compared one student with another, was norm referenced.

By extending her use of teaching and learning modes as well as the strategies and other tools students could use in sequences of tasks Megan changed both how she socially positioned young people about how they could author understanding and what she valued as achievements. Despite resistance she stuck with her approach because she believed in its efficacy and was prepared to engage in a struggle to learn how to teach using these approaches.

Her predominant teaching mode was facilitating the whole group to explore the case of *Wes Moore* through extended dialogic inquiry that was often dramatic. At the same time as she was strategically and tactically building community and expecting the group to work as much as possible as an ensemble she was also facilitating and instructing students individually and socially. She took a strong role as a director in the classroom leading tasks and providing information largely tactically in response to the students' needs or requests. And her teaching frequently shifted into dialogizing mode as she cajoled and pressed students to justify views and when she strategically planned tasks that challenged their perspectives.

Megan positioned students differently using all learning modes to open up alternative ways that they could author meaning, show understanding, and experience being successful. Throughout the *Wes Moore* work Megan consistently positioned students as critical inquirers—people who are expected to ask questions, question the status quo, compare and contrast ideas, go beyond the obvious and the superficial, and achieve as they explore questions in following a line of inquiry over time and in dialogue with others, that was at times dramatized.

In experiential and dramatic playing modes the students' sensual, social, as well as their current and past lived experiences were valued.

From simple games to exploring scenes as 'players' they could play with possibilities to open up meaning as if they were dialoguing as other people elsewhere. Dramatic playing releases students to try out ideas and possible actions to achieve new connections with other ideas often locked inside the pages of a book but that can be released by a teacher or student in role.

In performative and dramatic performance modes the students were positioned as 'performers,' as people who achieve when they initiate dialogue by showing others their current understanding. It took time for the students to become comfortable with shifting in and out of events to show exchanges and the leadership of peers was hugely significant.

In reflective and dramatic reflection modes when the young people were positioned as 'spectators' they achieved when they interpreted, analyzed, evaluated and respectfully critiqued the embodied presentations of other people's ideas. Some students were eager to be 'spect-actors' taking on roles in response to others' performances.

When people assess what they value in achievement they begin to achieve what they value. The insights I achieved about assessment practices, by working with Megan and the generous young people in her high school classroom, were unanticipated achievements that I treasure.

Yong Zhao provides an alternative vision to the current test-taking mania that hovers over this chapter. His books on globalization, technology, and innovation in education have caused a stir beyond the academy, in particular because Zhao (2009) believes that standardized testing "stifles creativity and innovation, [and] results in monolithic thinking." Active and dramatic pedagogies could thrive in, and support, the sort of dialogic future that Zhao proposes.

> As we enter a new world rapidly changed by globalization and technology, we need to change course. Instead of instilling fear in the public about the rise of other countries, bureaucratizing education with bean-counting policies, demoralizing educators through dubious accountability measures, homogenizing school curriculum, and turning children into test takers, we should inform the public about the possibilities brought about by globalization, encourage education innovations, inspire educators with genuine support, diversify and decentralize curriculum, and educate children as confident, unique, and well-rounded human beings.
>
> (Zhao, 2009, p. 198)

What would Bakhtin likely say about the largely authoritarian monologic current state of educational assessment? I think he would remind teachers as well as students, and those administrators who would listen, that as human beings in dialogue with one another *we* are the authors of meaning about whatever topic concerns us whether it is the dehumanizing effects of prison on an incarcerated man or of testing on an education system or classroom community. He would also remind us that in dialogue we are always authoring understanding about what we *value* in one another, our selves, our communities, and our world.

> To be human is to mean. Human being is the production of meaning, where meaning is further understood to come about as the articulation of values.
>
> (Quoted in Holquist, 1990, p. xli)

Chapter 7

Embrace the Complexity and Simplicity of Dramatic Pedagogy

> Art and life are not one, but they must become united in myself—in the unity of my answerability.
>
> (Bakhtin, 1990, pp. 1–2)

I've been in dialogue with Dorothy Heathcote and Cecily O'Neill, via their writing and in person, since I chose to be serious about becoming a better teacher about thirty years ago. I am still struggling to understand the complexity of their brilliant written and practical work.

Dorothy Heathcote (1984) once wrote, "Don't lobby for better dramatics, lobby for better learning … lobby for better schools" (p. 169). Yet she also wrote, "Theatre understanding is most necessary in classroom practice" (1972/1984, p. 31) and that we need classroom dramatic art to "reflect upon nature, people's affairs, ideas and behavior" (1984, p. 177). Dorothy's most well-known book in the field she tended to call 'drama in education' is titled *Drama for Learning* whereas Cecily introduced the term 'process drama.' Both also write about 'educational drama.'

I seek to be inclusive in my language, though I recognize that terminology can often be revealing of underlying assumptions about theoretical frameworks and practices. The recent term 'applied theatre' is clear about its location. In the introduction to *Drama Worlds: A framework for process drama*, Cecily O'Neill (1995) explained that she wanted to distinguish her approach from "less complex and ambitious improvised activities and to locate it in a wider dramatic and theatrical context" (p. xv). She had written the following in her 1978 MA thesis: "When the process of educational drama is recognized as an art form, teachers will be likely to help their pupils achieve the unique kind of knowing which can come from the experience of art … this meaning is likely to be concerned with human behaviour and its consequences" (quoted in Taylor & Warner, 2006, p. 72).

Dorothy Heathcote and Cecily O'Neill have parallel goals though they look at the classroom from different angles and foreground different intended outcomes. Heathcote is more concerned with the educational potential of dramatic pedagogy while O'Neill is more focused on drama as art. They bring two weighty resonant voices to the fields of arts/education and I join them in a desire to enter into dialogue with colleagues about the transformational potential of the artful process of teaching and learning through drama in the hands of adults ready and able to explore topics with young people.

When I was on the faculty at the University of Wisconsin-Madison I taught drama classes with both theatre and education undergraduates, whereas now at Ohio State I work with mostly K-12 practicing and pre-service teachers (some intending to be theatre teachers) as I explore the use of drama across the curriculum. I find that the terms 'dramatic pedagogy' along with 'dramatic teaching and learning' capture my core aim. Most teachers know that the term pedagogy combines teaching with learning but often not that there is a guiding theoretical framework which in my case is comprised of the social, cultural, linguistic, imaginative, and aesthetic theories alluded to in this book. For those who don't already know of my approach, their differing views of what it means to be 'dramatic' (for example, exuberant children's theatre, frivolous skits, or moments of classroom embarrassment) have tended to keep them away. But for those who know better, they appreciate that I teach teachers inductively through reflecting on non-threatening practical examples we create in the classroom, sometimes with young people. I create process drama work but mostly I stop to analyze tasks and later in a semester we plan for, and then reflect on, teachers' own classroom teaching experiences. My expectation is that they use dramatic approaches in their teaching initially for five to ten minutes. I want people to leave a course that I have led better teachers, more confident about being active and dramatic in the classroom. With returning teachers I begin to explore more of the subtleties of the artful process of dramatic pedagogy, a dimension of the work that I have barely addressed in this book but that is masterfully explored in Cecily O'Neill's work.

To understand the potential of dramatic pedagogy, in addition to studying the work of my peers, I find myself returning most often to the generative ideas of Mikhail Bakhtin. For over twenty years I have been in dialogue with what feels like the many voices, or consciousnesses, of this Russian scholar whose provocatively simple yet complex "truth" that I quoted at the outset has sustained me on the journey: "To live means to participate in dialogue."

Dialogue, inquiry, and dramatic art are the rhizomatic roots of my practice and of this book. The term dialogue, in English, can be over-applied and sometimes used to describe a process that Bakhtin would dismiss as monologic. It is monologue when one person is in charge of the meaning-making. In dialogue there must be two voices, two subjects, two consciousnesses, both struggling to take up the standpoint of the other's views on the topic of their exchange, which can of course include their relationship. Though the age or position of the people has social signifi-cance, these are only minimally relevant in terms of the actual dialogic process of listening and actively projecting into another's viewpoint in order to try to create understanding; often young children are more adept and sensitive than adults. Over time, the process is an inquiry struggle—not to reach an easy consensus but for each to author meaning that may be both harmonious and dissonant. There is a unity of purpose for everyone to author more understanding across a diversity of viewpoints while engaged in challenging but respectful dialogic inquiry, that may be dramatic.

All of that may be difficult to sustain, or even initiate, in many class-rooms for cultural, social, historical, and personal reasons, given the cur-rent testing and surveillance regimes of power, especially when a teacher is responsive to Bakhtin's desire for dialogue to be polyphonic, involving many voices struggling to understand one another in ongoing and never ending chains of meaning-making.

When a teacher adds dramatic art to the mix, intending to teach through dramatic inquiry, the task may seem too daunting. It's challeng-ing to enter and shape a polyphonic conversation that may now include embodied voices and viewpoints young people identify in fictional or factual texts that they are exploring. And what happens if the principal appears at the door?

Just as I was revising this chapter I heard a story reminding me that significant changes in *stance* can come before a substantial change in pedagogy. Dialogue, inquiry, and dramatizing are stances that can trans-form brief encounters in any classroom context and support ongoing conversations across tasks and sessions. Further, understanding the sig-nificance for learning in these ways creates a framework for explaining the value of work to any observing administrator.

Chris Ray is a first year teacher and Ohio State graduate who had just begun his first job in a high school in Columbus with young people from high-poverty homes. Chris was beaming one day in September 2012 as he told me how engaged the fifteen- to eighteen-year-old students were when the principal put his head round the door to check on how Chris was doing three weeks into the year. What was keeping them physically, men-tally, and socially engaged? Chris was using the strategy of **Consciousness Alley**. He had been strategic, working mostly with the whole group since beginning the year building community by working as much as possible as an ensemble. He'd reflected when the students had been disengaged by tasks and had promised to seek out engaging events as he had done that day. Just before the principal appeared the young people had used social imagination to enter an event that he had identified in a narrative text set on a school rooftop: an 'antisocial' high school girl, who always eats alone, sees an unknown boy walk toward the parapet. Dividing the class into two groups the students had dramatized the dialogue in which she discovers his plan to jump onto mattresses in order to face his fears. Stopping to analyze for meaning the ambiguity became apparent—could he be intending suicide? Chris directed the students to stand in two lines to create, on one side the consciousness that would press the boy on to jump, and on the other the consciousness that would hold him back from a permanent escape from his problems. The students took turns actively reflecting in dramatic action as they moved toward-and-away-from-the-edge-of-the-building in response to the intense voices of their peers-as-dramatic-performers. One boy blocked the path of a girl when she went to jump and the students moved into an animated discussion on the challenges of stopping people doing what they want when you believe it's not right. The principal had stayed to observe a sometimes high-energy but always focused and serious polyphonic conversation that engaged all students across sequenced active and dramatic tasks. Having been strategic in his planning, Chris could be tactical in his teaching as he listened and responded to what the young people said. He kept the conversation going, and the meaning in motion, as the students moved physically and then when they gathered on chairs in a circle. In dialogue, as the young people alluded to incidents in their lives Chris was respectful: people in despair; the difficulty in being a friend to someone they may not know is in trouble; how to reach out to help a stranger in need. At the door, as Chris thanked them for their contributions, the students could feel positioned as competent and resourceful, as being heard, able to work collaboratively, and being part of a community of dialogic and critical inquiry in which a teacher participated in creating authentic experiences in dramatised narrative events of significance in their lives.

Using Bakhtin's words from the quotation above, Chris had no difficulty "answering" the principal's questions about why he was using the art of dramatic pedagogy to enhance the academic and social lives of the students.

Conclusion: Being an Ensemble, Transforming Our Selves

> O chestnut-tree, great-rooted blossomer,
> Are you the leaf, the blossom or the bole?
> O body swayed to music, O brightening glance,
> How can we know the dancer from the dance?
>   (W.B. Yeats, from 'Among School Children,' 1973, p. 242)

On Sunday nights you'll invariably find me at Claddagh pub playing Irish music. The music transports me back in imagination to the mountains, the sea, and a landscape that I treasure. Just over a decade ago I retrieved my father's fiddle from my sister's home in Ireland and sought out a teacher. I'm an ensemble player. I do play alone for my own enjoyment, and occasionally for others, but what I value most is the ensemble experience of making music with other people who come together to play lively reels, jaunty hornpipes, and haunting airs. Especially in playing airs we improvise, adding harmonies. Together we can create something beautiful that not one of us can make alone. Whoever takes the lead makes a difference: when he or she establishes a 'lilt' this creates a rhythm to follow. Though we are always in a wordless polyphonic dialogue each listening to the whole of what is being created in-the-moment, feeling the rhythm mediates being more in sync with everyone else. Sometimes it feels as if everything else recedes leaving only us, making music.

On weekdays you'll often find me in classrooms in schools or at the university using dramatic pedagogy. One of the core reasons why I value, and teach, with the pedagogy I have described in this book is because I can create dramatic ensemble experiences in college classrooms and also with young people and their teachers. What Eileen Ivers (2004) says about Celtic music is similarly true in the classroom: "It is honest music, played by everyday people, and it evokes raw emotion" (p. xii). My job as an honest leader is to honor the affective, along with the sensual, the cognitive, the social, and the imaginative, as we create spaces of togetherness where matters of significance can be explored.

When I work honestly with a group, together we may encounter and experience moments from the lives of people in events as we transport ourselves into the imagined landscape of narratives to play with possibilities, perform ideas, and learn more about the complexity of the world and our selves. When we create collaboratively as an ensemble using the art of dramatic pedagogy, what is being formed is beyond what any of the individuals in the group could make alone. When I lead, I seek to create conditions in which a group may begin to gel and improvise together. Sometimes it feels as if everything else recedes leaving only us, creating an experience of being somewhere else. At times, to paraphrase the Irish poet, W.B. Yeats, I find myself asking, "How can we know the players from the playing?"

There are many examples, from previous chapters, of deep, though brief, ensemble experiences: celebrating Jack's recovery; meeting like whales from a pod having an exuberant family reunion; sitting in silence contemplating how to celebrate the end of the war now that a man has died. Being active in imagination and dramatic in our dialogue we can form collaborative possibilities for ensemble experiences, performances, reflection, and inquiry in which individual and collective understanding may be transformed.

The well-known phrase is true: the whole *is* greater than the sum of its parts. Going up a hill with Jack and helping him recover after his fall was a richer and more substantive experience for preschoolers than pretending alone. Embodying stories from the life of Wes Moore allowed high school students to help one another visualize, author understanding about, and critique what they had not previously seen in the text.

Those complex events could only be created collaboratively, and experienced collectively, when the participants in dramatic pedagogy simply worked in unity as an ensemble to create dramatic art. We were all transformed, not by me, but by us.

Attend

to the **energy** of learning:
moving back-and-forth
from motion to stillness
from sound to silence,
to feel the **rhythm** of our community.

to the **pulse** of dialogue:
keeping meaning in motion
opening up to the new
seeing the limits in the old,
to sense the **vitality** of our community.

to the **breath** of movement:
from whole to parts
from all of us to some of me and some of you
from parts to whole,
to shape the **coherence** of our community.

Attend

Afterword

Cecily O'Neill

In a speech given in 1978, Dorothy Heathcote asked "What do we mean when we say 'That is an excellent teacher?'" It is clear from the ways in which she defines the attributes of the excellent teacher that, for her, the relationship of teachers to their students is paramount.

According to Heathcote, the teacher who aspires to excellence must be able to:

- see the students as they really are.
- preserve an interest in them
- grasp something of their potential
- have the courage to meet them where they are
- refuse to be lessened by them
- withstand certain pressures
- bring power to the students and draw on their power.
- be slow to make judgments.

Heathcote acknowledges the unpredictable, reluctant and sometimes even hostile reality of students' responses and the constraints that are faced by the teacher who strives for a classroom based on ensemble and equality. But the list also reveals her core belief that teachers are made in the classroom during moment by moment encounters with their students. The qualities she values are visible in operation in every chapter of Brian Edmiston's book, and perhaps most forcefully in his thick descriptions and analyses of Megan Ballinger's teaching with her ninth-grade students. Megan demonstrates that the excellent teacher evokes her students' best selves by assuming the best in them.

When Heathcote was writing, more than three decades ago, there was a growing recognition that drama was a precise teaching instrument, a unique teaching tool. Since then, research studies in many different countries have confirmed the benefits of drama as an effective, enriching and motivating approach to teaching and learning. However, where the curriculum is characterized by prescribed goals and limited pedagogy and an increased emphasis on skills testing and instrumental learning, it is easy for teachers to move imperceptibly from an open, inclusive, intuitive approach to a mechanistic one, with a focus on decontextualized skills and inactive knowledge. Yong Zhao's warning in Chapter 6 about the trend towards bureaucratizing education, homogenizing the curriculum, demoralizing educators, and turning children into test takers is very timely.

Any teacher who is courageous enough to fight these influences and who aspires to excellence will find practical advice, reassurance, and affirmation on every page of this wise and truthful book. The classrooms that are brought to life here are real places, not utopian locations of perfect pedagogy. Too often, books about introducing active and dramatic approaches to the classroom offer lists of activities that make drama seem simple and foolproof. As Edmiston makes clear throughout this book, teaching through drama requires the teacher to take account of the complex social encounters that fill every classroom so that deeper learning becomes possible.

Students' learning is supported by active and engaging tasks that include spectatorship as a key element, for example when they create Macbeth's court, re-enact a traffic accident, help Jack to recover from his fall, or debate the guilt or innocence of a bank robber. The students are spectators of each other's acts, not as a passive audience but from an engaged perspective, where what is observed is available for interrogation and interpretation.

Positioned in an active performance mode, the students display and embody their ideas and imagination. They come to know themselves better, inhabiting a range of perspectives and seeing their achievements recognized and accepted by their peers.

In Shakespeare's *Troilus and Cressida*, Achilles puts it like this:

No man is lord of anything.
Till he communicate his parts to others:
Nor does he of himself know them for ought,
Till he behold them formed in the applause
Where they are extended.

When they are positioned as spectators in reflective mode, the students interpret, analyze, and evaluate what they observe. Whether the observation is of a piece of improvised dialogue, a tableau, a model of a street, a puppet, or the teacher in role, the students' insights and understanding is articulated and shared. A community of comprehension begins to be generated. Multiple perspectives and different ways of seeing the world are celebrated, where problems may have more than one solution, or none, and where questions may have more than one answer. Above all, the participants' perceptions, interpretations and imaginings will be accepted, honored, and embodied in these active and dramatic encounters.

Teachers who absorb the principles, advice, and examples offered here will become makers of knowledge alongside their students. They will inhabit a transformative community as they build classroom relationships in moments of authenticity. In classrooms based on mutual respect, equality and a sense of ensemble they will open up the materials of the curriculum to dialogue, critical inquiry and imaginative transformation. In the protected space offered by imagined roles and situations, they will invite speculation and negotiation and encourage discussion and debate. They will promote creativity, self-confidence and self-esteem as they accept and affirm their students' contributions to the dialogue—'the pulse of teaching.' They will enter the classroom as creative beings themselves and they will nurture classroom communities that allow their students a voice in their own learning.

References

Alexander, B.K., Anderson, G.L., & Gallegos, B.P. (2005). *Performance theories in education: Power, pedagogy, and the politics of identity*. Mahwah, NJ: Lawrence Erlbaum Associates.

Astin, A.W. (1991). *Assessment for excellence: The philosophy and practice of assessment and evaluation in higher education*. Lanham, MD: American Council on Education/Rowman & Littlefield Publishing Group, Inc.

Aukerman, M. (2008). In praise of wiggle room: Locating comprehension in unlikely places. *Language Arts, 81*(1), 52–60.

Ayers, W. (2010). *To teach: The journey of a teacher* (3rd ed.). New York: Teachers College Press.

Ayers, W. & Alexander-Tanner, R. (2010). *To teach: The journey in comics*. New York: Teachers College Press.

Bakhtin, M.M. (1981). *The dialogic imagination*. M. Holquist & V. Liapunov (Eds.). (V. Liapunov & K. Brostrom, Trans.) Austin, TX: Texas University Press.

Bakhtin, M.M. (1984). *Problems of Dostoevsky's poetics: Theory and history of literature*. C. Emerson (Ed.). (C. Emerson, Trans.) Minneapolis, MN: University of Minnesota Press.

Bakhtin, M.M. (1986). *Speech genres and other late essays*. C. Emerson & M. Holquist (Eds.). (V.W. McGee, Trans.) Austin, TX: Texas University Press.

Bakhtin, M.M. (1990). *Art and answerability: early philosophical essays*. M. Holquist & V. Liapunov (Eds.). (V. Liapunov, Trans.) Austin, TX: Texas University Press.

Bakhtin, M. M. (1993). *Toward a philosophy of the act*. V. Liapunov & M. Holquist. (Eds.). (V. Liapunov, Trans.) Austin, TX: Texas University Press.

Bateson, M.C. (1989). *Composing a life*. New York: Grove Press.

Beach, R. & Myers, J. (2001). *Inquiry-based English instruction*. New York: Teachers College Press.

Beach, R., Campano, G., Edmiston, B., & Borgmann, M. (2010). *Literacy tools in the classroom: Teaching through critical inquiry, grades 5–12*. New York: Teachers College Press.

Boal, A. (1979/1985). *Theatre of the oppressed*. New York: Theatre Communications Group.

Bodrova, E. & Leong, D.J. (2006). *Tools of the mind*. Columbus, OH: Merrill/Prentice Hall.

Bolton, G.M. (1986). *Selected writings on drama in education*. D. Davis & C. Lawrence (Eds.). London, UK: Longman.

Bolton, G.M. (1992). *New perspectives on classroom drama*. Hemel Hempstead, Herts: Simon & Schuster.

Bolton, G.M. (1999). *Acting in classroom drama: A critical analysis*. Portland, ME: Calendar Island Press.

Bowell, P. & Heap, B.S. (2001). *Planning process drama*. London: David Fulton.

Brand, R. (1995). Punished by rewards: A conversation with Alfie Kohn. *Educational Leadership, 53*(1), 13–16.

Brook, P. (1968). *The empty space*. New York: Atheneum.

Bruner, J. (1987). *Actual minds, possible worlds*. Cambridge, MA: Harvard University Press.

Burningham, J. (1978). *Would You Rather ....* New York: Thomas Crowell.

Cochran-Smith, M. & Lytle, S. (2009). *Inquiry as stance: Practitioner research for the next generation*. New York: Teachers College Press.

Cole, M. (1996). *Cultural psychology, a once and future discipline*. Cambridge, MA: Belknap Press of Harvard University Press.

Connery, M.C. (2010). The historical significance of Vygotsky's Psychology of Art. In M.C. Connery, V.P. John-Steiner, & A. Marjanovic-Shane (Eds.), *Vygotsky and creativity: A cultural-historical approach to play, meaning-making and the arts* (pp. 17–26). New York: Peter Lang.

Creech, S. (2003). *Love that dog*. (W. Steig, Ill.) New York: Scholastic.

Davis, O. (2010). *Jacques Rancière*. Malden, MA: Polity.

De Certeau, M. (1984). *The practice of everyday life*. Berkeley, CA: University of Los Angeles Press

Denton, P. & Kriete, R. (2000). *The first six weeks of school*. Turner Falls, MA: Northeast Foundation for Children.

Depalma, R. (2010). Toward a practice of polyphonic dialogue in multicultural teacher education. *Curriculum Inquiry, 40*(3), 436–449.

Dewey, J. (1897). *My pedagogic creed*. New York and Chicago, IL: Kellogg.

Dewey, J. (1997/1910). *How we think*. Mineola, NY: Dover Publication.

Dewey, J. (1938). *Experience and education*. New York: Collier Books.

Dyson, A.H. (1993). *Social worlds of children learning to write in an urban primary school*. New York: Teachers College Press.

Edmiston, B. (2003). What's my position? Role, frame, and positioning when using process drama. *Research in Drama Education, 8*(2), 221–229.

Edmiston, B. (2007). Mission to Mars: Using drama to make classrooms more inclusive for the language and literacy learning of children with disabilities. *Language Arts, 84*(4), 331–340.

Edmiston, B. (2008). *Forming ethical identities in early childhood play*. London and New York: Routledge.

Edmiston, B. (2012). Dramatic inquiry and anti-oppressive teaching. *Youth Theatre Journal, 26*(2), 105–119.

Edmiston, B. & Enciso, P. (2002). Reflections and refractions of meaning: Dialogic approaches to classroom drama and reading. In J. Flood, D. Lapp, J. Squire, & J. Jensen (Eds.), *The handbook of research on teaching the English language arts* (pp. 868–880). New York: Simon & Schuster Macmillan.

Edmiston, B. & McKibben, A. (2011). Shakespeare, rehearsal approaches, and dramatic inquiry: Literacy education for life. *English in Education, 45*(1), 91–106.

Edwards, C.P., Gandini, L., & Forman, G. (1998). *The hundred languages of children: The Reggio Emilia approach.* Greenwich, CT: Ablex Publishing, Corp.

Egan, K. (1989). *Teaching as storytelling.* Chicago, IL: University of Chicago Press.

Ellsworth, E. (1997). *Teaching positions: Difference, pedagogy, and the power of address.* New York: Teachers College Press.

Enciso, P., Cushman, C., Edmiston, B., Post, R., & Berring, D. (2011). 'Is that what you really want?': A case study of intracultural ensemble-building within the paradoxes of 'urbanicity'. *Research in Drama Education: The Journal for Applied Theatre and Performance, 16*(2), 215–234.

Fecho, B. (2011). *Teaching for the students: Habits of heart, mind, and practice in the engaged classroom.* New York: Teacher College Press.

Fey, T. (2011). *Bossypants.* New York: Reagan Arthur Books.

Goffman, E. (1986). *Frame analysis: An essay of the organization of experience.* Lebanon, NH: Northeastern University Press.

Goffman, E. (1990). *The presentation of self in everyday life.* Harmondsworth, Middlesex: Penguin.

Goncu, A. & Perone, A. (2005). Pretend play as a life-span activity. *Topoi, 24,* 137–147.

Greene, M. (1995). *Releasing the imagination: Essays on education, the arts, and social change.* San Francisco: Jossey-Bass.

Greenleaf, R.K. (1977). *Servant leadership: A journey into the nature of legitimate power and greatness.* New York: Paulist Press.

Harré, R. & Langenhove, L.V. (1998). *Positioning theory: Moral contexts of international action.* Malden, MA: Blackwell Publishers, Ltd.

Harré, R. & Moghaddam, F.M. (2003). *The self and others: Positioning individuals and groups in personal, political, and cultural contexts.* Westport, CT: Praeger Publishers.

Heath, S.B. (2012). *Words at work and play.* Cambridge, England: Cambridge University Press.

Heath, S.B. (2012a). The surround of artful science. Keynote address. *Worlds Together Conference.* London, UK. Retrieved from http://www.ShirleyBrice Heath.net/index.htm.

Heathcote, D. (1971). Subject or system? In L. Johnson & C. O'Neill (1984). *Dorothy Heathcote: Collected writings on drama and education* (pp. 61–79). London: Hutchinson.

Heathcote, D. (1972). Training teachers to use drama as education. In L. Johnson & C. O'Neill (1984), *Dorothy Heathcote: Collected writings on drama and education* (pp. 26–40). London: Hutchinson.

Heathcote, D. (1975). Drama and learning. In L. Johnson & C. O'Neill (1984), *Dorothy Heathcote: Collected writings on drama and education* (pp. 90–102). London: Hutchinson.

Heathcote, D. (1976). Drama as a process for change. In L. Johnson & C. O'Neill (1984), *Dorothy Heathcote: Collected writings on drama and education* (pp. 114–125). London: Hutchinson.

Heathcote, D. (1978). From the particular to the universal. In L. Johnson & C. O'Neill (1984), *Dorothy Heathcote: Collected writings on drama and education* (pp. 103–113). London: Hutchinson.

Heathcote, D. (1978a). Drama and the mentally handicapped. In L. Johnson & C. O'Neill (1984), *Dorothy Heathcote: Collected writings on drama and education* (pp. 148–155). London: Hutchinson.

Heathcote, D. (1978b). Excellence in teaching. In L. Johnson & C. O'Neill (1984), *Dorothy Heathcote: Collected writings on drama and education* (pp. 18–25). London: Hutchinson.

Heathcote, D. (1980). Signs and portents. In L. Johnson & C. O'Neill (1984), *Dorothy Heathcote: Collected writings on drama and education* (pp. 160–169). London: Hutchinson.

Heathcote, D. (1984). The authentic teacher and the future. In L. Johnson & C. O'Neill (1984), *Dorothy Heathcote: Collected writings on drama and education* (pp. 170–199). London: Hutchinson.

Heathcote, D. & Bolton, G. (1995). *Drama for learning: Dorothy Heathcote's mantle of the expert approach to education.* Portsmouth, NH: Heinemann.

Heathcote, D., Smedley, R., Eyre, R. (1972). *Three looms waiting* [television broadcast]. London, UK: BBC TV.

Heshusius, L. & Ballard, K. (Eds.). (1996). *From positivism to interpretivism and beyond: Tales of transformation in educational and social research (the mind-body connection).* New York: Teacher College Press.

Heston, S. (2011). Dorothy Heathcote: Larger than life teacher who placed drama at the heart of education. (Obituary). Retrieved from http://www.guardian.co.uk/education/2011/nov/17/dorothy-heathcote

Hicks, D. (1996). Learning as a prosaic act. *Mind, Culture, and Activity, 3*(2), 102–118.

Holland, D. & Cole, M. (1995). Between discourse and schema: Reformulating a cultural-historical approach to culture and mind. *Anthropology and Educational Quarterly, 26*(4), 478–489.

Holland, D., Lachicotte, W., Skinner, D., & Cain, C. (1998). *Identity and agency in cultural worlds.* Cambridge, MA: Harvard University Press.

Holquist, M. (1990). *Dialogism: Bakhtin and his world.* New York: Routledge.

Holzman, L. (2010). Without creating ZPD's there is no creativity. In M.C. Connery, V.P. John-Steiner, & A. Marjanovic-Shane (Eds.). *Vygotsky and creativity: A cultural-historical approach to play, meaning-making and the arts.* New York: Peter Lang.

hooks, b. (2003). *Teaching community: A pedagogy of hope.* London and New York: Routledge.

Hout, M. & Elliott, S.W. (Eds.) (2011). *Incentives and test-based accountability in education; Committee on Incentives and Test-Based Accountability in Public Education.* National Research Council. Retrieved from: http://www.nap.edu/catalog.php?record_id=12521

Ivers, E. (2004). Foreword to F. Richie. *The NPR curious listener's guide to Celtic music.* New York: Perigree Books.

James, G. (2005). *Finding a pedagogy.* (Doctoral dissertation) University of East Anglia. Retrieved from http://www.solution-support.co.uk/index_htm_files/GJ-Finding%20a%20Pedagogy.pdf

James, G. (2012). Personal email correspondence. September 12–15.

James, M. (2009). Assessment and learning. Position Paper on Assessment for Learning from the *Third International Conference on Assessment for Learning*. Retrieved from http://www.mantleoftheexpert.com/.

Janesick, V.J. (2006). *Authentic assessment*. New York: Peter Lang.

Janks, H. (2010). *Literacy and power*. New York: Routledge.

Johnson, L. & O'Neill, C. (Eds.) (1984). *Dorothy Heathcote: Collected writings on drama and education*. London, UK: Hutchinson.

Johnson, M. (1997). *The meaning of the body: Aesthetics of human understanding*. Chicago, IL: Chicago University Press.

John-Steiner, V. (1987). *Notebooks of the mind: Explorations of thinking*. Oxford University Press.

John-Steiner, V., Connery, M.C., & Marjanovic-Shane, A. (2010). Dancing with the muses: A cultural-historical approach to play, meaning-making and creativity. In M.C. Connery, V.P. John-Steiner, & A. Marjanovic-Shane (Eds.). *Vygotsky and creativity: A cultural-historical approach to play, meaning-making and the arts*. New York: Peter Lang.

Johnston, P.H. (2004). *Choice words: How our language affects children's learning*. Portland, ME: Stenhouse Publishers.

Kalantzis, M. & Cope, B. (2008). *New learning: Elements of a science of education*. Cambridge, CT: Cambridge University Press.

Kittredge, W. (2000). *The nature of generosity*. New York: Knopf.

Kliewer, C. (1995). Young children's communication and literacy: A qualitative study of language in the inclusive preschool. *Mental Retardation, 33*(3), 143–152.

Kohl, H. (1998). *The discipline of hope*. New York: Simon & Schuster.

Kohn, A. (2005). Unconditional teaching. *Educational Leadership, 63*(1), 20–24.

Landay, E. & Wootton, K. (2012). *A reason to read: Linking literacy and the arts*. Cambridge, MA: Harvard Education Press.

Langer, S. (1977). *Feeling and form*. Upper Saddle River, NJ: Prentice Hall.

Lankshear, C. & Knobel, M. (2002). *Steps toward a pedagogy of tactics*. Keynote presented at the *National Council of Teachers of English Assembly for Research Mid-winter Gathering*. New York. Retrieved from http://everyday-literacies.net/files/pedtact.html

Lankshear, C. & Knobel, M. (2011). *New literacies: Everyday practices and social learning*. Maidenhead, England: Open University Press.

Makri-Botsari, E. (2001). Causal links between academic intrinsic motivation, self-esteem, and unconditional acceptance by teachers in high school students. In R.J. Riding & S.G. Rayner (Eds.), *International perspectives on individual differences: Self perception* (pp. 209–220). Westport, CT: Ablex.

Medina, C. (1994). Drama wor(l)ds: Explorations in Latina/o realistic fiction. *Language Arts, 81*(4), 272–282.

Menaker, D. (2010). *A good talk: The story and skill of conversation*. New York: Hachette Book Group.

Metcalf, L. (2003). *Teaching toward solutions* (2nd ed.). Carmarthen, Wales, UK: Crown House Publishing.

Moore, W. (2011). *The other Wes Moore: One name, two fates*. New York: Spiegel & Grau Trade Paperbacks.

Morson, G.S. & Emerson, C. (1990). *Mikhail Bakhtin: Creation of a prosaics.* Stanford, CA: Stanford University Press.

Neelands, J. (1990). *Structuring drama work: A handbook of available forms in theatre and drama.* T. Goode (Ed.). Cambridge, England: Cambridge University Press.

Neelands, J. (2009). Acting together: ensemble as a democratic process in art and life. *Research in Drama Education: The Journal of Applied Theatre and Performance, 14*(2), 173–190.

Neelands, J. (2010). The art of togetherness. In P. O'Connor (Ed.), *Creating democratic citizenship through drama education: The writings of Jonothan Neelands* (pp. 131–142). Stoke on Trent, UK: Trentham Books.

Neuman, S.B. & Dickinson, D.L. (2011). *Handbook of early literacy research* (Vol. 3). New York: The Guilford Press.

Newmann, F.M. & Associates (1996). *Authentic achievement: Restructuring schools for intellectual quality.* San Francisco, CA: Jossey-Bass.

Nieto, S. (Ed.) (2005). *Why we teach.* New York: Teachers College Press.

Nikulin, D. (1998). Mikhail Bakhtin: A theory of dialogue. *Constellations: An International Journal of Critical and Democratic Theory, 5*(3), 381–402.

Noddings, N. (1984). *Caring: A feminine approach to ethics and moral education.* Berkeley, CA: University of California Press.

Noddings, N. (1991). Stories in dialogue: Caring and interpersonal reasoning. In C. Witherell & N. Noddings (Eds.), *Stories lives tell: Narrative and dialogue in education* (pp. 157–170). New York: Teacher's College Press.

Norris, P. (Ed.) (1994). *The Bakhtin reader: Selected writings of Bakhtin, Medvedev, Voloshinov.* London, UK: Arnold.

Nystrand, M., Gamoran, A., Kachur, R., & Prendergast, C. (1997). *Opening dialogue: Understanding the dynamics of language and learning in the English classroom.* New York: Teachers College Press.

Ogle, D.M. (1986). K-W-L: A teaching model that develops active reading of expository text. *Reading Teacher, 39*, 564–570.

O'Neill, C. (1995). *Drama worlds: A framework for process drama.* Portsmouth, NH: Heinemann.

Paley, V.G. (2007). On listening to what the children say. *Harvard Educational Review, 77*(2), 152–163.

Palmer, P. (1997). *The courage to teach: Exploring the inner landscape of a teacher's life.* San Francisco: Jossey-Bass.

Pelo, A. (Ed.) (2008). Introduction. *Rethinking early childhood education.* Milwaukee, WI: Rethinking Schools.

Pinar, W. (2011). *What is Curriculum Theory?* (2nd ed.) New York: Routledge.

Project Zero, Cambridgeport Children's Center, Cambridgeport School, Ezra H. Baker School, & John Simpkins School. (2003). *Making teaching visible: Documenting individual and group learning as professional development.* Cambridge, MA: Project Zero.

Project Zero and Reggio Children. (2001). *Making learning visible: Children as individual and group learners.* Reggio Emilia, Italy: Reggio Children.

Rancière, J. (2007). *On the shores of politics: Radical thinkers.* (L. Heron, Trans.) N/A: VersoBooks.com

Rilke, R.M. (1903/1993). *Letters to a young poet.* (H.M.D. Herter-Norton, Trans.) New York: W.W. Norton.

Rimm-Kaufman, S.E., Larson, R., & Baroody, A. (2012). Efficacy of the *responsive classroom* approach: Results from a three year, longitudinal randomized control trial. *Presentation at Society for Research on Educational Effectiveness Fall Conference.* Washington, D.C.

Rodgers, C. (2002). Defining reflection: Another look at John Dewey and reflective thinking. *Teachers College Record, 104*(4), 842–866.

Royal Shakespeare Company (RSC). (2010). *The RSC Shakespeare toolkit for teachers: An active approach to bringing Shakespeare's plays alive in the classroom.* London: Methuen Drama.

Ryan, M.J. (2000). *The giving heart: Unlocking the transformative power of generosity in your life.* Berkeley, CA: Conari Press.

San Souci, R.D. & Comport, S.W. (Ill.) (2002). *Brave Margaret: An Irish adventure.* New York: Aladdin.

Sawyer, K. (2004). Creative teaching: Collaborative discussion as disciplined improvisation. *Educational Researcher, 33*(2), 12–20.

Sawyer, K. (2007). *Group genius: The creative power of collaboration.* New York: Basic Books.

Sipe, L.R. (2008). *Storytime: Young children's literary understanding in the classroom.* New York: Teachers College Press.

Sizer, T. (1984). *Horace's compromise: Dilemma of the American high school.* Austin, TX: Houghton Mifflin Harcourt.

Skiba, R. & Peterson, R. (2003). Teaching the social curriculum: School discipline as instruction. *Preventing School Failure, 47*(2), 66–73.

Smith, T. E. & Knapp, C.E. (2010). *Sourcebook of experiential education: Key thinkers and their contribution.* New York: Routledge.

Soja, E.W. (1996). *Thirdspace: Journeys to Los Angeles and other real-and-imagined places.* Malden, MA: Blackwell.

Steig, W. (2009). *Amos and Boris.* New York: Square Fish.

Taylor, P. & Warner, C.D. (Eds.) (2006). *Structure and spontaneity: The process drama of Cecily O'Neill.* Stoke on Trent, UK: Trentham Press.

Traugh, C. (1986). In North Dakota Study Group on Evaluation (1986), *Speaking out: Teachers on teaching* (pp. 109–112). Grand Forks, ND: University of North Dakota.

Turner, V. (1974). *Drama, fields, and metaphors: Symbolic action in human society.* Ithaca, NY: Cornell University Press.

Vygotsky, L.S. (1930/2004). Imagination and creativity in childhood. *Journal of Russian and East European Psychology, 42*(1), 7–97.

Vygotsky, L.S. (1933/1976). Play and its role in the mental development of the child. *Soviet Psychology, 5*, 6–18.

Vygotsky, L.S. (1934/1986). *Thought and language.* (A. Kozulin, Trans. rev. ed.) Cambridge, MA: MIT Press.

Vygotsky, L.S. (1978). *Mind in society: The development of higher psychological processes.* Cambridge MA: Harvard University Press.

Wells, G. (1999). *Dialogic inquiry: Towards a sociocultural practice and theory of education.* Cambridge, England: Cambridge University Press.

Wells, G. (2000). Dialogic inquiry in education: Building on the legacy of Vygotsky. In C.D. Lee & P. Smagorinsky (Eds.), *Vygotskian perspectives on literacy research: Constructing meaning through collaborative inquiry.* Cambridge, England: Cambridge University Press.

White, E.J. (2011). Aesthetics of the beautiful: Ideological tensions in contemporary asssessment. In E.J. White & M.A. Peters (Eds.), *Bakhtinian pedagogy: Opportunities and challenges for research, policy, and practice in education across the globe.* New York: Peter Lang.

Wiggins, G. (1993). Assessment: Authenticity, context, and validity. *The Phi Delta Kappan, 75*(3), 200–214.

Wiggins, G. (1998). *Educative assessment: Designing assessments to inform and improve student performance.* San Francisco, CA: Jossey-Bass.

Wiggins, G. & McTighe, J. (2005). *Understanding by design* (2nd ed.). Alexandria, VA: Association for Supervision and Curriculum Development (ASCD).

Yeats, W.B. (1973). Among school children. *Collected poems.* London: Macmillan.

Zeichner, K. (1999). The new scholarship in teacher education. *Educational Researcher, 28*(9), 4–15.

Zhao, Y. (2009). *Catching up or leading the way: American education in the age of globalization.* Alexandria, VA: Association for Supervision & Curriculum Development (ASCD).

Index

References to figures and photographs are shown in *italics*. References to tables are shown in **bold**. References to detailed descriptions of specific strategies are shown in ***bold italics***. References to notes consist of the page number followed by the letter 'n' followed by the number of the note, e.g. 67n1 refers to note no. 1 on page 67.

tool 24; performance as public utterance 45; play and imagining 17; polyphonic author 33; polyphonic dialogue 94, 309; reading and individuality 14; selfhood 186; utterances, decoding of 17; utterances, responses to 28, 32; utterances and speaker's attitude 231; utterances and speech 7–8; ventriloquating of words 34
Ballinger, Megan: assessing achievement (oral and writing) 296–297; assessing achievement (organizing meaning-making) 295–296, 295; assessing achievement (shifting viewpoints) 298–303, 301, 302; assessing achievement (taking up alternative viewpoints) 297–298; assessing disciplined inquiry (dialogue about text) 285–289, 286, 288; assessing disciplined inquiry (reading and critical inquiry) 289–294, 290, 291; assessing discipline inquiry 283–284; assessing discipline inquiry (reading) 284–285; assessing engagement with topic 277–283, 279, 280, 281; assessing what we value 303–306; authentic assessment 263–265, 267–273, 268, 271, 274–275, 276; building background knowledge 193; caring and dealing with conflicts 109; community building 79–80, 79, 82, 84, 95; community building and leadership 92–94, 92, 93, 94; ensemble tasks 85, 88; ensemble tasks, students' resistance to 112; generosity 107–108; "hopeful teacher" 124; inclusion 117–118, 119–123; O'Neill on 313; professional development program 124n1; teaching and agency 255–256; teaching as a journey 259
Bateson, Mary Catherine 230–231;
Beach, Richard 217
beginning collaborative tasks and negotiations 132–135;

Behaviorism: and assessment 276; cooperation vs. caring 109
bifocal vision 228, 229, 231, 233, 243, 255, 259
Bigler-McCarthy, Tracey 73, 75–76, 80, 84, 98, 124
Big Wind Blows /Sun Shines on All Who active strategy 79, 89, 174, 283
Boal, Augusto 20, 221n2
Bodrova, Elena 15
Bolton, Gavin 16, 67n1, 137
Bowell, Pam 125–126;
Boyd, Michael 84
Brave Margaret (Robert San Souci) session: Consciousness Threes dramatic strategy 181; dramatic inquiry 59, 60–62, 62; dramatic performance 47–49, 48; dramatic playing 42; facilitating performances 49–50; Hotseat Teacher-in-role 54–58, 55; model of Black Castle 57; narrative events, identification of 140; narrative events and dramatic tension 137; 'OIA' inquiry questions 127; polyphonic conversations 34–38, 35, 36, 37; reflective learning 52; teacher performance for student reflection 53
Brook, Peter xiii, xv
Brown University, ArtsLiteracy Project 101
Bruner, Jerome 3–4;
Burningham, John, *Would You Rather ...* scenarios 69

caring: and community building 98, 100; for individuals 108–110, 110; and "real conversations" with group 111–112; with Solution Focus approach 113–115; see also community
Certeau, Michel de 229
Choral Reading active strategy 149, 198, 285; see also L2L Reading active strategy; P2P Reading active strategy; Reading-in-role dramatic strategy

An environmentally friendly book printed and bound in England by www.printondemand-worldwide.com

PEFC Certified

This product is
from sustainably
managed forests
and controlled
sources

www.pefc.org

PEFC/16-33-415

This book is made entirely of sustainable materials; FSC paper for the cover and PEFC paper for the text pages.

#0009 - 230415 - C0 - 229/152/20 [22] - CB